Link/Age

WHAT FIFTY SAID

When I was young my teachers were the old.
I gave up fire for form till I was cold.
I suffered like a metal being cast.
I went to school to age to learn the past.

Now I am old my teachers are the young.
What can't be molded must be cracked and sprung.
I strain at lessons fit to start a suture.
I go to school to youth to learn the future.

—Robert Frost

Link/Age

Composing_in_the
_Online_Classroom

Joan_Tornow

UTAH STATE UNIVERSITY PRESS
Logan, Utah

Utah State University Press
Logan, Utah 84322-7800

The poem "What Fifty Said" from *The Poetry of Robert Frost*, edited by Edward Connery Lathem. © 1956 by Robert Frost. © 1928, © 1969 by Henry Holt & Co., Inc. Reprinted by permission of Henry Holt & Co., Inc.

Typography by WolfPack

Library of Congress Cataloging-in-Publication Data

Tornow, Joan C. (Joan Clark)
    Link/age : composing in the online classroom / Joan C. Tornow.
        p.   cm.
    Includes bibliographical references and index.
    ISBN 0-87421-221-9
    1. English language—Rhetoric—Study and teaching—Data
processing. 2. Academic writing—Study and teaching—Data
processing. 3. English language—Computer-assisted instruction.
4. Online data processing—Study and teaching. I. Title.
PE1404.T67 1997
808'.042'0285—dc21   96-45822
                                                    CIP

To Nicholas and Alexander,
my links with the future . . .

Contents

Acknowledgments

WHILE I'M NOT NECESSARILY READY TO SEND IT ON ITS WAY, I CAN SEE THIS book is ready to leave home. Over the past several years, I have done my best to raise it. There have been times of conflict, frustration, and uncertainty, but also times of surprise, laughter, and joy. Ultimately, the book had to take its own path, and I simply tried to be as understanding and supportive as possible. Of course, I did not raise this book alone. It took a village to raise this book.

It took friends, relatives, colleagues, editors, copyeditors, professors, librarians, pilots, conference organizers, taxi drivers, computer technicians, print shop staff, mail deliverers, coffee importers, CD manufacturers, UPS drivers, local service providers, and a host of others to assist me in the raising of this book. I am grateful for this opportunity to acknowledge at least some of them.

The director at Utah State University Press, Michael Spooner, saw a very early version of this book and encouraged me to persevere. He has remained monumentally supportive throughout my myriad revisions over many moons. His unwavering belief in the project has made it possible for me to shape and reshape the book until—at this point—I am willing to finally let it go.

My friend and colleague, Susan Romano, read several early versions of the manuscript and offered invaluable insights. Our conversations, whether over coffee or via email, were probably more multi-themed than any of the "polylogues" that appear in this book. She and I both recognize that the nurturing of children, manuscripts, cats, dogs, and turtles is more fun when one has a friend who can "relate."

Other readers of the early project upon which this book is based included Doug Foley, Diane Schallert, Hugh Burns, Gail Hawisher, Charles Moran, Carolyn Handa, and Cynthia Selfe, all of whom contributed their keen insights.

The students enrolled in E309, "Writing, Thinking, and Learning" consented not only to my online lurking, but also to my continuing interviews over the years. A special thanks goes to "Lora" who allowed me to track her for most of a day, observing her post-college life.

My parents filled my childhood home with books and conversations and instilled in me at an early age a special fondness for words.

My most special thanks goes to my husband, John, and my sons, Nicholas and Alexander. My conversations with them helped to sustain me during some of the more challenging days as major caretaker of *Link/Age*. When blizzards kept us indoors during our winter vacations, or rainstorms on our summer ones, I shamelessly exploited the situation by tasking them with reading chapters. Always, their insights were profound. My husband helped in a thousand other ways, too, and consistently conveyed his steadfast conviction that when the book left home, it would be responsible and independent.

These are some of the people in my village. I am humbled by their kindness and grateful for their generosity. This book is my attempt to give back to them some small measure of what they have given me.

N.B. "It takes a village to raise a child" is an African proverb I have been using in my teaching for several years.

@1

Introduction

THE STUDY ON WHICH I REPORT IN THIS BOOK BEGAN WITH MY FASCINATION
with language—specifically online language I discovered in a networked
college composition classroom. Although the study began with language,
it took me on a journey through many other issues related to the "computer revolution." In trying to understand the significance of online language, I found myself examining notions of authority, power, knowledge,
quantum physics, the university, and the workplace. I quickly discovered
that the networked classroom can be understood only in the context of a
networked society and its careening complexity.

Computer networks are changing the ways people work, play, and
learn. They are changing the ways people write and—because our symbol
systems are tools of thought—they are changing the ways people think.
New conventions are evolving and blurring the past distinctions between
writing and talking. The "talk" that occurs on networks is written talk, a
relatively new mode of language with its own peculiar qualities. This new
form of language even has a new name—electronic text or e-text. E-text is
changing the patterns of *when* we talk to others—and *how* we talk. New
social webs connect people and institutions in new ways, and information
that was formerly sequestered or confined to a select few is now accessible
to a larger number of people. As a result of this and of other changes in
society, hierarchical self-contained bureaucracies are giving way to fluid
interactive webs.

The interactions of people within institutions and between institutions
are becoming increasingly independent of geographic locations; people can
now easily be in immediate contact with others who share their interests,
regardless of location or of institutional affiliation. While these changes foster certain democratic ideals, they threaten other ideals. Computer access

can give voice to those who have been silent, silenced, or ignored. It can lead to grass-roots initiatives. On the other hand, the existing "computer culture" supports existing power structures in many ways. Those in power can use computers to monitor people and to censor their communications. Moreover, access to computers and to electronic information sources is not equitable, and computer use is certainly not consistent across American society. For example, a 1994 study for the National Telecommunications and Information Administration found that while 28.6 percent of white households had computers, only 11.1 percent of African-American households had them. On a global scale, developing nations lag far behind the United States and Europe in computer technology. These inequities are serious and should be addressed.

Despite ongoing problems with inequitable access, it is the premise of this book that the global changes brought about by computer networks will radically affect all our institutions, including our educational institutions. Writing classes have already been impacted and, in fact, have a key role to play in the transformation that is occurring. Writing teachers simply cannot afford to ignore the fact that writing is increasingly an activity that occurs online. In our country, a growing number of elementary school and high school students are already at home on the information superhighway through the Internet. By the time they get to college, they are apt to be doing most of their writing on computers—and probably on computer networks. They will consider the World Wide Web (WWW) to be at least as important as the campus library. Right now, twenty million households are connected to the Internet, and the number of connections has been tripling every year. Young people growing up in this environment will expect their computers to be linked so that they can readily access an ever-expanding web of computer networks.

Students are preparing for careers in institutional settings far different from those in which we, their teachers, have worked. Accustomed to writing on networks, students now anticipate pursuing careers in environments that are heavily network-dependent. They see their writing in this context and increasingly find traditional composition curricula to be out of pace with their world.

Scholars and teachers in rhetoric and composition are, of course, noting these changes. Richard Lanham writes, "In university literature courses, we will soon have to teach students who have been brought up on interactive electronic 'texts,' and we will have to prepare them for a world of work that relies on the electronic word. I don't think we can sit out this technological revolution; why not use it?" (Lanham 1993, 10). Gail Hawisher says, "How we go about this work—how we adapt our teaching and research to meet the demands of electronic writing spaces—will largely determine the success with which we are able to serve coming generations of students in the virtual age" (Hawisher 1991, 96). And Carolyn Handa notes of today's students, "The world we learned to write in is not the world they will be living and writing in" (Handa 1990b, 182). Seymour Papert, author of *The Children's Machine: Rethinking School in the Age of the Computer,* notes "Like any other social structure, School needs to be accepted by its participants. It will not survive very long beyond the time when children can no longer be persuaded to accord it a degree of legitimation" (Papert 1993, 6).

Sherry Turkle, a professor of the sociology of science and author of *Life on Screen: Identity in the Age of the Internet* (1995), refers to this time in history as a "liminal moment." She attributes this phrase to anthropologist Victor Turner, and explains

> It means a moment when things are betwixt and between, when old structures have broken down and new ones have not yet been created. Historically, these times of change are the times of greatest cultural creativity; everything is infused with new meanings.

She goes on to say that "Liminal moments are times of tension, extreme reactions, and great opportunity" (quoted in McCorduck 1996, 109).

The changes occurring in our modes of communication are embedded in a larger shift affecting the way we perceive and organize reality. In the field of composition, this is generally referred to as the shift from modernism to postmodernism—a new foregrounding of fragmentation along with a collapsing of coherence and of the "autonomous" individual.

While humanities disciplines tend to frame this shift as one from modernism to postmodernism, science disciplines frame it as one from a mechanistic and predictable Newtonian world view to a dynamic and unpredictable quantum world view. People in both the humanities and the sciences are apt to refer to such radical changes as "paradigm shifts"— especially after the influential, though controversial, book by Thomas Kuhn, *The Structure of Scientific Revolutions*.[1]

Some frown on nonscientists using terms like "paradigm shift" and "quantum world view." However, I do use these terms—and others from science and math domains—in my explorations of changes which seem to be affecting us all. I at first assumed that scientific "truth" was filtering down from the "hard sciences" to the humanities. Later, I realized that changing perspectives in both the humanities and the sciences are evolving simultaneously in what literary theorist N. Katherine Hayles calls "feedback loops" which "help to create the context that energizes the questions they ask" (Hayles 1991, 7). Shifting cultural contexts enable physicists to ask new questions just as they enable philosophers, mathematicians, artists, writers, and teachers to ask new questions. Although writing teachers may feel that the discipline of physics is far from the discipline we inhabit, it's important to keep in mind that physicists and writers are engaged in a common endeavor to describe and interpret experience.

Most of us aren't aware of how much in our culture can be attributed to a Newtonian world view. We take this world view for granted because it is transparent and seems normal or "real." Although this world view is anchored in Newton's *physics*, it impacts our economics, our research methodologies, our bureaucracies, and so forth. For several centuries it has provided metaphors which, as tools of thought, affect our very perceptions. As this world view is supplanted by a "quantum world view," all this is changing. Perhaps postmodernism is one part of this shift. After all, postmodern theorists do refer to postmodernism as, in part, a shift in "sensibilities" (Faigley 1992; Susan Sontag 1966).

One physics experiment, in particular, has become well known across disciplines. This is the pivotal experiment that shows that, at the subatomic level, our world is not composed of finite and observable particles as Newton thought. Rather, our world is composed of subatomic entities which may appear as either particles or waves—depending on what the observer is looking for. This finding has shaken the foundations of "objective quantitative research" by demonstrating that the notion of the researcher observing reality "out there" is illusory. Observer and observed are intrinsically linked. As the implications of this finding in physics become absorbed into common understanding, there is a greater appreciation of the fact that all researchers are, in a sense, simply telling stories from particular points of view. Such an understanding certainly validates ethnographic studies such as this one.

In this text, I have decided to employ the particle/wave dichotomy in additional ways. In a purely playful manner, I have used this dichotomy as a "tool of thought" which has helped me to foreground contrasts between dynamic and static features in cultural artifacts—for example, the dynamic nature of electronic text as opposed to the static nature of printed text. I also use it to contrast varying stances or styles in my writing—contrasting narrative sections as "wave" versus analytic sections as "particle." In other words, the narratives are wavelike in their attempt to describe an ongoing experience, whereas the theoretic sections in a sense "pin down" the experiences and make them hold still like *things* while I analyze them. I realize that subatomic particles do not hold still any more than do waves. Nevertheless, there is a sense in which the wave reality appears, in certain circumstances, to be caught up into relatively finite particles. I ask my readers to recognize the tentative way in which I use these quantum concepts throughout this study. I am using them as tools for *exploration*, not *explanation*. I am describing what I believe to be an emerging sensibility.

I am admittedly taking poetic license in applying scientific terms in this way, and I am mindful of Stephen Toulmin's warning about the misapplication of scientific terms. As Toulmin points out, one can easily create scientific myths by taking terms out of their original contexts (Toulmin 1982). I respectfully request forbearance from scientists who have devoted their lives to precisely defining terms which I now use for mere play. But I think that now, in this "liminal moment," it is important to explore new metaphors. There are new ideas in the air and already the young are trying them on for size. Certain terms have already made it into common parlance—terms such as "black hole," "chaos," "emergence," "resonance," "Schrodinger's cat," and "quantum leap." The popularity of science fiction also represents a cultural need to play with some of the new concepts emerging from physics and other sciences.

As conversations within fields become more accessible across disciplines—one of the changes coming about through networking—I expect to see increased borrowing and using of terms among disciplines. However, like Toulmin, I am concerned about the risk of perpetuating scientific myths which distort scientific findings through ignorance or expedience. For example, Darwin's concept of "survival of the fittest" was intended by Darwin to mean "the most well adapted to existing ecology," yet it has been distorted by nonscientists to justify triumphs of force and of Machiavellian deeds, claiming that such acts of brutality and cunning are somehow inevitable or natural.

I suggest three antidotes to the dangers of (mis)applying scientific terms. First, that we consider these terms as metaphors only. Second, that we strive to learn more about the sources and original contexts of the concepts that we use metaphorically. Not only will this accord scientists the respect they deserve, but it will no doubt provide us with better metaphors. Third, I suggest that we find ways to engage more often and more thoughtfully in conversations across disciplines. The Internet is one place where such conversations can occur.

Even if physics and math provide us only with compelling metaphors, I believe these images are contributing to an emerging mind set. For example, there is an increasing tendency to see patterns as fluid, emerging, and self-organizing—not as static "givens."

Naturally, language is playing a significant role in this paradigm shift since we rely on language to create meaning. As more and more writing occurs online, and as we move away from mechanistic Newtonian thinking, new genres are emerging and displacing traditional forms of the essay and the research paper. Newly emerging genres tend to be polymorphic, imaginatively including the diversity of voices which we experience when we write and read via computer network. Indeed, the championing of the *solitary* author is on the wane.

Writing teachers should take heart that language is currently foregrounded in this age of computer networks and is playing a major role in this paradigm shift. While images and sound are increasingly added to the mix, language has a secure position at the moment. Printed text remains the major medium of exchange on computer networks. Even in MUDs[2] (Multiple User Domains), one of the newest cyberspace applications, Michael Day notes that everything "must be uttered, created, or described in *text*" (Day 1996). As Sherry Turkle points out, "Online communication is in many ways a return to print—to reading and writing" (*Technology Review* 1996, 45), especially when compared with television. However, electronic text is quickly evolving its own conventions in a myriad of overlapping online discourse communities. Should we rejoice at the vitality of this new kind of text and the enthusiasm surrounding it? Or should we try to lure students back into writing the standard academic prose with which we are more familiar and in which we have so much vested? These are questions I explore in this text.

I discovered computer networks several years ago while attending a class that met online. I was beguiled and fascinated by this environment in which people's minds seemed to become so instantly and spontaneously linked. Here, it appeared, was a community constructed almost entirely through language. I immediately began to wonder if what I was seeing and experiencing had the potential to radically change classrooms.

As a parent of two high school sons, I had a visceral sense of what today's students have already endured by the time they reach the academy. If they are like my sons, they have trudged through years of instruction in large bureaucratic public schools, completing year upon year of busywork. Sometimes English classes have been among the bright islands of humanity in which students could explore their opinions or feelings, candidly talking about what is really on their minds. But far too often, overcrowded classrooms and overly-prescriptive curriculum mandates have prevented even the best teachers from engaging students in genuine dialogue. Today's high school students, on the verge of burnout, look toward college with hope and fear. They hope it will be different from high school, but they fear it will not be.

Even before I undertook this study, I was aware—from observations of my own children and of my peers in graduate school—of a smoldering student rebellion against the academy and its conventions. I could see that a growing number of students resent the expectation to revere the canon and the faculty. While adolescents have always been noted for a certain independent spirit, I sensed that we were on the brink of a more serious revolt. The students who registered for the course described in this book were like students everywhere. What was different, was that in this online class they could act out the fact that they were tired of "doing school" in the same old ways. They seemed eager to be done with school so they could move on.

As schools struggle with change, so too do corporations and other work places. In fact, many work places have come to resemble campuses because of their emphasis on education. This new age, dubbed the age of information, puts more emphasis on what we do with our brains than what we do with our hands. (Of course, this concept should be tempered by an awareness that people still work with their hands, but increasingly we delegate such work to labor forces in developing countries, a disturbing detail of our "postmodern" world.) Furthermore, the rate of change is so fast that, in this country, no one can safely depend on only twelve, sixteen, or twenty years of schooling to acquire the knowledge necessary for a lifetime. This is all the more true when so much of current schooling is based on what Gatto (1991) calls "prepackaged" knowledge—both static and stale.

The notion of education as *preparation* for life was challenged by John Dewey in 1916 and is now widely regarded as absurd. Just as Dewey argued that schooling should be considered life itself, students increasingly want school to be fulfilling in and of itself (Dewey 1916). Similarly, they increasingly expect their jobs to provide more than just a livelihood. We would hope that students see education not simply as job training, but as a means of developing civic responsibility necessary for ethical life in a democracy. All these issues are affected by the pedagogic choices we make in our classrooms.

When I embarked on this study, I was still in graduate school and straining at bureaucratic constraints which at times stood in the way of my learning. I was drawn to the language communities taking shape in the English department's computer lab because here I found faculty and students who were willing to take risks and question traditional means of education. I found the candid and free expression refreshing. I sensed that the network was not just a new gimmick, but that it signaled a radical change in the way university classrooms are configured and run. Intrigued by the social webs that were created online, and fascinated by the playful use of language, I decided to systematically study an undergraduate class meeting on a network. I simply wanted to listen to the students and see how the network embodied their diverse voices and opinions. What content and style would appear in the writing? Would the students be comfortable or uncomfortable in this environment? What kind of community, if any, would emerge?

I was fortunate in finding a writing class, meeting in the English department's Computer Research Laboratory, which was ideal for this study. The writing instructor, Hugh Burns, had a fascination with the networked classroom which paralleled my own. Moreover, his teaching style in this environment was experimental and relaxed. I was primarily interested in hearing student voices, and Burns created an environment where these voices could be heard. Unlike some teachers who teach in networked classrooms, he was not threatened by student candor, originality, and wit—even on those occasions when he himself was the target. Burns was interested in the process of writing; he was especially interested in invention and brainstorming and the ways these processes pay off in later writing. It was this combination of factors which enabled me to obtain a wealth of data.

This group of students was also ideal. None of them had experienced network conversation before, and only a few had ever used email. Only one had a modem at his home. Some had never used computers before, even for word processing.

In her book, *In the Age of the Smart Machine: The Future of Work and Power*, Shoshana Zuboff explores human and organizational issues arising in the face of computerization. She notes that we are "on the edge of a historical transformation of immense proportions, as important as that which had been experienced by the eighteenth and nineteenth century workers" (Zuboff 1988, xiii). Having earlier studied the industrial revolution, Zuboff had noted the unfortunate fact that the available data

> offered inadequate insight into the subtleties of human experience. Constructing an idea about the inward sensibilities of ordinary people during those volatile times required painstaking effort and imagination . . . I was fascinated by the ways in which older sensibilities are lost to a kind of social amnesia, crowded out by our adaptations to the demands of changing times. (xi)

Zuboff's insights on sensibilities echo those of Susan Sontag, who wrote that "The sensibility of an era is not only its most decisive, but also its most perishable, aspect" (Sontag 1966, 278). Zuboff notes that on the brink of such transformations as the industrial revolution, or the computer revolution, there is but a brief "window of time" in which we can harvest the sensibilities of people responding to change. She says of her study, "The jolt of unfamiliarity had to be exploited for the heightened sensibility it brings." She adds, "I wanted to discover the flesh and blood behind the concepts, the interior texture rather than the external form" (Zuboff 1988, xiv).

I am indebted to Zuboff because she expressed so eloquently the tacit ideas I was struggling to make explicit as I wrestled with the data in my own study. It was, indeed, the "jolt of unfamiliarity" I was trying to capture—in order to garner insights on how students respond to networked classrooms. Zuboff was studying factory workers and managers implementing computer technology and then reeling from the changes—with elation, dismay, or some combination of the two. I was studying students and teachers. Yet, I discovered that many of the issues were parallel. Both the work world and the academic world are parts of a larger world which is rapidly changing as we move beyond the age of information and into, as Fred Kemp notes, the age of ideas (Kemp 1993).

As Zuboff and Turkle each did in their respective studies of technology and culture, I chose an ethnographic approach, and simply immersed myself in the class as a participant-observer. From this vantage point, I looked for patterns in what students were saying and writing online. I also interviewed the students and the instructor from time to time, studied the computer transcripts, and conducted a final attitude survey. In reporting my findings, I have used narrative to capture the feel of a computer classroom and to get at the sentient experience of the students. I have designed the theoretical sections to provide frames, i.e., to construct meaning. The "wave sections," if you will, are more intuitive while the "particle sections" are more analytic.

I have included observations from a wide array of academic sources, including experts in composition as well as experts in biology, physics, and business. I have also included the voices of those outside of academia, including—for example—journalists, filmmakers, and artists. This eclectic and holistic approach stems from my sense that evolving genres will tend toward just such a medley and away from the intense specialization with which we are more familiar.

Many educational innovations begin in humble environments, and the computer classroom described here was no exception. The classroom herein depicted had begun on a proverbial shoestring. Housed in a desolate room in the basement of a library, it was surrounded with the clutter and confusion that typically accompanies change. This solitary lab has since evolved into a complex of computer classrooms. Having earned a central place in the University of Texas Division of Rhetoric and Composition, these classrooms have acquired the budgetary wherewithal to shed, for the most part, any former experimental trappings. The Division headquarters are now accessed via a quick walk down a grassy slope to a stately stone building which houses not only a complex of faculty offices, but the newest networked classrooms and workrooms. Here students still engage in the LINCs (Live Interactive Network Conversations) described in such detail in this book. But now they also access the World Wide Web, construct home pages, engage regularly in MUDs, and compose hypertexts.

Several years after I had collected my original data, I returned to the site of my study to access some additional electronically archived texts. The changes I observed in this library-basement environment were striking. As I walked down the hallway, I noticed that the whole wing had been remodeled. A bright ribbon of encased fluorescent lighting illuminated the gleaming tiles below. At the end of the hall, where once there had been but one (IBM) computer classroom, now there were two—an IBM and a Mac. The classrooms were newly painted in bright vanilla and were in immaculate condition. Every computer station had a new swivel chair. Upgraded air conditioning kept the rooms cool despite the heat relentlessly generated by the computers and printers. The printers were new, silent lasers.

Adjacent to the classrooms was a room which served as the hub for the teachers and lab administrators. This administrators' room housed the staff mailboxes along with an array of computers and printers used for brainstorming, planning, and printing. Tacked to the door of this room was the now famous *New Yorker* cartoon picturing a dog working at a computer as he chatted with a second dog peering over his canine shoulder. The caption read: "On the Internet, nobody knows you're a dog" (Steiner 1993).

A newly-hired assistant helped me access the data I needed. It seemed amazing to me that on the hard drives of the computers in this small room were stored virtually all the written words of all the students who had taken classes in these labs for the past five years! I soon walked back down the long corridor, the archived information now electronically duplicated on a small plastic disk tucked in my purse.

I noticed that the hall, unlike two years before, was remarkably clear of clutter—with one exception. At the end of the hall farthest from the computer classrooms—where the more traditional faculty offices were located—cardboard boxes sat on the floor outside each door. I examined a couple of these boxes closely. They were whiskey boxes crudely cut in half and labeled with composition course names such as E306, E309K, and E316K. In one, students had deposited their final papers—papers with titles like "A Feminist Perspective on Hamlet" or "Religion: God or No?" In another, students had deposited a stack of "Blue Books," containing handwritten final exams. I wondered how long such artifacts of college life would survive. Would student essays change dramatically to reflect changes in online literacy conventions? And would the paperless classroom, predicted by many, actually come to pass? Or would student essays sound much the same, and would faculty continue to frequent liquor stores in search of cardboard boxes?

It is impossible to predict the composition classroom of the future or even of next year. Technology appears to be escalating our move into postmodern sensibility, and it is bringing about many changes which few, if any, could have anticipated even a short time ago. In E309, however, I could begin to get a feel for some possible directions of change. In immersing myself in the language which surrounded me in this online class, I could begin to detect subtle patterns in how the students wrote, what they wrote, what metaphors they used, how they related to each other, how they related to texts, how they related to the academy, how they envisioned their futures, and how they related to authority. In the world of E309, the students and teacher interacted almost entirely through language alone. It was a curious world indeed.

Notes

1. Thomas Kuhn's *The Structure of Scientific Revolutions* was originally published in 1962. A second enlarged edition was published in 1970. This second edition includes a Postscript which responds to criticisms and sketches new directions in the author's thoughts.
2. A MUD is a Multi-User Domain. A MOO is a MUD, Object Oriented. A MUSH is a Multi-User Shared Hallucination. All three are online virtual environments, but of the three, MOOs are currently the most commonly used in writing classes. A MOO gives every participant the opportunity to congregate in a constellation of virtual spaces and to interact through language.

@2

The_Room_in_the_Basement

Appealing workplaces are to be avoided. One wants a room with
no view, so imagination can dance with memory in the dark.
—Annie Dillard, "Schedules" (1989, 74)

THERE HAS ALWAYS BEEN A MYSTIQUE ABOUT CLASSES THAT MEET IN BASE-
ments. The classes which meet in the basement of the undergraduate
library at the University of Texas are no exception. The library is situated
next to the Union Building and between the two are an assortment of
tables, chairs, and benches where on nice days (almost always) students
can bring their lunches from the Union cafeteria. After eating, students
linger here, tilting their young faces up toward the omnipresent Texas sun.
Only yards away are the wide cement stairs leading to the library basement. In the foyer, if a basement can be said to have a foyer, recruiters are
sometimes permitted to set up lobbying stands. On one day each year, for
example, a student trying to reach a basement class must maneuver
through a maze of pamphlet-laden tables and suited men and women
espousing the good life awaiting one in the FBI.

It was in this basement that space was found for an experimental computer classroom for the English department. In the early days of this
"experiment," a student entering the library through this basement door
entered a quiet, even monastic environment. A dim hallway in the basement of the library stretched back into cavelike space. It was dim because
only every third overhead light was illuminated. Where the hall reached a
dead end, an ever-changing array of brown metal trash cans, freshly fitted
with black plastic, was stacked against the wall like children's blocks. No
one seemed to know, or care, why these cans were here. But since the hallway was the only authorized smoking area in the basement, the cans came

in handy for discarded cigarette packages and spent match folders. On the wall above the trash cans, and obscured by them only on certain days, was the label, "English Department Computer Research Lab." Predictably, this label was spelled out on four strips of computer paper taped to the cement wall.

To the left of this dead end, a door opened into the room used to administer the computer classroom and to store the electronic data which accrued. To the right, a door opened into the computer classroom itself. In contrast to the shabby hallway environment, this classroom demanded respect. Twenty-six IBM computer terminals sat on collapsible tables flanking the four walls—forming a square donut of technology. Thirteen IBM ProPrinters, dot matrix printers, were wedged between the computers. Inside this high-tech donut was a low-tech donut, a cluster of conference tables pushed into a jagged square. In contrast to the clean homogeneity of the computers, the furniture appeared to have been scavenged from garage sales: few of the chairs matched, the wheeled chairs were missing wheels, the swivel chairs no longer did so, and the wooden chairs wobbled and creaked.

The walls were a smudged and faded chartreuse, except for one which was a burnt sienna. They were bedecked here and there with recklessly placed posters, freebies from various computer hardware and software companies. When the teaching assistants had prepared the room for class, thirteen panels of fluorescent lights buzzed and flickered overhead. Four fans on stands created a steady breeze of white noise. The monitors of the computers selected for use that day emitted a sapphire light. They seemed to hum, in anticipation, the siren song of the nineties.

@3

A_History_of_the_Computer-Networked_Classroom

When we weren't crying, we were dancing around doing high fives. When the classroom worked, it bristled with activity and student energy. When it didn't, the room died and the instructors felt helpless. Those of us who weren't teaching hugged the doorway to the classroom, intent on how our software, our machines, were helping or hurting what the instructors were doing.
—Fred Kemp (1993, 165)

WHEN ONE ENTERS A ROOM IN WHICH COMPUTERS ARE NETWORKED, instead of stand-alone, one enters an environment very different from the first computer classrooms. In the first classrooms, students worked in isolation at their terminals. But in networked classrooms, students interact via computer. As Denise Murray notes, with networking the computer becomes the "medium" rather than the "means" of communication (Murray 1985, 205). I like to think of the distinction in terms of opacity. When a stand-alone computer becomes networked, it's as if it suddenly shifts from being opaque to being transparent. The user may have the sensation of looking not *at* a machine but *through* a machine to one's peers, or to information sources beyond the machine itself. (This differs significantly from Lanham's concept of looking either *at* or *through* a text [Lanham 1993, 5] as will be explained in chapter 20.) Participants using a network for discussion for the first time invariably react to the novelty of the experience. With networking and the social interaction that ensues, there has been a shift from seeing the computer as a technology for writing to seeing it as a technology for "talking" in print.

The computer classroom described in this book was, at that time, a rarity. Just how did such a classroom come to exist in this time and place?

The first computer conferencing system was designed by physicist Murray Turoff in the 1960s for use by the President's Office of Emergency Preparedness (Taylor 1992, 138). In the 1970s the Department of Defense sponsored ARPANET, a wide-area network that would allow communication, command, and control even in the midst of nuclear war. The network was designed as a web without a central control so that it could not be disabled by a single bomb. These first networks were designed to send data, not words. Yet once the technology was in place, the sending of words became easy.

Howard Rheingold notes that networks were quickly used for dispersed decision-making by U.S. policymakers (Rheingold 1993b, 7). He notes, as well, that the first networks were deliberately designed without a central control, and while this provision was for national security, it later came to be an essential characteristic insuring democratic participation. Science fiction writer Bruce Sterling notes the irony in the way that something designed as a cold war military command grid quickly became harnessed for more pleasurable pursuits:

> When I look at the Internet, I see something astounding and delightful. It's as if some grim fallout shelter had burst open and a full-scale Mardi Gras parade had come out. I take such enormous pleasure in this that it's hard to remain properly skeptical. (Sterling 1995, 10)

The adoption of computer networks in English classrooms is best understood by looking at the personal stories of teachers and students who first attempted to use this new medium. In tracing the roots of electronic conferencing at the University of Texas, we need to go back to the early eighties and the story of Trent Batson, an English professor at Gallaudet University, an institution dedicated to the education of the deaf. Even when he earlier worked with hearing students, Batson had never enjoyed the "game" in which "I was on stage and the students were judging me; then they took their turn when they wrote a paper that I judged. We took turns performing for and judging each other." What Batson valued instead was "anything that seemed like genuine interaction, or genuine engagement, and not a game." He liked "good discussions, one-on-one conferences, dialogue journals" and other activities which emphasized dialogue (Batson 1993, 87).

While on sabbatical in 1983, Batson began using a computer for the first time and states that his enthusiasm was "nearly unbounded—I came to believe that the computer could be my ally in the writing classroom. I didn't know how yet, but I could sense the potential" (90).

Meanwhile, at Gallaudet, Batson was aware of the "many attempts that had been made to bring deaf people into the flow of living English, its spoken form . . . " (97). The typical deaf college student uses American Sign Language (ASL) as his/her "social language"; English is a "school language"—typically experienced in static written form, divorced from a live social context (95). Batson noted that teachers of the deaf, addressing this problem, had used such strategies as giving each student an overhead projector so that "the projected writing, encircling the room like a ring of wisdom, would be real-time communication in English" (97). Teletype devices for the deaf (TDDs) were also common, but had not worked well with a whole class of people. Batson noted:

> My English department colleagues and I were [more] primed to see different kinds of opportunities with microcomputers than were writing teachers at other colleges. . . . People *typing* to each other over the wires in a room full of computers could simulate a spoken conversation and thus, for the first time ever, allow deaf people to directly experience and participate in a live group discussion in English. (98–99)

Batson's first networked class met in the spring of 1985 under the acronym ENFI (English Natural Form Instruction). Students responded with "glee," he reported. One of them wrote, "Wow, look at this Ping-Pong English" (99). At the end of that year, Batson noted the irony that the computer, "perceived as anti-human, a tool of control and suppression of human instinct and intuition, has really humanized my job" (13). Joy Peyton, a linguist, soon joined Batson and contributed a Bakhtinian theoretical framework to Batson's work.

Meanwhile, in 1985, the University of Texas established the Computer Research Lab with English professor Jerome Bump as director and Fred Kemp, at that time a graduate student, as associate director. This lab, originally part of an IBM Project Quest grant program, began with twenty-five stand-alone (un-networked) IBM PC computers which students used for word processing. Kemp was soon joined by two other English graduate students, Paul Taylor and Locke Carter. Kemp notes that the three of them were committed to "the development of innovative instructional practices," as specified by Project Quest (Kemp 1993, 162). One innovation was the heuristic software TOPOI, based on Aristotle's *topoi*, which had been developed by Hugh Burns (the teacher in this book, then a doctoral student) some six years earlier. Still, there was a restless dissatisfaction among these graduate students as they watched students toil away in isolation at their respective workstations. A remarkable breakthrough was about to occur—based in part on serendipity and in part on the blending of the diverse talents of a group of graduate students.

In 1987, Kemp, Taylor, and Carter heard a conference presentation by three other University of Texas students—Valerie Balester, Wayne Butler and Kay Halasek. This presentation was on the collaborative pedagogy of Kenneth Bruffee (Kemp 1993, 163). Kemp, Taylor, and Carter immediately realized that collaboration was what was missing in the computer classroom. More serendipity was to follow. Soon afterwards, Kemp attended a Conference on College Composition and Communication (CCCC) in Atlanta and heard Trent Batson describe the synchronous electronic discourse that he was using with deaf students at Gallaudet. Chance, as the saying goes, favors the prepared mind, and Kemp recognized instantly that synchronous electronic discourse was exactly what he was looking for to foster collaboration in the computer classroom.

The Computer Research Lab could not afford the networking software which Batson and Peyton were using, but within two days, Taylor, a self-taught BASIC programmer, had achieved a major breakthrough and designed a workable networking program similar to that which Kemp had seen in Atlanta. The lab coordinators promptly transformed the computer classroom into an "ENFI classroom" (Kemp 1993, 165) in which students could conduct synchronous online conversations.

Soon, the graduate students who had been implementing Bruffee's collaborative theories in their noncomputer classes asked if they could teach a summer class in this embryonic networked classroom. Kemp, Taylor, and Carter welcomed this idea; Kemp describes that first summer class as "the most active intellectual period of my 20-year teaching experience" (Kemp 1993, 165).

I have included the very personal story behind the development of the computer classroom featured in this book because I think it is important to recognize that this technology evolved from grass-roots yearnings for more collaborative writing instruction. This was a "bottom-up" development, if you will, in that a group of English graduate students were motivated to somehow bring a group of computers into harmony with collaborative theory. It is noteworthy that this software was designed *by* students and *for* students. Rheingold observes, "it wasn't the mainstream of the existing computer industry that created affordable personal computing, but teenagers in garages" (Rheingold 1993b, 68). In a similar vein, it was a group of students in a basement who solved the electronic puzzles that would enable students at the University of Texas to converse and collaborate via computer about their lives, their ideas, and their writing.

Meanwhile, Batson and Peyton became increasingly aware of the potential for network discussion within higher education in general. In 1987, Gallaudet joined with four other institutions (Carnegie Mellon, The University of Minnesota, New York Institute of Technology, and Northern Virginia Community College) to form the ENFI Consortium. At this time, ENFI changed its name to Electronic Networks for Interaction, keeping the acronym but changing the words to which the acronym referred. This new name encompassed network implementation among either deaf or hearing students. The ENFI Consortium was a three-year demonstration project sponsored by the Annenberg Corporation for Public Broadcasting. It did much to disperse the concept of local area network use in college writing classrooms.

In 1982, the first Computers and Writing Conference was held at the University of Minnesota. This soon evolved into a national conference which, with one two-year hiatus in the eighties, has met annually ever since. Originally a conference attended by only about a dozen academicians, it now draws about three hundred people. By 1990, many sessions of the conference reflected the growing interest in the theory affecting and evolving from this emerging field (Gerrard 1995).

The 1990 conference was held in Austin, co-hosted by the University of Texas and Texas Tech, and co-chaired by John Slatin and Fred Kemp. I vividly recall a brunch presentation by Lester Faigley in which he had volunteers read a transcript of an online discussion generated earlier in one of his classes. The volunteers stood at microphones strategically placed throughout the banquet room and read the student comments as an oral reading. There was much laughter as the attendees heard for the first time what I now consider a new genre. Some of the messages were funny in and of themselves, but I think the laughter resulted from people hearing, for the first time, a new use of language. Laughter is a natural response to something that blends the familiar and the strange.

Lisa Gerrard points out that the growing attendance at this annual conference indicates that the field of computers and writing has come of age. She alludes, as well, to the closing brunch presentation in 1994 in which Cynthia Selfe, Gail Hawisher, and Charles Moran traced the history of the field from the late 1970s. I was there, and I remember that they closed their polyvocal presentation by passing out papers and pens to everyone and inviting us to record some of our turning points in the field. As we shoved our omelets and coffee aside to reflect in writing on our experiences in the field, there was an almost palpable feeling in the air that we had come of age. For the first time, many of us realized the significance of our unique history. The personal testimonials collected that morning later appeared in the margins of *Computers and the Teaching of Writing in American Higher Education, 1979–1994: A History* (Hawisher et al. 1996)—a text which I recommend to all who want to delve deeper than is possible in this brief chapter.

By 1990, when the ENFI Consortium completed its three-year stint, the use of networked computer classrooms for writing instruction was an accepted, if still relatively rare, practice. A new arena for educational research was born, and professional journals were receptive. In 1991, for example, *Written Communication* devoted a "Special Issue," to "Computers, Language and Writing" and the four feature articles in this issue were devoted to the use of *networked* computers. And in 1992, one issue of *College English* included three reviews of books relating to English studies and technology. The category "Computers and English" even appeared on the journal's cover.

In 1989, Kemp started an online discussion list, or "listserv," called Megabyte University (MBU). This has helped to develop a sense of community among rhetoric teachers and researchers both in the United States and abroad. Meanwhile, the graduate students (now graduated) and professors who developed the software for networked discussion at the University of Texas formed a company to further develop and market their software. Several other companies have developed similar software.

The two software applications which are the focus of this book are real-time interactive writing and email. The former has gone by various names—including ENFI (coined by Trent Batson) and InterChange (coined by The Daedalus Group). There are other versions now on the market; each product has its own features but each provides for what I call Live Interactive Network Conversation. In this book, I have chosen to use my own term, LINC, to identify this software in a generic manner. I want to make clear that I am not endorsing any particular product or company. Rather, I am exploring a new kind of talk which can be facilitated by a growing number of software applications. (Similarly, the students in my study used CONTACT for email, but I use the generic term, email.)

A new journal, *Computers and Composition: A Journal for Teachers of Writing*, evolved in 1985 from a newsletter started two years earlier by Cynthia Selfe and Kathleen Kiefer. In 1988, Gail Hawisher followed

Kathleen Kiefer, and Hawisher and Selfe have continued to co-edit. *Computers and Composition* was the earliest journal devoted to computers and composition studies, and it has continued to play a key role in this relatively new discipline. Its first issue included no articles about networked computers, and by the time the class in this book met, about one out of five of its articles was about networked computers. In 1994, this journal expanded its scope and circulation as it evolved into *Computers and Composition: An International Journal for Teachers of Writing*. Editors Hawisher and Selfe said of this new journal: "We begin a new adventure as the only international academic publication focusing on the use of computers in writing instruction and dedicated to bringing together, within its pages, a worldwide community of teachers, scholars, and technology users" (Hawisher and Selfe 1994, 1). The first issue of the international journal included seven articles, five of which were based on networked or online classrooms, thus reflecting the overall shift from word processing concerns to networking concerns.

In 1993, Trent Batson and Fred Kemp founded the Alliance for Computers and Writing, a hub of professional support in the field. The ACW has sponsored workshops, created Its own listserv and WEB page, and recently become a co-sponsor—along with the Annenberg/CPB Project, Gallaudet University, and George Mason University—of the Epiphany Project, designed to support pedagogical change in networked college classrooms

By 1993, many of our professional activities were moving online. For example, the 1993 Computers and Writing Conference had an online version which was "attended" both by people who could not get to the "physical" conference and people who wished to engage in dialogue before and after the physical conference itself. Online conferences have now become a standard adjunct to annual conferences. The National Council of Teachers of English (NCTE) Conference on College Composition and Communication (CCCC) implemented their first online conference in 1995; this *virtual* conference included abstracts of presentations, real-time online meetings, and a number of MOOs (Hawisher et al. 1996, 251).

Online journals have begun to proliferate, beginning in 1991 with Ted Jennings's *EJournal* which quickly drew international subscribers. This has been joined by ACW's peer-reviewed online journal, *Kairos: A Journal For Teachers of Writing in Webbed Environments* (edited by Mick Doherty) which announces on its home page that it is addressing both "individually and syllogistically" the new and different ways we are writing, reading, and teaching. Still another e-journal, *RhetNet: A Cyberjournal for Rhetoric and Writing*, is edited by Eric Crump, who states that it is "as much a place to play around with the notion of academic publishing as it is an actual publication . . . It is a place where we may explore the possibilities for publishing online the kinds of written conversations that occur online" (*RhetNet* home page, July 1996). These are just a few of the e-journals that are being published through the Internet.

The Internet has now become well known, and with the advent of the World Wide Web (WWW) and various Web "browsers," it is now accessible to thousands of people who had previously shied away from the technical hurdles of "Net surfing." Using Netscape or another browser, people can now readily link up with databases and people around the globe. Web sites have made hypertext a familiar concept. In hypertext, one clicks on an icon or highlighted word or phrase imbedded in a text to access a different layer of information. Each click on such a hot spot connects the reader or user with a new screen of information that is in some way linked with the prior text. Netscape and other browsers enable one to click on a "back" icon, thus returning backwards along whatever path one took through a series of clicks. Of course, one need not click on icons and often has the option of simply reading a given text in the familiar linear way. However, hypertext—and especially as applied on the WWW—has introduced a sort of third dimension into the written text.

Professional organizations now find it easy to homestead in "cyberspace" and are now developing "home pages" with hypertext links to webs of information. Home pages are typically linked to other home pages, resulting in a labyrinth of information and ideas. Home page sites of interest to composition teachers include NCTE (<http://www.ncte.org>) and ACW (<http://english.ttu.edu/acw.html>). A Composition Course Database (<http://moo.du.org:8888/00anon/cybercomp>) provides a listing of composition instructors using the Internet in their classes (Leslie Harris, Project Director, Composition in Cyberspace). Meanwhile, NCTE founded the NCTE Assembly for Computers in English in 1984, becoming a Council Assembly in 1985.

As the WWW has entered popular culture in recent years, one can scarcely open a newspaper without seeing a new article on it or without seeing an http address. Even cartoonist Scott Adams includes his http address on his weekly comic strip, *Dilbert*, so that people can email him ideas for future strips. In the last few years, composition teachers have begun incorporating the WWW into their writing classes. Rebecca Rickly and Wayne Butler, for example, had a Web-based course founded on a hypertextual "syllaweb." In a post to the ACW list, Rickly explained that this web included a section which logs

> all of the text generated by the students in the course: their email from the class email list, and InterChange [LINC] discussions. We also have links to each student's home page, which includes a copy of their Webfolio: a webbed port-folio of all the writing they've done for the course, along with a self-assessment essay which links to work they've done as part of the classroom community. (Rickly 1996)

Thus, networking has worked its way into college writing classrooms, and those writing in classrooms now write, as well, beyond the classroom through the WWW. From its inception, classroom networking was not simply a "new tool" or a "new technology" but a major breakthrough which teachers saw as enabling radical changes in classroom pedagogy. These changes all began with online communication on relatively simple local area networks. And it is the premise of this book that the initial redirection, the radical shift, began there. In this primal text-based form, we saw the harbingers of change.

@4

Lora

Wow, am I confused. Should I continue this adventure in computer chaos? This class was recommended to me by Kate Frost. She felt like I had a lot to say, but didn't know how to say it. That is why I'm here. God help me! The people next to me are going so quickly. AHHHHHHHH!

—Lora, LINC (first week)

ON A HOT DAY DURING THE SECOND WEEK OF THE SEMESTER, STUDENTS clustered at rustic tables on the patio of the Union Cafeteria. Some wolfed down lunches of pizza or hero sandwiches. Others simply "hung out," nursing stale colas and enjoying the September sunshine. Most students wore T-shirts which, in addition to making fashion statements, made quite literal black-and-white statements, such as "Party Naked," "Bo Knows Your Sister," and "Friends Don't Let Friends Go to A&M."

The students at one table cast anxious glances upward as a flock of grackles landed in the tree overhead. Said one student, "Oh, shit, look!" All grabbed food and drinks, jumping back as the grackle fulfilled the prophecy. With no empty tables in sight, the students dispersed to the cement stairway that led to the library. Some resettled on the warm steps, but as the tower bell was now gonging, others muttered that they'd better get to class.

From this group, Lora and Tammy emerged, hoisting backpacks onto narrow shoulders and heading down the remaining steps to the library basement.[1] They were on their way to English 309M, "Writing, Thinking, and Learning" which met in the computer classroom and was taught by Hugh Burns. Lora told Tammy how overwhelmed she was feeling by this semester's demands. As she talked, her dark features turned even darker, and she said she was afraid she was going to have to drop one of her courses.

Arriving at the trash cans at the end of the hall, Lora deposited her Pepsi cup and entered the computer classroom. She went directly to the terminal she had sat at the first day, and logged-on, entering her secret password. The screen flashed from sapphire blue to swimming-pool blue. She knew that her first task was to read the day's assignment entered earlier by the professor. Like the others arriving and logging-on, Lora momentarily ignored everything but the monitor, which read:

CLASS ASSIGNMENT —English 309M Dr Hugh Burns Lesson 3— 6 September
CLASS THEME: Getting to Know [the System], continued.
GENERAL INSTRUCTIONS: By now, you have completed the Lab's User's Manual. This class will be another exploration of how to use the network effectively, especially using [LINC] and [email].
ASSIGNMENT DETAILS:
1. CLASS ASSIGNMENT (5 min.): Print out a copy of this assignment.
2. INSTRUCTIONAL SYSTEM REVIEW (10 min.): Take a few moments to review the basic operations of the computer network and the computer keyboard.
3. CLASS DISCUSSION (9 min.) I will go over the official class roster and the syllabus for any of the new people who have added the course. I also have an announcement or two.
4. [LINC] (40 min.): Under Message Systems, enter the [LINC] program. From the MAIN conference, you will be led to the HERMES conference. There we will learn the ropes of online class discussion and discuss some of the ideas about "knowledge" and "writing across the curriculum."
5. [Email] (5 min.): Mail me a message about your experiences in the class thus far. How are you doing? Do you have any questions for me or for the staff. What are your goals for this class? [pick up thread somewhere, re; goals]
6. LOG-OFF (1 min.)
NEXT LESSON: Our first online discussion of Zinsser's ideas.
Scavenger Hunt "Preparation." Next Tuesday, you will bring to class the products of your Scavenger Hunt—your search for the best writers in your major area of study. You'll have to find five authors and have one prose sample for each author. [Xerox two copies—one for you and one for me.] Pick wisely, you will be learning to love the writers you select. You may

ask your professors, fellow students, me, lab assistants, or President Cunningham. Please assemble your collection, put a cover sheet on the package, and have it ready to turn in at the beginning of the period.

After scanning these pixelated instructions, Lora stared at step one: Print out a copy of this assignment. Tammy, who sat next to Lora, had already succeeded in activating her printer, so Lora asked her how she did it. Tammy pointed to a succession of keys on Lora's keyboard, and Lora pressed each in turn, her eyes anxiously darting between keyboard and monitor. The printer swung into noisy action and Lora sighed with relief, muttering, "Next time I think—I hope—I can remember all this!"

Waiting for the cacophony of printing to conclude, Lora and Tammy now turned in their chairs, propped their feet on the rungs, and continued their conversation. As students eventually activated all the dot matrix printers in the room, they either stared vacantly at their monitors or talked to their neighbors. Unlike traditional classrooms, this classroom made conversations easy; the room noise rendered quiet conversations confidential.

Lora told Tammy about a professor she had last semester who, as Lora recalls, had told her that she was an "external" person, one who could express herself beautifully when speaking, but not in writing. Lora continued her narrative, telling Tammy how this professor, Kate Frost, in giving a speech on campus, had used one of Lora's introductory sentences as an example of bad student writing. (In fact, Frost was referring to undergraduate papers in general.) The representative sentence, quoted later in a campus newspaper's article about Frost's speech, was "Beowulf is definitely a hero." *(The Daily Texan.)*[2] On hearing Lora's report of this speech, Tammy smiled benignly and then turned her attention once more to her terminal. "Anyway," continued Lora, "That's why I'm here. I've got to learn how to write."

The class assignment was now printed on a scroll of perforated computer paper which Lora folded hurriedly and tucked under her keyboard. There were two parts to the assignment. First, the students were to learn to use LINC for synchronous "real-time" conferencing. Lora had heard about this but had never tried it. She knew that in "real-time" conferencing, she and her classmates would conduct what amounted to written conversations. They would "talk" by using the keyboard to compose messages that would be instantaneously transmitted to everyone's computer screen.

The other part of the assignment was to send Burns an email message. Lora read the assignment again, this time in hard copy. Her slight body was coiled in a knot as she pulled at her ponytail. They had learned to send email to other class members and to Burns last week, and this hadn't been too hard. She had managed to successfully compose and send the following message to Burns:

IVE HEARD GOOD THINGS ABOUT YOU[3]

Most students had sent messages like "Hi!" Several students, anxious about computers or course-overload or both, had expressed an interest in dropping the class; Lora wondered if she should, too.

When Burns entered the classroom, he sat at the "center donut" and looked through his notes until he saw that most of his eighteen students had printed the daily assignment. Then he directed the students to bring their chairs to the center for a meeting. Students dragged and scooted their ragtag chairs to the conference area and sat with practiced nonchalance, not looking up till someone spoke. Burns, six foot three inches, got comfortable by sliding deeper into his chair, some of his height disappearing under the table.

Burns told the students that as they read the first text, *Writing to Learn* by William Zinsser (1988), they should begin reflecting on what this book implies about thinking and writing in their own fields. Soon they would be expected to relate this book to books by writers in their respective areas of study.

Today, Burns noted, they would be learning to use LINC, the synchronous conferencing program. He briefly went over details of the class assignment printout with them, but explained that in future classes they would need to get in the habit of getting the assignment directly from the computer. Lora, and others, appeared nervous—perhaps victims of "technostress," the "fear and avoidance of computer use" (Heim 1987, 201). The computer classroom was still intimidating to many.

Burns reiterated that before the end of class they would each need to send him an email message, telling about their experiences in class so far and describing their personal goals for the class. Most of the students in the class, including Lora, admitted they were not accustomed to defining or articulating their own goals in composition studies. Thus, the email assignment was worrisome. Lora, the youngest member of the class, was a sophomore and had listed her major as "undecided." The other seventeen students were seniors, four of whom were in their fifth year. Yet even these students stated that they were uncomfortable with too many choices. Too much independence, as one student remarked, resulted in a state of being "SOBB—Stressed Out Beyond Belief."

As the students returned to their terminals, some frowned, brows knitted. Several asked their neighbors, "Do you know what we're supposed to be doing? I wish he would just say what he wants!" Burns, when interviewed, said he believed that a certain amount of paradox and ambiguity would compel students to think and to collaborate. He believed that a certain amount of freedom would engender creativity. He was trying to induce students to take ownership over their own learning.

During today's class, Lora and her classmates mastered LINC, thanks to the coaching of Burns and his two teaching assistants. To do this, students logged-in to MAIN CONFERENCE and found a message from Burns welcoming them to LINC, giving them some brief online instructions on how to navigate, and asking them what they thought about writing across the curriculum. Lora read the message and then, following the instructions given, pressed a key which introduced a split screen on her monitor. On the top screen she composed a message of her own, looked it over, and sent it to the scroll of messages which was forming moment by moment on the lower screen as students responded at their own pace. Lora quickly mastered "scrolling," or scanning up and down through the tapestry of messages created by her and her classmates. Insecure about her writing abilities, and about her abilities to master computers, she spent most of her time reading the messages of others rather than composing messages of her own.

Lora entered the following message in her obligatory email message to Burns:

> Wow, am I confused. Should I continue this adventure in computer chaos? This class was recommended to me by Kate Frost. She felt like I had a lot to say, but didn't know how to say it. That is why I'm here. God help me! The people next to me are going so quickly. AHHHHHHHHH!
>
> Anyway, I'll continue now. I found out in my freshman year of college that I didn't know how to write a correct essay. What a discomforting thing to realize about yourself.
>
> Especially when your desire is to be an English major. Eventually, I would like to teach high school English. Are you scared for me or what? I'm hoping to better my writing with practice and help from you and the others in the class. Also, I'm a doof with computers, so I'm wanting to be enlightened in the computer world.

Class, which had begun at 3:30, was officially over at 4:45, and around this time students began logging-off and departing. There was no dismissal per se, nor were there good-byes, except among the handful of developing friendships.

"What are we supposed to do for next week?" Lora asked Tammy. Tammy pointed to the assignment on the bottom of the printout and said, "You know, the scavenger hunt for authors in our field."

"Oh, right," said Lora, stuffing the computer printout in her book bag and rolling her eyes. "Can I call you? I'm not sure I'm getting this. God, this is the semester from Hell!"

Lora then turned back to her computer and, with intense concentration, pressed a series of keys until she saw the message, "Do you want to log-off?" "Si! Si!" she called out emphatically and punched one more key. The screen now returned to its original shade of sapphire blue. Grabbing her book bag, Lora said a quick "Hasta mañana" to Tammy, and headed for her part-time job at a health food grocery store.

Notes

1. Pseudonyms have been provided for all students.
2. Kate Frost's speech had included this passage:
   Historically, most English departments have taught writing as the core of their endeavor, balanced with courses in literature, and many colleges and universities still adhere to this practice. But most faculty who teach writing publish about literature. And publication gets raises, tenure, promotion, and perks at this University. It is, after all, very difficult to concentrate on the implications of Shakespeare as a radical Marxist feminist when you've got fifty undergraduate essays on your desk, all of which begin: "Beowulf is definitely a hero."
3. Throughout this book, computer messages will be printed exactly as they appeared on the screen, including all typos, misspellings, and usage errors. Editorial comments will be added only if the meaning is especially unclear.

@5

First_Online_Conference

You type therefore you are . . .

—Tim, LINC

Burns structured the course around reading and responding to three texts: William Zinsser's *Writing to Learn* (1988), Robert Grudin's *Time and the Art of Living* (1982), and Geoffrey Wolff and Roberta Atwan's (eds.) *The Best American Essays 1989*.

Students had several weeks to read each text. During this time, they would engage in two parallel activities: First, they would respond to given chapters during in-class online conferences (LINCs) with their peers, and second, they would begin constructing an essay related to the reading of each respective text. My emphasis in this book is not on the course structure per se, but rather on the quality of the classroom dynamics when class goals were pursued online via computer network. This chapter, for example, explores student response to *Writing to Learn* by William Zinsser.

In order to contextualize specific student responses to Zinsser's book, it is first necessary to highlight the parts of this text to which students referred in their own writing. Zinsser, a nonfiction writer who has taught nonfiction writing at Yale and other colleges, states in *Writing to Learn* that his aim is "to demystify writing for the science types and demystify science for the humanities types" (Zinsser 1988, viii). He gives vivid examples of writing across the curriculum, including writing from professors "who cared about good writing even though their subject wasn't English" (35). He adds, "I've discovered that knowledge is not as compartmented as I thought it was. It's not a hundred different rooms inhabited by strangers; it's all one house" (11).

Zinsser confesses his earlier mistake in defining himself as a humanities person and subsequently avoiding the sciences, an avoidance that threatened to extend his undergraduate days at Princeton even after he had served in World War II. Returning to campus after the war, Zinsser met with Princeton's white-haired and revered Dean Root. To Zinsser's surprise, Dean Root took a personal interest in him and apparently waived standard requirements so that Zinsser could graduate. This episode is one that apparently struck a chord among several students in Burns's class who felt frustrated with various degree requirements in their fields. Zinsser states that although he avoided science as an undergraduate, he later discovered its bounty and in so doing became convinced that students could overcome their apprehension about certain disciplines by 1) finding accessible writings in the discipline and 2) using one's own writing "to wrestle with facts and ideas" (49).

Students were also impressed with Zinsser's compelling story of Willie Ruff's interdisciplinary seminar on rhythm. Ruff, a professor of music and African-American studies at Branford, pioneered a seminar which included artists, an art historian, a drummer, a dancer, a poet, a Bach scholar, a metallurgist, a geologist, a zoologist, and a physiologist—each contributing a perspective on *rhythm* as it figured in his or her respective discipline. Burns's students apparently liked this vivid example of interdisciplinary studies.

In a chapter on "Crotchets and Convictions" Zinsser spells out his consternation with the "pompous bureaucratic language of our times" (70). This notion also struck a chord with the students who, in their online talk, frequently expressed disdain for obscure academic prose.

As mentioned in chapter 4, Burns had directed students to read the first part of *Writing to Learn* and then to go on a "scavenger hunt" to find writers of quality in their respective fields. Economics majors were to find exemplary writers in the field of economics, psychology majors were to find exemplary writers in psychology, and so forth. The first essay would consist of each student's critique of the texts he or she had discovered, relating these texts to the idea of "writing to learn."

Again, when students logged-on at the beginning of the class, they found a well-organized class assignment previously entered into the network by Burns.

To launch the first online class discussion (LINC), Burns had entered the following instructions into the class computer system:

CLASS ASSIGNMENT—English 309M Lesson 4—
CLASS THEME: Writing to Learn

GENERAL INSTRUCTIONS: Today, we will use [LINC] to discuss Zinsser's ideas about writing to learn. Then, you will use [email] to write me a short note about the class [LINC].
ASSIGNMENT DETAILS:
1. CLASS ASSIGNMENT (5 min.): Print out a copy of this assignment.
2. (50 min.): Under Message Systems, enter the [LINC] program. From the MAIN conference, join the ZINSSER conference. There we will participate in an online class discussion on some of the ideas about "writing to learn" and "a liberal education."
4. [Email] (10 min.): As usual, please mail me a message about your experiences in the class thus far. Since I am writing these days about computers in education, would you please write me a short note about how you think these machines might be used in the future to teach writing and reading and speaking and business and art and whatever. Can I quote you? Let me know. If you are having any problems, please let me know.
5. LOG-OFF (1 min.)
ADMINISTRATIVE NOTES: Again, BAE *[Best American Essays]* has arrived at the Coop [a local bookstore].
NEXT LESSON: Finish Zinsser's WTL *[Writing to Learn]*. Think about some of your own "crotchets and convictions" and come prepared to share them.

The following LINC was composed by the students in response to the class assignment. (The transcript includes sequential numbers and senders' names.)

MAIN CONFERENCE, Lesson 4
1 Burns: Now that you have arrived over here, let me ask you to share some of your reactions to Writing to Learn. What did you think about his ideas? What is the feeling you have about the differences between "learning to write" and "writing to learn"? Let's get this first electronic conversation off to a flaming start, shall we?
2 Kara: HAS ANYONE READ THE MATERIAL FOR THIS CLASS?
3 Angela: I thought Zinsser was correct in saying that the responsibility for teaching students to write should not be solely on the Eng. department.
4 David: as hey
5 Kara: David, what does "as hey" mean?
6 Tammy: I think that he is correct when he says that writing is thinking on paper. The only problem I have is that I do not think clearly or in sequence. I jump around in my mind.

7 Tim: I really liked what Zinsser wrote about most writing based on literature having little to do with reality. I always hated reviewing old texts in high
school. Coercion rarely produces good writing.

8 Kara: As a future teacher, I think that computers are a fun as well as educational tool for learning. Does anyone think that computers should be the
sole teacher? I feel computers can be used to teach subjects, but not become
the sole administrator of information.

9 David: It seems that Zinsser's thoughts on the subject of writing reached
the University in last couple of years. I say this because of the emphasis
placed on writing components just like Gustavus Adolophus did. [This is a
reference to Zinsser's discussion of a college, Gustavus Adolphus,
which designated seventy-five courses, across the curriculum, as writing component courses and required three of these for graduation.]

10 Sandra: In the "real" world we're expected to write in our field of work,
but we never get any practice doing that in school.

11 George: After reading Zinsser's ideas of our approach to learning writing,
I felt that his approach has a great deal of potential. As he says, "It's by writing about a subject we're trying to learn that we reason our way to what it
means."

12 Tammy: As one who was thinking of entering the education field I agree
with Kara's point. The computer should not be the sole teacher, but can and is
used today to supplement our education and raise our level of learning . . .
hopefully.

13 David: Kara: I don't know what "as hey" means the TA typed it in.

14 Kara: The ideas mentioned of writing about a subject seem ideal in an
elementary classroom. It would help to write your own ideas and feelings
about a subject instead of "parroting" back what the teacher or author says.

15 Angela: I thought Zinsser made a good point when he said that students
writing for Eng profs are oftentimes "fuzzy and verbose" because they reach
for a literary style that they think the teacher wants. (Zinsser 1988, 13-14)

16 Todd: I feel that at college level, the idea of "learning to write" should still
be an ongoing process, but we should now be able to use writing as a key
to the learning process. It is sort of a continuous circle type thing; writing
to learn to write to learn to write . . . and so on. thank you.

17 Tammy: My research field for authors was in history and the authors I
chose have a way of writing to where you are able to picture the scene
instead of just reading facts about event that shaped our lives.

18 George: In essentially any field of study, communication is an integral
part of success. By being exposed to writing in various subjects during our

formal education, it can become second nature by the time we begin our professions.

19 Todd: all we are is dust in the wind . . .

20 Tammy: As of now I am going to use my degree and go to law school so being able to clearly communicate what I am thinking and trying to say is going to be invaluable in my profession.

21 Tammy: Todd: Like sands through the hourglass so are the days of our lives.

22 Casey: I totally agree with the concept that the teaching of writing should not lie solely in the hands of the English teacher. Students interests vary. Writing about these interests in the different subject areas only increases the desire to write. We have to be realistic, not everyone likes to write about literature. For so long the emphasis was placed in the English classroom to write about literature. It was not until recently, when people like Zinsser, started to explore the concept of writing across the curriculum. I think it's great. While students are learning how to become better writers, they are also learning about new subjects.

23 Sandra: I agree with Zinsser when he says that in an English class, students "reach for a 'literary' style that they think the teacher wants and that they assume is 'good English.' But this style is no part of who they are." [Quoting Zinsser 1988, 13-14]

24 Tim: I researched authors writing about business management. It was refreshing to find authors who wrote about the reality of business and got away from talking about organizational models and other such items which never exist in actual practice. An example of such writing comes from Robert H. Waterman: Our tools are measured toward measurement and analysis. We can measure the costs. But with these tools alone we can't really elaborate on the value of a Frito-Lay salesperson going that extra mile for the ordinary customer.

25 Sharon: I have really enjoyed the book so far. I agree with his ideas of writing to learn. I do believe that understanding of a topic comes easier when you are forced to put what you know down on paper. I think for one thing that after writing down what you know, you can actually "see" what you know. You will then be able to decide what more you need to learn about a topic, or, what it is that you do not understand about a topic. Writing also lets you get your thoughts down on paper; it helps to organize your thoughts so that they won't be so confused. I guess that ties in to what I said before. Once you get down what you know, your thoughts, you will be able to put them down in order so that you can figure out what it is that you do know. I think his idea that a liberal education include all the fields of study, that is, one that includes math, chemistry, etc., is a good notion. All people must be acquainted with these fields. Unfortunately, like he so aptly points out in his book, not all of us are equipped to understand all of these topics well. That is where writing to learn comes in handy. Besides helping a person become a better writer, employing writing in all courses will help a person better understand a topic. They will be able, in math, for instance, to write out a theory in their own words, sort of explain it to themselves, in order to obtain a better grasp of what it is they are having trouble with. This will also help a teacher in realizing what it is a student does not understand. Also, it takes the burden of teaching students how to write off the shoulders of the English teacher.

26 David: I think that the most important point that Zissner makes is that riting can be an enjoyable and valuable learning experience.

27 Josh: I think that Zinsser is right to say that writing shouldn't be left completely to the English department, however, I don't think that it should be included in every subject outside of one's own field. I do think that the early stages of writing (grammar, and comp.) do need to be taught by the English department. As far as writing in a specific discipline, I feel that writing should only be required or included in the upper levels of a person's specific field.

28 Holly: Actually, I really enjoyed the reading assignment in Writing to Learn. Mr. Zinsser is an interesting man who has obtained a dictionary of knowledge through his ability to communicate his own experiences to other people. His passion for his writing was obvious in that I was lured farther and farther into the piece. I, like Mr. Zinsser, have always feared (and therefore been turned off by lessons of the science origin. However, Mr. Zinsser's vivid descriptions about his research on the subjects were absolutely incredible. Unfortunately, I was unable to find an equally stimulating author in my field during my scavenger hunt on Thursday. The author that was most recommended to me was one named Veblen who wrote a book in the twenties. However, this book has escaped the U.T. library system. Due to this disappointing fact, I found myself starting all over. I was then recommended to look for the authors Deborah Abbott, Mary Galpin, and Zandra Rhodes, all of whom are frequent writers in fashion designers' magazines such as Threads, Women's World Daily, and Sew News. I found all of these authors, and some of the material was quite interesting. On the other hand, a lot of the material was dull and boring. I have decided to use these authors as models, but I hope to add more before we turn in our papers.

29 Tim: Todd: you type therefore you are . . .

30 Kara: My topic of study was language acquisition in young children. In education, teachers are often more limiting on the children's growth. One article was written by Edwin Newman, a former newscaster [in *Strictly Speaking*]. His style of writing was fun to read because it wasn't formal, he spoke with current vernacular of the 70's which helped me understand his points more clearly. "There remained the question of what bald men and women two feet tall would be wearing while the earth was going dry." Newman's sense of humor did not distract from his information, but added a daily something to parallel to the new knowledge he is sending us.

31 George: tammy—currently I am also planning on attending law school when I graduate. hopefully the ideas I encounter in this class will aid in my future occupation

32 David: golly Sharon you sure did write a lot!!! I guess you did enjoy the book.

33 Tiffany: I agree with Zinsser in that writing is definitely becoming a requirement for college classes and that motivation is crucial for successfulness. In regards to writing, I, too, feel that it is difficult to begin writing. I liked the terms "writing across the curriculum" as well as the "three R's." Overall, I thought it was amusing.

34 Angela: My areas of interest are Sociology and Law. The authors I found were Peter Berger, Harry Sullivan, and Bartlett Stoodley. The excerpt from Berger's book, The Noise of Solemn Assemblies, I used is entitled "The Task of Disestablishment." From Sullivan's book, The Fusion of Psychiatry and Social Science, I copied from the chapter entitled "A Note on Formulating the Relationship of the Individual and the Group." Finally, I used Stoodley's essay entitled "Social Class and Sociability in Fraternity Pledging."

35 Irene: My feeling, or more like my thoughts, are that "writing to learn" implies the discovery a writer makes as he/she is writing that he/she may still have something to learn before he writes about it. In other words, it needs to be clear, and if it's not clear in the writers mind, how can it be clear in the readers? Learning to write is just that . . . understanding what is necessary to put in and what should be left out.

36 Sharon: Yes, David, I did enjoy the book. So I am a little long winded, I can't help it, I have a habit of talking too much.

37 Holly: I agree with the aspect that learning to write is an ongoing process, and I feel that writing to learn should be used as a tool in all phases of education. If writing to learn begins when children are in grammar school, by the time they reach the college level, they will be clear, logical thinkers whose thoughts do not just jump around.

38 Josh: Anyone find any good authors on Economics? I got one, that's it.

39 Burns: Have any of you had a special teacher like Dean Root? You know the kind who let you discover what it is you know and why you know it? Writing is the key that opens the door, but so is conversing with others about our experiences.

40 Burns: Josh, who did you find?

41 Todd: I began researching an area of communications, specifically communications as they relate to interpersonal interaction and the notion of teamwork in todays busines sector. It is interesting to note how management theories have evolved over the years, beginning first with the traditional model which is demeaning and often cruel to the worker. Today, there are many different management styles, each with it's own agenda for completeing it's task. One thing that becomes obvious is the need for a certain amount of teamwork and personal interaction to get the job done properly. Thus, our communication skills are called upon if we are to interact with a team or group successfully. According to Herbert G. Hicks, from THE MAN-AGEMENT OF ORGANIZATIONS, "It has been demonstrated throughout human history that most individuals can achieve more of their goals or achieve them faster, easier, more completely, or more efficiently through organizations."

42 Angela: This is really cool!

43 George: although I am planning on attending law school, right now I am currently studying psychology. the 3 articles i found dealt primarily with the concept of perception. E.H. Gombrich writes: "What we get on the retina, whether we are chickens or human beings, is a welter of dancing light points stimulating the sensitive rods and cones that fire their messages into the brain."

44 Josh: Robert L. Heilbroner

45 Burns: Sharon, Long-windedness is well rewarded in this class. Efficiency is the first goal: faster, faster. Am I concerned about the quality of the ideas? Of course, but what I need to see first is that the ideas are ample, large, encompasssing, engaging, and worth hearing about.

46 Kara: Casey: I like the idea of a "desire to write". That is one thing that is important to me as a future educator. How can "writing to learn" motivate you to write? Tiffany: You did a great job starting this [LINC] session. Have more confidence—I like your ideas. Irene: How do you determine what is important or not important enough when writing?

47 Holly: I think that computers are probably the key to learning to write in the future. They are easy to use and seem as if they make the job easier.

With a word processing program, they allow you to move information around if your thoughts get all jumbled up.

48 Tammy: My authors in history are Barbara Tuchman, Bruce Catton, and Daniel Boorstein. Are there any other history majors out there with a more interesting author than Boorstein?

49 David: George: which psychology professors did you talk to? I talked to Dr. Thiessen and Dr. Horn

50 Todd: to tim and tammy: "We're just two lost souls swimming in a fish bowl, year after year, running over the same old ground, what have we found, the same old fears . . . "

51 Josh: Tammy—Are you a "DAYS" fan?

52 Angela: Lots of people going to Law School. So am I. When are y'all graduating, and where do you want to go to Law School. I am graduating this May, but I don't know yet where I want to go.

53 Burns: Tiffany—you are write, errrrr, right. The toughest thing about writing is beginning to write. Listen to all of these keystrokes today. Pretty weird for a "writing" class to actually be writing. Amazzzzzing!

54 Tiffany: By the way, I found some great writers over the weekend: David Elkind, Claire Cherry, and Louise Derman-Sparks. One of my professors recommended them, and coincidently, the first two were some of my personal favorites. I enjoy them because they present their material in a clear, concise, informative, as well as entertaining way.

55 Tim: I hope that all of us will begin to let our individuality show in our writing. We should all try to avoid trying to "sound learned" or strive for a style that we feel is expected of us. Let yourself come through.

56 Tammy: Josh: Of Course!! Todd: What drugs are you on? Where do you come up with this stuff?

57 Burns: You write, therefore you are. Well put, Tim.

58 Casey: I am an education major. I decided to research information on mainstreaming since that is such a big issue today. I found lots of info, but the authors I chose were Judy W. Woods, Rena B. Lewis, and Joseph R. Jenkins. I particularly liked the way Woods opened her first chapter, "Mainstreaming is a way to teach handicapped students in environments that do not restrict their educational potential, including placing handicapped students in the regular classroom with their nonhandicapped peers. \mainstraming is not only a reality of today's educational system but an educational standard as well. Responding to this mandate requires cooperation between regular and special education personnel as well as the ability to adapt to new roles and responsibilities."

59 Josh: I am also hoping to get into law school, mabye South Texas in Houston. It's supposed to be 'up and coming.'

60 Sandra: Writing to Learn gave me new hope! As a math major, the thought of having to write terrifies me. I always hated analyzing stories in English. I never knew what to write. Zinsser's approach to writing in one's own field makes a lot of sense. As Zinsser says,"Students will write far more willingly if they write about subjects that interest them and that they have an aptitude for." [Quoting Zinsser 1988, 13-14]

61 Holly: Kara: I think "writing to learn" can motivate people to write by letting them explore their own horizons and letting them write about their explorations. As someone said earlier, you can't coerce people to write, but if there is a subject that excites someone, they usually want to tell others about it. So, why not tell others through writing?

62 Tammy: Depends on the grades. I graduate next May and would like to attend either UT, Texas Tech, or Virginia. UT and Virginia are going to be a reach though

63 Burns: Holly, see if you can find this Veblen person. It sounds really interesting. What is fashion design? I mean, what are "fashion designer's magazines"? Vogue? McCalls? Like that?

64 Todd: tammy: don't you listen to p. floyd? you know, "we don't need no educatin, we don't need no thought control" that kind of stuff.

65 Jake: I did my research on legal writing, and I was able to find a number of books specifically devoted effective legal writing. The interesting thing was that all of the authors preached strongly against the unnecessary use of legal jargon and archaic lawerly phrases such as: "hitherto the party of the first part . . . " etc . . . Instead, they suggested a "plain and direct style."

66 Kara: My other two authors are Roger Brown and Jean Berko Gleason. I want to check on Howard Gradner's work, too. Brown and Gleason both are research informationalists. I enjoy statistics and details, things that can be used as solid proof of the unknown.

67 Josh: In defense of Todd, you can't beat Pink Floyd.

68 Sharon: In my search for authors, I found three that represent good writing in my field. I am aspiring to be an English teacher so I looked for books on how to teach writing. My favorite book is Writing with Style. He [John Trimble] has a chapter on people he calls "literary prudes." People who diligently adhere to rules, such as,"never end a sentence with a preposition." A favorite passage of mine is when he describes these people as belonging to a sect and gives their "Articles of Faith" and the rules they abide by. He even calls grammar books their "Sacred Texts." Now, if

humurous, well-thought out, easily understood writing is not good writing,
I don't know what is.

69 Tiffany: Kara, I agree!! I think computers are great for reinforcement of
learning but should never replace the teacher.

70 Angela: What books did you find? Those sound great!

71 Josh: Does anyone know if it is required that you go to law school in
Texas, to be able to practice here??

72 Tammy: O.K. guys. Whatever you say. I'm not really into p. floyd but I'll
take your word for it.

73 Steve: I am studying economics and I wasn't expecting to find much in
the way of good writing in that field. At least not good writing in the way in
an English professor would be looking for. I talked to a couple of econ professors and they echoed my feelings, though my regional econ prof told me
two he admired. So I have only two writers, at least for the moment. These
two are Robert Heilbranner and John Kenneth Goldbraith. I'm planning on
using Heilbranner's "Worldly Philosophers." I'm not sure what I'll use from
Goldbraith.

74 Holly: Mr. Burns: NO! Fashion design magazines are more like Women's
World Daily and Thread News. Although Vogue is a good inspirational tool,
McCall's is more like Better Homes and Gardens—for the housewife!

75 Angela: Josh: No, you do not have to go to Law School in the state in
which you plan to practice. You just have to pass that state's Bar Exam.

76 Todd: Another important aspect of teamwork, is the structure and goals
of that particular team. It makes no sense to have uneccesary or extraneous
members on a team. A clear cut goal and purpose are vital to meeting a
team objective. A key aspect to a successfully functioning team is leadership
and trust among the teams members.

77 Irene: I'm back again (I know you've all been waiting) to let everyone
know what I found on the `scavenger hunt'. To tell you the truth, I was a little
confused about what I was looking for in the first place. But what I did finally
come up with was writing on writing, and it turned out to be quite amusing.
The first author, Kurt Vonnegut, wrote what he called an autobiographical
collage. In it, I found a chapter in which he shared some valuable opinions
on writing. Here's a little ditty "When you yourself put words on paper,
remember that the most damning revelation you can make about yourself is
that you do not know what is interesting and what is not." I also got some
good stuff from Wayne C. Booth and John Trimble, of the University of Texas.

78 Lora: Yes, I actually read the material. Zinsser says that the reader doesn't
have to be familiar with the subject he/she is reading about. He also says

that the writer must be able to present the info in good narrative order. I agree with him. When I opened the book, I didn't know what I would be reading. I certainly didn't expect cocaine or heroin. [This is an allusion to Zinsser's providing an example of an article written by a doctor but accessible to the general public.] because of the way the material was presented, it was easy for me to understand and really get a feel for. i especially liked the jazz musican and the neurologist getting together to study rhythm. they helped each other understand more about what one another were doing and how their studies compliment each other. ok now on to so of the "good stuff" i found. at first when you announced this assignment i thought immediately about a professor i had last semester.her name is kate frost im using a speech she gave last semester about how much we as students are getting robbed of our education.

79 Sharon: Todd, you seem to have many philosophical ideas. Have you by any chance seen "Bill and Ted's excellent adventure," and are you an adament follower of "Days of Our Lives?"

80 Denise: I thought Zinsser did an excellent job of explaining that if a subject has some "avenue" which leads to humanity, it can be found interesting. I am pre-med and have had to read many dry readings. The only way I made it through physics was to remember that one day I will be helping people. I can also relate to his indecisiveness during his years at Princeton University. His sentences are very clear and easy to understand. He points out that one of the greatest problems with writing is understanding the language. I think too many writers try to write in an "intelligent" way and often confuse the reader. He points out that it is also important to only give necessary information; brevity has always been a problem for me. Other problems in writing are keeping the reader interested and following a logical order. These sound easy, but I think most of us know it's not. The authors I found are mostly literary critics since my major is Spanish and I have to criticize lots of literature.

81 Tony: Just letting all of you know that I do exist.

82 Steve: I got a couple of econ writers my regional econ prof gave me, let me know if you're interested.

83 Kara: The books I skimmed are "Studying Language Development" and "A First Language." I LOVE CHILDREN AND I WANT TO TEACH NOW!

84 Jake: As to lawering, I once heard some interesting advice. Unboubtably you have read some fine print. How would you feel about writing it.

85 Casey: Kara, A desire to write comes through writing on topics of interest. And learning comes from enhancing knowledge of these interests.

So ended the first online discussion in 309M, "Writing, Thinking, and Learning." Perhaps the major point about this LINC is best expressed by Burns's message (53) above: "Listen to all of these keystrokes today. Pretty weird for a 'writing' class to actually be writing. Amazzzzzing!"

@6

Participation_in_Discussion

Survey question: The kinds of "conversations" I liked best on LINC:

The ones that went wild—very funny and really outrageous
—Holly

Watching people try to make heads or tails out of the Grudin book
—Josh

Light hearted brawls of opinion disagreement
—Kara

IT'S EASY TO FAULT THE LINC SESSION PRESENTED IN THE PREVIOUS chapter for all the things it was *not*. It was not a well-organized discussion with a beginning, middle and end leading to a consensus or conclusion. It was not tightly coherent; there was not a clear flow from one idea to the next. Persuasive elements were not clearly delineated, and students did not stay "on task." Indeed, by traditional standards, this discussion was chaotic and lacking in many respects.

Let's now shift perspectives and consider what it *was*. One startling fact is that in this half hour discussion, all nineteen of the students in the class spoke up. The plurality of voices contributed to its chaotic quality. Yet, the fact is that all the players ran out onto the field. No one remained on the bench. This is all the more significant when one considers that each student spoke voluntarily without being "called on" or given permission by an authority.

The conversational topics emerged from student response to Zinsser's *Writing to Learn* (1988) and the scavenger hunt relating to it. Student comments seemed more candid than is the norm for class discussion, particularly early in the semester when students are typically trying to "read" the teacher and shape their comments accordingly.

Students, for example, engaged readily in critiquing common school experiences. Tim mentioned that he "always hated reviewing old texts in high school." Sandra noted that "In the 'real' world we're expected to write in our field of work, but we never get any practice doing that in school." Kara made a pejorative remark about the common "parroting" of what the teacher says. Continuing in this vein, Casey noted that "not everyone likes to write about literature." Sandra picked up on this saying, "I always hated analyzing stories in English. I never knew what to write." While these criticisms were fairly safe in that they were directed toward *previous* schooling, Lora took a risk by extending the critique to this university. She referred to a professor who, in a recent talk, told students they were getting "robbed" of an education. In my experience, it is highly unusual for a student to introduce a topic like this in the midst of a college class discussion.

Students also critiqued jargon and stilted language. Angela paraphrased Zinsser (1988, 13–14) in her comment that students are "'fuzzy and verbose' because they reach for a literary style that they think the teacher wants." Jake alluded to the fact that the authors in his field of legal writing "preached strongly against the unnecessary use of legal jargon and archaic lawerly phrases such as: 'hitherto the party of the first part . . . '" Instead, they suggested a 'plain and direct style.'" Sharon referred to John Trimble's chapter on rule bound "literary prudes"—"People who dilegently [sic] adhere to rules . . . " Denise noted that "too many writers try to write in an 'intelligent' way and often confuse the reader." Kara spoke highly of Edwin Newman whose style she appreciated because "he spoke with current vernacular of the 70's which helped me understand his points more clearly."

Although the assignment directed students to relate their major field of study to writing, it is interesting that the students took this a step further and directly addressed their anticipated professions. Law school emerged as a topical thread when Tammy, George, Angela, Josh, and Jake all discovered this common goal. Kara announced her intention of becoming an elementary school teacher, and Holly announced her interest in fashion design.

Students asked for help and received it: Josh asked if anyone could recommend authors on economics, and Steve responded. Josh also asked whether it was required to go to school in the same state in which you intended to practice, and Angela provided the answer. Tammy asked if anyone could recommend a history writer more interesting than Boorstein. It was clear that networking—in the sense of asking acquaintances for good leads—had occurred in the scavenger hunt as well; several students mentioned that they had asked professors to recommend books in their fields of specialty. Holly and Kara discovered a common interest in motivation. Said Holly to Kara, "If there is a subject that excites someone, they usually want to tell others about it."

The sheer number of ideas and concepts on the conversational table added up to a smorgasbord. In this one discussion, students had access to a wealth of information about each other. They also shared thoughts about approximately fifty different authors considered to be exemplary writers in their fields.

At the 1994 Computers and Writing Conference, conference organizer Eric Crump referred to a creative person on the planning committee as an "idea hamster." When I later queried him via email as to the origin of this phrase, he said he had found it in the "Jargon Watch" section of *Wired Magazine* (2.06): "Idea hamster—Someone who always seems to have his or her idea generator running. That guy's a real idea hamster. Give him a raw concept and he'll turn it over 'til he comes up with something useful." When network discussions are at their best, they appear to transform an entire class into idea hamsters.

John Goodlad, in his 1984 study of high schools, found an "emotional flatness" and an absence of "overt expressions of joy, anger, and other feelings" (Goodlad 1984, 243) in the classrooms he studied. In the college classes I have attended and observed, I have noticed a similar pattern. It is significant, then, that overt expressions of emotion *did* occur in the network discussion presented here. For example, Angela exclaimed, "This is really cool!" (apparently referring to network discussion) and Kara virtually shouted (by using all capitals) "I LOVE CHILDREN AND I WANT TO TEACH NOW!"

The expression of strong emotion on networks has, in fact, been noted by many teachers and researchers, and not always with glee. Indeed, the expression of negative emotions, and open hostilities, is so common that it has received the label "flaming" and is widely considered a serious problem in network discussion. (Flaming will be discussed in chapter 18.) In the network conversation just presented, negative emotions were not expressed in antisocial or hostile ways. However, the reader may have noticed some strange conversational twists having to do with Pink Floyd and *Days of Our Lives*. Just what was *that* all about? This occurrence is part of underlife. While many have considered such underlife comments to be trivial and disruptive, I find them to be of central importance. Underlife represents the struggle of students to define themselves and to expand the curriculum to include questions of special interest to them. (Underlife will be discussed more fully in chapter 13.)

Since wide-based participation is one of the features of networked discussion most often noted, I'd like to discuss class participation in general, then turn to class participation in the networked environment.

In earlier times, when classroom discourse was typified by teacher lecture, there was plenty of talk—but most of it was teacher talk. The lecture mode of education fit a transmission model in which the teacher's task was to announce and explain knowledge. The students, in turn, wrote down the "facts" which comprised this knowledge, memorized them, and reproduced them during written tests or oral recitations. The lecture has largely been replaced by whole-class discussion and—to a lesser extent—small-group discussion. While both forms of discussion provide opportunities for active dialogue, the research indicates that there are often problems in the way discussion is implemented. Even when teachers value student-centered discussion, teacher-centered patterns persist for a variety of reasons.

Opportunities to develop personal responses to texts, or to selected topics, and to share and build upon these responses in a social context, are rare. The student is generally cast in a passive mode, with the task of learning "about" something. James Marshall studied the class discussion of six high school English teachers selected on the basis of their reputations for excellence. In interviewing these teachers, he identified two conflicting purposes many of them had for class discussion:

> On the one hand, teachers felt discussions were an opportunity for "interaction," a chance for students' "self discovery" . . . On the other hand, though, teachers also felt that discussion should "go somewhere," should stay "on track" and away from "irrelevancies." (Marshall 1988, 41)

Along with these conflicting purposes, teachers also expressed contradictory pedagogical strategies. On the one hand, these six English teachers felt they should function as interpretive guides; on the other hand, they thought they should eventually be able to "remove themselves, disappear, and 'watch it happen'" (44). Despite their professed goals, these exemplary teachers "dominated most of the large-group discussions" (42) and wove both student and teacher comments together so as to fulfill a teacher-determined "interpretive agenda" (44).

In 1979, Hugh Mehan found class discussions he observed were most often teacher led and characterized by what he termed the traditional pattern of IRE, i.e., teacher Initiates, student Responds, teacher Evaluates (Mehan 1979). The consensus of Marshall, Mehan, and others is that students have only rare opportunities to construct their own interpretations alone or in dialogue with their peers. In missing out on an opportunity to forge their own interpretations, students also miss out on opportunities to emotionally connect with texts.

John Dewey was one of the first to deplore the absence of opportunities for students to actively participate in constructing knowledge: "That education is not an affair of 'telling' and being told, but an active and constructive process is a principle almost as generally violated in practice as conceded in theory" (Dewey 1916, 38).

Why do teachers persist in the IRE sequence even when they want to create a different kind of discussion? It is only fair to mention the constraints within which teachers typically work. For example, John Goodlad notes, "Society expects teachers to be in charge of their classrooms" (Goodlad 1984, 109) and "the demands of managing a relatively large group of people in small space may become a formidable factor in determining and limiting pedagogy" (111). The IRE sequence surely reinforces teacher control of classroom talk. Douglas Barnes hypothesizes that teachers may use a "rapid series of questions" as a means of control and behavior management (Barnes 1990, 81) because to allow time for exploration is also to allow time for misbehavior. He suggests that teachers may cling to a transmission model of education because it enables them to survive in the classroom.

Courtney Cazden notes that teachers need to hold the attention of a large number of diverse students. This need leads teachers to confine the contributions of individual students to brief and quickly-delivered comments. She observes that requirements for conciseness and speed are not necessarily issues in out-of-school conversations, and students may not understand or welcome these artificial restraints. Furthermore, she points out that in class discussion, students must obtain the floor while their comments are still precisely relevant. Timing restraints can operate against the nurturing of tacit thought, especially among students who need time to think and compose their comments (Cazden 1988).

Catherine Krupnick also notes the constraints of timing issues in discussion. She found Harvard instructors to be concerned with

> . . . keeping the flow of discussion going by getting most of their contributions from the first students to volunteer. As a result, classroom discourse is biased toward assertive students who have the quickest response time. Participation becomes based on quick thinking instead of deep or representative thinking. (Krupnick 1985, 22)

Krupnick also found that the quick responders and slow responders soon comprise dominant and subordinate conversational groups.

It is generally assumed that a key feature of a good discussion is vocal participation by all attending. The group as a whole benefits from hearing a wide spectrum of perspectives. Individual students benefit because they can make their own tacit knowledge more explicit, and they can benefit from the questions, challenges, and information their talk elicits from others. There is also evidence showing that self-esteem and self-confidence are related to active participation in classroom discussion (Krupnick 1985; Welch 1984).

Large classes make it impossible, even under ideal circumstances, for every student to have abundant opportunities for talk. While it would be a mistake to equate not talking aloud in whole-class discussion with passivity, still some researchers suggest that heavy reliance on whole-class discussion fosters passivity and "spectatorhood" among some students. This occurrence is of special concern in light of evidence that some students are *consistently* quiet, or even silent, during whole-class discussions (Sadker and Sadker 1986; Tornow 1993). Teacher and researcher Margaret Cintorino reflected on her own schooling: "We learned to still our young, clamorous voices, to be quiet, and to remain quiet for much of the school day. We inherited, from the beginning of our school years, a legacy of student silence" (Cintorino 1993, 23). Similarly, Anthony Adams noted the prevalent reluctance of teachers to appreciate "the natural rebellion and vigor" of student expression (Adams 1984, 121).

Some students may simply choose not to talk; they may not be negatively affected by choosing silence. However, as Robert Probst notes, "the ideas of the more vocal student are likely to command attention while the equally valuable ideas of more timid students may wither away unnoticed" (Probst 1984, 45). A study by Joan Long suggests that the tendency not to talk in classrooms increases as students get older (Long 1986). And Krupnick finds that quiet people are less noticed in the workplace and thus less apt to be promoted (Krupnick 1992). Thus, silence in discussion may not only hamper the exercise of talk for the reasons outlined earlier, but also may foster habits of silence which limit one's opportunities later in life.

Another problem with standard teacher-led class discussion is gender bias which acts in two principal ways. First, it has been reported that teachers may unwittingly respond more often to boys than to girls and to provide boys with more elaborated responses than they do girls (Sadker and Sadker 1986; Krupnick 1992). Second, boys may, in general, be more comfortable than girls in speaking in the public arena of a whole-class discussion (Tannen 1990). Sadker and Sadker found that in both elementary and secondary school classrooms, boys are ten times as likely to call out and demand the teacher's attention. Moreover, teachers respond differentially to boys and girls:

> When boys call out, teachers tend to accept their answers. When girls call out, teachers remediate their behavior and advise them to raise their hands. Boys are being trained to be assertive; girls are being trained to be passive— spectators relegated to the sidelines of classroom discussion. (Sadker and Sadker 1986, 513)

Krupnick also found that boys get called on more often than girls and they participate more in teacher-led class discussions. She attributes this to the fact that they are quicker to raise their hands even if they don't know the answer. She believes that those who remain silent, mostly girls, constitute a "silence ghetto" and learn habits of silence which they carry into their adult lives (Krupnick 1992).

In summarizing research on gender bias in classroom discussion, Krupnick notes that "talkativeness studies in general have concluded that men dominate mixed discussion groups everywhere—both within the classroom and beyond" (Krupnick 1985, 19). She notes that in mixed-sex conversations, women are interrupted far more frequently than men, and that once interrupted they may refrain from participating in the discussion for the remainder of the class period (20). In a study of Harvard classrooms, she found that discussion frequently proceeded in "runs" of all-male talk or all-female talk. The men tended not to interrupt each other, and thus the men's runs were longer. The women spoke in "bursts" and frequently interrupted, or overlapped, each other. She concluded that females were "at the bottom of the conversational heap—some passive, others competing for the scarce resource of conversational space" (20).

Cheris Kramarae and Paula Treichler conducted an ethnographic study of gender and power in a graduate course at the University of Illinois taught by three white, male instructors. They found that the discussion was dominated by a small group of (predominantly male) students, and that students perceived that "authorization to talk depended on certain credentials, including the quality of the product (*what* was said, *how* it was said), expertise, disciplinary training, and ability to engage comfortably in 'little professor' talk" (Kramarae and Treichler 1990, 45–46). They found that females typically saw talk as fulfilling a different role than did males. Males, including the instructors, tended to see talk as a way to communicate and defend a position, whereas females were more apt to see talk as a form of exploration. Said one female student:

> Because the discussion tends to occur on two levels, I find it cautionary not to join in. At the surface level there is a call to interact freely and openly, but there seems to be an underlying tension or competition over which reading will emerge victorious. . . . Students don't explore each other's positions on ideas so much as they vie for attention and compete to get their own ideas to be heard. (49)

In their post-class interviews, females in this study frequently expressed a desire for an opportunity to discover their meaning as they talked, whereas the males often made critical remarks about the voicing of ideas that were "ill-conceived or unclearly expressed" (47).

Ethnicity is another factor which can affect patterns of participation. Differing cultures foster a variety of stances toward class discussion as well as widely varying norms and strategies for participation. When a student's expectations and norms differ from those of the dominant group in the class, or of the teacher, problems can arise. Several researchers have found that certain discourse communities are accustomed to collaborative and/or overlapping speech as opposed to solo performances. (Tannen 1990; Au 1980; Philips 1972). Both L.W. Fillmore and Valerie Pang in separate publications discuss the reticence many Chinese-American students exhibit during class discussions due to their strong respect for authority (Fillmore 1990; Pang 1990). A multicultural student population is going to respond differentially to the talk norms and expectations in the typical American classroom.

Some, though certainly not all, of the participation problems common to class discussion are mitigated in network discussion. Trent Batson notes the sense of "engagement" students typically exhibit when using the network (Batson 1989a). Jerome Bump noted that the network discussion in his college classes was "truly egalitarian" and "student-centered" (Bump 1990, 41).

He found the most remarkable result of his study to be that network discussion was "more popular than small face-to-face and whole-class discussion combined" (54). Marshall Kremers conducted conventional class discussions with basic writers three hours a week and network discussions with the same students two hours a week. He noted:

> In conventional class discussions—these students were shy, reticent, unwilling to engage me or each other in dialogue. Yet during the ENFI [network] sessions (which they attended more faithfully than the conventional meetings), they wrote with enthusiasm. (Kremers 1990, 38)

Participation factors of particular interest include 1) turn-taking and timing, 2) participation by the shy, 3) participation by ethnic minorities, and 4) participation by women. I will address each in turn.

Turn-Taking and Timing

Networked discussion typically brings every student into active participation, perhaps because a student need not wait for a turn, but can *speak* at will. Also, a student can take as much time as desired to complete a thought without fear of being interrupted. One of Bump's students wrote on an evaluative questionnaire, "I also felt like everyone had more of a chance to say what they wanted and however much they wanted without having someone interrupt them" (Bump 1990, 54). This may in part account for Wayne Butler and James Kinneavy's finding that, on the network, responses "were considerably longer than oral responses typical of students in the traditional classroom" (Butler and Kinneavy 1991, 100).

Michael Spitzer noticed that students were not under pressure to make a comment at a precisely relevant moment:

> If you choose, you can comment on the earlier topic, the one everyone has left. By so doing, you may spark new ideas among those who have moved on, or new users, and so that topic is resurrected with a new vigor. In computer conferencing, topics become "hot" like this all the time. (Spitzer 1989, 193)

Similarly, Cynthia Selfe noted that, "In the electronic environment of my class, those quieter members and those who wanted to mull over their responses before they contributed were no longer silenced or marginal in our discussions" (Selfe 1990, 127). Denise Murray concurred: "There is no need to negotiate for time to express an utterance" (Murray 1985, 213).

Mehan was a co-investigator in a study comparing face-to-face discussion and computer-network discussion in his course, "Classroom Interaction." In this study, Quinn, Mehan, Levin, and Black found that an IRR (Initiation, Response, Response) sequence tended to replace the traditional IRE sequence because many students had an opportunity to respond to each question posed. Additionally, the linear pattern that typified classroom discussion was replaced by simultaneous discussion of multiple topics (Quinn et al. 1983).

Participation by the Shy

Because network discussion reduces the effect of static cues (gender, race, other aspects of appearance, artifacts such as clothing and furniture, etc.) and dynamic cues (nonverbal behavior such as nodding, frowning, etc.) (Sproull and Kiesler 1986, 1495), it appears to provide a comfort zone in which a wide range of students choose to participate. Batson believes networked interaction gives shy students a chance to speak up and be heard. He elaborates, "Since I myself was a shy student in college and didn't speak up much, I can't help thinking of all those like me out there who maybe have good ideas but are afraid, in face-to-face conversations, to take the risk of saying something" (Batson 1989a, 13).

One of the students in Bump's study wrote: "Even the people who don't talk as much in class find it very easy to communicate through the computers" (Bump 1990, 55). Shoshana Zuboff, observing network interaction in corporate settings, noted:

> People who regarded themselves as physically unattractive reported feeling more lively and confident when they expressed themselves in a computer conference. Others with soft voices or small stature felt they no longer had to struggle to be taken seriously in a meeting. (Zuboff 1988, 370–71)

Participation by Minorities

Network discussion has also been reported to foster increased participation by minorities. Bump, for example, found computer discussion restored voices to all students, regardless of "sex, race, class, or age" (Bump 1990, 55). Faigley reported that a student from Sri Lanka wrote that the computer removed his foreign accent. A Hispanic student in Faigley's class wrote, "One comment had no more impact than another because the computer has only one color and the same print" (Faigley 1992, 182).

However, Susan Romano found that Hispanic students in her LINCed class who spoke up did not fulfill the "egalitarian narrative" as described by proponents of networked classrooms. For example, one woman claimed that it was worth losing her "hispanic identity" if that was the price to pay in getting a higher education (Romano 1993). Hispanic students spoke, but either supported the dominant discourse or challenged it circuitously. In cases like this, LINCs certainly do not dissolve prejudices, but perhaps open limited opportunities for examining them.

Participation by Women

There have been mixed findings about participation by women. Some informal studies have indicated that women in mixed groups speak more on the network, and are more apt to maintain a minority or unpopular position than in a face to face discussion. However, Paul Taylor analyzed discourse in a networked class he taught and discovered he wrote "more messages to male students and that those messages were longer than the ones I wrote to female students" (Taylor 1993, 97), thus indicating that online discourse can echo the teacher gender bias found in the traditional classroom discourse studies cited earlier. Moreover, Pamela Takayoshi found that network communication can silence women by ignoring or disregarding their contributions (Takayoshi 1994).

Some women, however, have been outspoken about finding "netspace" to be a welcoming space. Kathleen Yancey wrote of online space as:

> A place where the rules are still being made, and arguably the one place I've been in my entire life that wasn't completely mapped and interpreted and governed by men first. A place where there isn't an ideal posited on the masculine so that from the get-go I am different at best and pathological at worst. Put differently, a place where women can talk. (Yancey 1996a, 2)

Sherry Turkle found that the Internet is "a significant social laboratory for experimenting with the constructions and reconstructions of self that characterize postmodern life. In its virtual reality, we consciously construct ourselves" (quoted in McCorduck 1996, 160). Having found the ideas of Jacques Lacan, a French psychiatrist, to be helpful to her in her own self-explorations and self-constructions, she said of him:

> I think he'd have been very excited by the idea of this new space for the weaving of the symbolic order, as he called it. The Web is a very Lacanian idea—chains, knots, weaving, tissues of meaning, people building meaning out of

linking and association, not linearly but associatively—these are all his metaphors. (160)

She goes on to say, "But I did not live these ideas until I had experiences on the Internet. Then they became far more real to me" (161). Turkle notes, "Perhaps the single most underreported aspect of our time is that the most compelling and serious discourse about new technologies and cultural change proceeds from women" (109). Elsewhere, she says, "Computer technology is moving in a direction that makes it easier for women to see it as something that is culturally theirs" (*Technology Review* 1996, 46). Her research reveals that girls were never so much phobic about computers as they were merely reticent; this reticence was based on the fact that computers were "culturally constructed as male." Now, Turkle says, "The Net is all about chatting with people, being with people" (46).

Lester Faigley notes that in one of his online classes, the women participated freely and, because of this, began to wonder why it was so difficult to speak in conventional classes. This observation also caused the teacher and male students to confront the issue of silencing (Faigley 1992, 198).

Some have begun to question the utopian claims that were at first made for participation in networked classrooms (Romano 1993; Hawisher and Selfe 1991; Regan 1993). In particular, the claims for egalitarian discourse must be put in perspective. While participation levels are to be applauded, the content of the discussions can be disturbing at times. Romano's point is well-taken when she says instructors need the freedom to not measure up to utopian claims so they "notice what it is that students do with words without trying to fit these words into a grand narrative." She asks, therefore, "What are the multiple phenomena—positive, negative, and polyvalent—that networking facilitates or mandates?" (Romano 1993, 27)

Teachers in these new classrooms are alternately delighted and dismayed with what occurs. Time and space for reflection and debriefing with peers is important. The increased participation brings incredible complexity into the classroom. This new environment is not for the faint of heart. It is part playground, but also part town meeting, bull session, sensitivity training, and talk radio—as well as college classroom. In computer-network discussion, the teacher no longer mediates the conversation by calling on students and responding to their comments with a direct or indirect evaluation. He or she no longer controls the conversation (Bump 1990; Faigley 1989; Moran 1990; Peyton 1990).

While many teachers welcome this shift in pedagogy that places increased responsibility on students to conduct their own explorations, virtually all teachers nevertheless find this new kind of discussion disconcerting—at least initially. Says Batson, "Even teachers who claim to prefer 'student-centered' education are bothered when it actually happens" (Batson 1989b, 252). Burns's response to these changing patterns of participation will be addressed later.

@7

Irene

Ask yourself when was the last time you laughed so hard that a tiny tear started to dribble out of the corner of your eye.
—Irene, "Fun and the Art of Living"

My convictions about how to write in my style have grown stronger. i am not as afraid, or even ashamed to put my voice on paper.
—Irene, email

IRENE WAS A TALL, SHY, SENIOR MAJORING IN ENGLISH. WITH HER IVORY skin, delicate features, and gray-blue eyes, Irene had an almost waiflike presence. Her gutsy language on the computer, therefore, came as somewhat of a shock. But language was something that interested Irene intensely. In fact, she planned to write for a living.

On the first day of class, Irene happened to sit next to Lora, and since Lora saw Irene as a role model, she pumped Irene for information about good courses in the English Department. On this day, Irene—nervous about computers—sent the following email message:

I might drop this course

At the next class, Irene sat on the other side of the room where she remained for the rest of the course. When directed in CLASS ASSIGNMENT to post her goals to email, she included the following:

I don't think I'll ever get to the point where I feel I know it all, ie. "I'm a writer, by God, and you can't possibly tell me anything useful . . . I'm an 'artist!' Ha!" Consequently, I think using computers as a forum for discussion is excellent for someone like me. And: I digress. I have found in all the writing classes

I've taken at UT, that it's almost stiflingly frightening to criticize peer's work. Not only that, but the fear of asking for advice from peers and teachers often turns me away from suggestions that could have otherwise changed my writing for the better. Thus, with this silent exchange, I expect a (for lack of a better word) wimpier way to get help

A week later, she sent the following message to Burns:

Well, Hugh, (if I may be so informal as to use your first name), I'm not feeling too creative today, so I may not be able to come up with "ideas for the future" right now. But I will be thinking. I guess on a broader note, I think computers are much easier than I once thought. It may be a less personal way of teaching, but its clandestine quality makes it kind of fun. You know. . . sort of a mystery.

Irene, like many students, addressed Burns as "Hugh" on the network, yet never addressed him by his first name on other occasions.

A week after sending the above message, Irene found herself confused about the major assignment relating to Zinsser's *Writing to Learn*. As mentioned in chapters 4 and 5, Burns had explained that students were to read Zinsser's book and then go on a "scavenger hunt" to find authors relating to their major field of study. Students would base their first paper on their readings of these authors, focusing on the idea of "writing to learn." Irene wrote an email message to Burns, stating her frustration in no uncertain terms:

O.K. I'm going to try to make this as simple as possible. I find this assignment highly problematic, because my field is supposedly writing; and not only writing, but writing fiction, and the assignment requires that we get quotes from non-fiction. The way I solved this was to get work from Wayne C. Booth, who sometimes writes on writing, from Kurt Vonnegut, who talks and writes on writing, and from John Trimble, who teaches at UT and has a stylebook. . . . Prithee, give me a clue as to what direction I need to go now!

While scanning the electronic mailbox for a response from Burns, Irene came across this message sent two days previously by Lora:

Hey Irene. I'm lora. We sat next to each other the first day of class. You said you were thinking about dropping, but you didn't. Good for you. Stick out this journey through computer choas [*sic*]. I'd like for you to read some of my stuff, if and when i get any so-called stuff. Okay? Let me know. I would also like to talk to you about some profs. See you. Bye!!!

And, minutes later, an answer from Burns, including the following:

Booth, great! Vonnegut, wonderful! Trimble, a stroke of sheer genius. Prithee is not dry. It shows some flash, some enthusiasm and warmth. That's what I want. I am not in this class to be bored by student writing. And I wasn't bored by your message today. So do it like that.

Irene, meanwhile, answered Lora:

well, lora if i remember correctly you sit in the corner and i would be glad to read your stuff. but why, praytell, choose me? just curious. anyway i guess you can tell how much i hate using the "change case" key. remember how i told you i was taking a course with trimble. well it's turning out to be a very personal kind of course, and if you enjoy a class and a teacher that isn't hung up on pretension, bullshit literary theory, and self-righteousness, you'll like trimble a lot. how do you feel about this anonymity stuff? i mean isn't it weird to talk to people through computers? sure you know who the people are, but its almost like telepathy. like you dont even have to be here (modem) for instance.

And Lora answered Irene:

hey, i chose you because it seems like you and i are interested in the same sort of stuff. as far as how i feel about the anonymity stuff, well, hell, i'mup to trying anything new, i guess. anyway, let's talk face to face next time. like i said the only reason i wrote to you on this was because i was just trying it out. good luck.

Together, the two students had established a new usage convention. First, Irene had used capitals for sentence beginnings in her messages to Burns; but when writing to Lora, she had used all lower case. Lora apparently liked this convention, because from this point on, she used virtually all lower case for all her computer messages.

Irene's next message to Burns was a long one, describing her admiration of Vonnegut. She wrote about "the silent relationship that goes on between the author and the reader" and of the way a reader sometimes feels after finishing a book, wishing "simply to call him (the author) up."

In Irene's first paper, entitled "What I Missed the First Time," she described the process of going back to two favorite authors—J.D. Salinger and Kurt Vonnegut—and analyzing their appeal. She concluded that they validated her, as a writer and a reader, by using a natural style. She paraphrased Vonnegut's advice to the author: "Stick to simplicity even though it's tempting to be mysterious or sound smart."

Irene credited Vonnegut with helping her understand her fondness for Salinger. It was Vonnegut's discussion of the way that a writer reveals himself to the reader through style that provided the insight. She continued:

> I understood partly what it was about Mr. Salinger that I was so excited about. He seemed a lot like me—somewhat confused, but full of idealism and a sense of humor. It dawned on me that I admired him, and with my low self-esteem, I began to like myself a little more.

Later in the paper, Irene referred to a class "in which I was able to see what my classmates wrote in their papers. I discovered that their problems were my problems. We all seemed to have a problem with 'noise' or useless sentences and words."

Irene said that at first she resisted any use of computers. "I'm the kind of person," she said, "who likes to write in little notebooks—unlined." As someone who even found typewriters "impersonal," her resistance to computers was predictable. Yet, once her initial anxiety about computers had abated, she actually liked using the network. She admitted that she found the relative anonymity of LINC to be more comfortable than traditional class discussions. She found that it did away with the "tension to sound intellectual," and that in fact a student who tried to sound that way would be quickly chided back to a more informal tone.

Irene later wrote that she had rarely spoken in her previous college English classes, and that in the majority of such classes she had not spoken even once.

> I was terrified to speak. I guess I felt like I had nothing intelligent to say. Sometimes I thought maybe I would speak, but most of the things I say I'm emotionally attached to, so I'll lay low because I might have to defend what I say and there's a chance I might start crying in class.

At the eighth class session, Irene sent the following message to Lora:

> hey, i guess it's time to meet you, ready or not

@8

The_Shifting_Paradigm

At the moment physics is again terribly confused. In any case, it is too difficult for me, and I wish I had been a movie comedian or something of the sort and had never heard of physics.
—Physicist Wolfgang Pauli (quoted in *Kuhn 1970*, 84)

ALTHOUGH THOMAS KUHN DID NOT COIN THE TERM "PARADIGM," HE DID, in his 1962 book, *The Structure of Scientific Revolutions*, propel the term into public discourse. Now, almost thirty-five years later, there is wide use of the term along with confusion as to what it really means. The term is variously used to mean theory, schemata, point of view, world view, etc. While I can't disentangle the semantic web now surrounding this word, I can at least address some of the contexts in which it is being used and specify the one way I choose to use it. Although the word is not always used with precision, I think that its frequent use—especially preceding the word *shift*—is an index of the degree to which people are sensing radical changes in the way we structure knowledge, meaning, and value. The shifts include those from modernism to postmodernism, from positivism to phenomenology, from structuralism to poststructuralism, from Newtonian mechanics to quantum mechanics, and so forth. At some level, all these shifts must be related since they are all arising within the same cultural matrix.

In this chapter, I will address Kuhn's notion of paradigm and explore the way it has been applied to describe shifts in writing pedagogy. I will go on to briefly discuss postmodernism, ending with the suggestion that we cautiously extend our discussion of postmodernism by linking up with some of the notions and conversations that are evolving in the sciences. Indeed, I choose to limit my own use of the word paradigm, when applied to *present-day* transitions, to what I consider to be a shift from a Newtonian world view to a quantum world view. I will grapple more with this in chapter 21. My background is in education, not physics, so my discussion of these issues is limited—perhaps even presumptuous. But, as I said in the introduction, my attempt to understand e-text has led me into many areas of inquiry. I share my travels through this theory because I have found constructs there to be illuminating.

Kuhn's primary interest is the history of science and the way this history is misrepresented in science textbooks. That is, he claims that science does not proceed by steady increments of knowledge, but rather by periods of stability followed by crisis and eventual adoption of a new organizing construct or world view.

While Kuhn's theories have not been universally endorsed by science historians, many in the humanities have found the concept of "shifting paradigm" to be useful in describing certain fundamental shifts in a variety of disciplines. This is one example of the way people in diverse disciplines borrow constructs, metaphors, and language from each other to describe change. Kuhn, in his second edition of *The Structure of Scientific Revolutions* (1970), responded to criticism of his first edition, addressing in particular the way he had used the word paradigm to mean several different things. Nevertheless, despite the semantic flaws in his basic work, Kuhn deserves credit for providing academicians and others with some powerful schemata for conceptualizing and discussing various kinds of shifts.

For example, Kuhn posits that knowledge in a particular discipline is not cumulative in the sense of adding brick after brick to a building. Rather the building must sometimes be rebuilt from the base up. Or, perhaps the bricks need to be used to construct something entirely new: "Within the new paradigm, old terms, concepts, and experiments fall into new relationships one with the other" (Kuhn 1970, 149). Kuhn compares this shift to a visual gestalt: "The marks on paper that were first seen as a bird are now seen as an antelope or vice versa" (Kuhn 1970, 85, quoting Hanson). Historian Herbert Butterfield, quoted by Kuhn, describes the reorientation as "picking up the other end of the stick" (85). In this part of Kuhn's book, he seems to be describing a sudden insight—such as recognizing a cause to actually be an effect. This is akin to the experience one has in viewing an Escher drawing in which one can elect to see black birds flying to the left or white birds flying to the right by simply switching one's visual gestalt.

In addition to highlighting gestalt shifts, Kuhn also describes the more gradual process whereby paradigms reign supreme for a time before entering a crisis stage. During the time that a paradigm is generally accepted within a scientific community or a society, people tuck their observations into the categories the paradigm provides. With time, however, anomalies arise and the categories no longer serve. Ad hoc modifications are made to the reigning paradigm in an attempt to account for these anomalies. But as more and more incongruities arise, competing paradigms may be proposed and seriously considered until one seems to provide a better fit with current observations.

Of course, the classic example of this kind of paradigm shift is that from Ptolemaic astronomy to Copernican astronomy. When Ptolemaic astronomy was accepted, observations of celestial bodies were interpreted according to the paradigm that the earth was the center of the universe. When, over time, observations of certain celestial bodies could not be accounted for, these phenomena were considered to be anomalies. "Ad hoc modifications" to the Ptolemaic paradigm sufficed for awhile, but eventually the model, or paradigm, proposed by Copernicus provided a better fit with newer observations. As we know, everyone did not accept this new model overnight; and, to this day, we still talk of the sun "rising"—thus showing how tenacious old paradigms can be in our thinking.

Indeed, Kuhn delves deeply into the process by which one paradigm gradually gives way to another in the community at large. He says of early "converts" to the new paradigm that "if they are competent, they will improve it, explore its possibilities, and show what it would be like to belong to the community guided by it" (Kuhn 1970, 159). Gradually more scientists are converted and, in their research, they present more evidence for acceptance of the new paradigm. For some the conversion to a new paradigm is painful. Albert Einstein, for example, responded to some aspects of quantum mechanics with the comment: "It was as if the ground had been pulled out from under one, with no firm foundation to be seen anywhere, upon which one could have built" (quoted in Kuhn 1970, 83). And, as can be seen in the epigraph of this chapter, physicist Pauli wished he were a movie comedian instead of a physicist so he could be spared all the confusion.

Eventually, though, if it can provide a plausible explanation for observed data, a new paradigm brings a kind of relief. Five months after his anguished lament, Pauli wrote, "Heisenberg's type of mechanics has again given me hope and joy in life. To be sure it does not supply the solution to the riddle, but I believe it is again possible to march forward" (quoted in Kuhn 1970, 84).

In the field of composition, it was Maxine Hairston who is credited with bringing Kuhn's ideas of paradigm shift into the discussion about college composition pedagogy. Her 1982 article, "The Winds of Change: Thomas Kuhn and the Revolution in the Teaching of Writing," is considered to have marked a turning point in the field.

Hairston alerted the profession to the fact that the tensions writing teachers were experiencing in the profession were not simply the workings out of old problems (analogous to what Kuhn would call "normal science"), but rather the gradual adoption of an entirely new approach to writing instruction (shifts analogous to what Kuhn would call "extraordinary science").

Hairston pointed to the steady movement toward "a process-centered theory of teaching writing" as the first stage of a paradigm shift in composition instruction (Hairston 1982, 77). She noted the attention given to process by researchers such as Mina Shaughnessy, Janet Emig, Donald Murray, and others. The heart of Hairston's argument lies in the following statement:

> We cannot teach students to write by looking only at what they have written. We must also understand *how* that product came into being, and *why* it assumed the form that it did. We have to try to understand what goes on during the internal act of writing and we have to intervene during the act of writing if we want to affect its outcome. We have to do the hard thing, examine the intangible process, rather than the easy thing, evaluate the tangible product. (84)

Hairston stated that the paradigm shift probably began in the 1950s with changes in other fields, including linguistics, anthropology, and clinical and cognitive psychology. She noted that Donald Murray may have been the first to admonish "Teach Writing as a Process not Product" in his 1972 article by that name (84).

Alluding to the burst of new research on the composing process, Hairston noted that we have learned that writers "develop their topics intuitively, not methodically" and that "usually the writing process is not linear, moving smoothly in one direction from start to finish" (85). In listing twelve principal features of the new paradigm, she included this one: "It is holistic, viewing writing as an activity that involves the intuitive and nonrational as well as the rational faculties" (86).

Hairston herself exhibited considerable intuitive skills in assessing the winds of change so accurately fifteen years ago. However, she admitted that "complex developments" were beyond her "current state of enlighten-ment" (80). For example, she had no way of knowing the degree to which computers—and especially networked computers—would change writing environments in schools and in society at large. She saw computers only in terms of "computer-assisted instruction" and dismissed their application as a relatively useless ad hoc measure used to "patch the cracks" of the old paradigm (82).

While Hairston applied the term paradigm to *teaching*, Janet Emig applied it to *research*. Her article "Inquiry Paradigms and Writing" (1982) appeared in the same issue of *College Composition and Communication* as Hairston's. Emig drew on Kuhn's work and contrasted the "gaze" of the positivist with that of the phenomenologist. She criticized positivists for engaging in "what [Elliot] Mishler calls context-stripping." The phenom-enologist, she noted, takes a more holistic view with a gaze "wide enough to include the field" (Emig 1982, 66–67).

Nancie Atwell, in her landmark book about writing process in the mid-dle school, did not use the word *paradigm*, but instead employed a para-digmatic metaphor to describe a basic shift in her approach to teaching writing. She wrote, "I confess. I used to be a creationist," explaining that in the past she would create a curriculum and stick to it. But in the next paragraph, she claims, "I've become an evolutionist, and the curriculum unfolds . . . " (Atwell 1987, 3).

As theorists began examining writing *processes*, their view of process began to expand. Some in the field suggested that teachers and theorists were overemphasizing the *how* of composing, while giving short shift to the *why*. Patricia Bizzell (1982), Lester Faigley (1986), and Linda Brodkey (1987), for example, identified a need to expand notions of *why* beyond cognitive fac-tors so as to include the contexts of history, culture, and social position that motivate any writer's choices. They noted that writing processes, like other behaviors, occur within hierarchies of power. Faigley questioned the notion that the individual is autonomous and suggested, rather, that "the individual is a constituent of a culture" (Faigley 1986, 46). This view resonates with scientific field theory as described by N. Katherine Hayles:

> In marked contrast to the atomistic Newtonian idea of reality, in which physical objects are discrete and events are capable of occurring indepen-dently of one another and the observer, a field view of reality pictures objects, events, and observer as belonging inextricably to the same field. (Hayles 1984, 10)

In other words, the paradigm shift occurring in composition studies seems to parallel that occurring in physics. Just as physics theories no longer view atoms, objects, and events as autonomous, neither do recent composition theories view writers as autonomous. Both atoms and authors are now viewed within their context or the *field*. For each writer, the *field* includes language itself which, as now acknowledged, not only *fosters* thought but also directs and constrains it.

The changing focus from product to process is indeed a sign of a major shift in composition studies, but I think it is just the beginning of a larger shift whose shape we are just beginning to discern. I find this larger shift to be the broad cultural transition from the mechanistic certainty of Newton to the chaotic uncertainty of quantum physics. However, scholars in the humanities have been more apt to frame this shift as one from the certainty of modernism to the uncertainty of postmodernism.

For example, in *Fragments of Rationality: Postmodernity and the Subject of Composition*, Lester Faigley explores composition studies within postmodernism. He quotes novelist Don DeLillo who said in an interview (DeCurtis 1991): "We seem much more aware [these past 25 years] of elements like randomness and ambiguity and chaos . . . " (Faigley 1992, 3). Faigley asserts that this awareness is expressed not only in novels, "but in the work of many other artists, musicians, choreographers, film makers, and architects, and even in the productions of advertisers, fashion designers, sports promoters, and politicians" (3).

Author Pamela McCorduck, also writing about postmodernism, finds the contrast between the certainty of the past and the fragmentation of the present to be played out in the closing lines of two broadcast newscasters. She comments that "Modernist Walter Cronkite could end his newscast with 'That's the way it is.' Dan Rather, however, ends more tentatively with 'That's part of our world tonight'" (McCorduck 1996, 108). Dan Rather, with apparent postmodern sensibility, recognizes the limits of his subject position.

Susan Sontag spoke of the alleged conflict between the two cultures of the scientific and the literary-artistic during times of "profound and bewildering historical change":

> What we are witnessing is not so much a conflict of cultures as the creation of a new (potentially unitary) kind of sensibility. This new sensibility is rooted, as it must be, in our experience, experiences which are new in the history of humanity—in extreme social and physical mobility; in the crowdedness of the

human scene . . . in the availability of new sensations such as speed . . . and in the pan-cultural perspective on the arts that is possible through the mass reproduction of art objects. (Sontag 1966, 296–97)

New sensibilities foster new concepts just as new concepts foster new sensibilities. In both the humanities and the sciences, common notions are emerging simultaneously and seem to indicate a paradigm shift. These notions include order emerging from chaos, unpredictability, non-linearity, open systems, ecology, etc. Along with these notions, new sensibilities draw the human gaze toward flow, turbulence, and dynamic unpredictability. Within the humanities, these observations appear both in discussions of postmodernism and in discussions of electronic text. Water metaphors mirror certain conversations occurring in the sciences. Specifically, the turbulence of water, like that of wind, is often mentioned as a system for which Newton could not provide predictive theories.

We can readily find examples of water metaphors, for example, in Faigley's description of postmodernism. [Note: In this paragraph and the following two paragraphs, all italics are added.] He states that there has been a "*sea change* in cultural, artistic, political, and economic practices during the past three decades" (Faigley 1992, 4). He titles one of his chapters "In the *Turbulence* of Theory" and quotes David Harvey who said, "postmodernism *swims*, even *wallows*, in the fragmentary and the chaotic *currents* of change as if that is all there is" (quoted in Faigley 1992, 4).

Referring to electronic conferencing, Faigley mentions that "The movement of discourse in InterChange [LINC] is more *wavelike*, with topics *ebbing and flowing* intermingled with many *crosscurrents*" (183). He goes on to say that "Not only do the many voices act out Bakhtin's principle of multiaccentual nature of the sign, but the movement recalls the opposition he described between the monologic centripetal forces of unity, authority, and truth and the dialogic *centrifugal* forces of multiplicity, equality, and uncertainty" (183). Even the reference to "centrifugal" is consistent with images of whirlpools. In an earlier essay, Faigley claims that "A written message in InterChange [LINC] is not an isolated container of meaning but part of a *constantly moving stream* of communication" (Faigley 1989, 310).

Others writing about electronic conferencing employ similar metaphors. For example, Gail Hawisher refers to the way that research on e-text seeks "to examine the conference as a contextual change that *ripples*

through the whole of the environment rather than as a treatment that creates a particular effect" (Hawisher 1991, 94). James Catano (1985) refers
to "*navigating* the *fluid* text." Lanham remarks that e-text has a fluid quality in which type is *poured* rather than *set* (Lanham 1993, 36). Diane
Balestri (1988) refers to e-text as *softcopy*. And almost everyone is familiar
with the phrase, "*surfing* the Net." All of this emphasis on *flow* signifies, at
the very least, something about postmodern sensibility.

I certainly can't claim to have a grasp of all the changes that surround
us. It would be impossible, in any case, since I am part of the change and
can never observe it as "out there." I'm at least as confused as Pauli, quoted
in the epigraph at the beginning of this chapter. But I can't help wonder-
ing if the changes have something to do with a shift away from the
Newtonian metaphors that have shaped Western thinking and toward
quantum metaphors which are similarly working their way into our thinking. Perhaps now, in the final few years of the century, we can peer even
further than Hairston did fifteen years ago. The winds of change are
indeed blowing, and we are experiencing a sea change as well.

It is not surprising if many of today's students find linear academic
prose to be out of sync with their own aesthetics of language and structure.
They live in the postmodern world of MTV and the World Wide Web.
They are accustomed to the fragmented interwoven story lines that course
through television programs such as *Seinfeld*, *Friends*, and *E.R.* Increasingly, they are accustomed to eclectic electronic conversations over the
Internet—rivers of thought that seldom result in closure. As French
philosopher Jean-Francois Lyotard said, postmodern knowledge "refines
our sensitivity to differences and reinforces our ability to tolerate the
incommensurable" (Faigley 1992, 41). Students are, to varying degrees,
living out a postmodern sensibility.

Some of us teachers inhabit the "modern" world to such an extent that
we can scarcely comprehend MTV, let alone enjoy it. The channel surfing
of our teenagers, considered an act of composition by some, leaves us
exhausted and annoyed. Compared to this teeming chaos, this crowded
bazaar, the stolid linearity of academic prose feels safe and familiar. We
may find it hard to understand the tension and sense of misfit students
might experience in reading—much less writing—such prose. To compli-
cate matters still further, students give us mixed messages; although they
may feel quite comfortable in the postmodern world of art, movies, and
"the strip"—when they walk into a college classroom, they still seem to
expect the merely modern.

Students appreciate the sameness and predictability of school at the same time that they mock it. Their intuitive sensibilities and their previous school experiences are at odds. Moreover, since this tension is largely intuitive, they do not try to explain. Caught between the modern and the postmodern, negotiating both worlds within each day, they seem to be in a continual state of discomfort. With postmodern zest, they aim to turn even this discomfort into a *cause celebre*. Nevertheless, this tension between academic requirements (as one sort of everyday student reality) and their sensibilities reminds me of the *New Yorker* cartoon which depicts two people talking at a bar. Says one to the other, "I reside in New York, but my mind is based in L.A." (Schoenbaum 1996). The students I studied in Burns's class seemed to say by their demeanor, "We reside in modernism, but our minds are based in postmodernism."

The process movement jolted us from our complacent gaze at products and forced us to consider writing as part of a dynamic system including the writer in the context of his or her space and time. We are still, to use Kuhn's terms, apparently working out the "normal science" of elaborating on what this process entails. Remnants of the Newtonian mindset have led some to view even the writing process as a mechanistic series of steps including, for example, prewriting, writing, and postwriting. But for the most part, our current sensibility, to which some might apply the label *postmodern*, induces us to view writing as an activity as complex as whitewater turbulence. We will toss this stick into the river and retrieve it downstream in chapter 21.

@9

Todd

One lesson I have learned from this writing is that it is important to have a method of self-reflection. I have learned, and re-learned, much about myself in the process of writing these words . . . if we don't re-examine where we have been, what we have done, and who we have met, much will be lost in the vast vacuum of time that, as Grudin says, "gently mocks us."
                                            —Todd, "Special Places and the Art of Living"

TODD WAS A COMMUNICATIONS MAJOR AND A MICHAEL DOUGLAS look-alike. Beginning with the second week of classes, Todd approached the LINC sessions playfully, sometimes inserting comments such as:

All we are is dust in the wind—

or:

Like sands through the hourglass so are the days of our lives.

or:

Where am I? What is all of this strange and wonderful stuff? How does it all work? Who are all you people?

While students in the class had immediately responded to Todd's online wit, Lora was a relative latecomer. She had not responded directly to any of his LINC comments and, over a third of the way through the semester, still did not know who Todd was. But during the seventh LINC session, she began to direct rather personal messages to Todd. It all started when the class was discussing the second text of the course, Robert Grudin's *Time and The Art of Living*. Students were to write a paper in which they imitated Grudin's style and substituted a concept of their choosing for his concept of "time." Thus, Casey had selected the concept of "trust" and her paper would be, "Trust and the Art of Living." During a topic brainstorming session, Casey asked the group:

Hey yall, I'm doing TRUST, any ideas?

After receiving some ideas, she solicited still more input from her peers:

Can anyone think of a good analogy for TRUST?

Todd wrote:

TRUST IS LIKE A SANDCASTLE . . . WHEN THE TIDE COMES IN IT'S GONE FOREVER.

And Lora responded:

Todd, you're too cool

Characteristically, Lora said, "Todd you're too cool!" out loud to her computer before typing in these words. By message 66 in the class discussion, Lora was so enamored with Todd, that she wrote:

Todd, if you ever want a travelling companion, give me a call.

Although Todd did not respond to that particular message, he later responded to a message Lora had directed to Irene who had asked peers to join her in brainstorming on "fun and the art of living," the topic of her second paper. Lora had written:

irene eating ice cream is fun. having sex is fun. vacationing is fun. reading shakespeare is fun. dissecting a pig can be fun. driving is fun. shall i go on?

Todd did not know who Lora was, or where she sat. But eight messages after Lora's brief commentary on "fun," Todd's response appeared on the screen:

LORA PLEASE, GO ON.

Lora picked up the thread, and her response appeared some thirteen short messages later:

fun is reading what todd writes in this network.

Another student wrote:

LORA DO YOU HAVE A FIXATION FOR TODD'S WRITING, OR IS THERE SOMETHING YA'LL AREN'T TELLING US?

Todd later read this LINC message from Lora:

yo todd are you married? i know you said you have kids, but . . .

Lora asked Tammy if she knew who Todd was, and Tammy pointed to someone who she thought was Todd.
Todd chose to answer Lora's question about marriage via email:

Dearest Lora,
I am happy to say that NO, I am not married at this point in time . . . at least as far as I know. There are some hazy memories of a hot, sweaty, drunken mexican vacation that i'm not to sure about, though. Howza bout you? Your single pal, TODD.

The transcript indicates that this message was read twice by Lora, once by Todd, once by Burns, and once each by three other women in the class. Todd could have put a security code on this so that no one but Lora would read it, but he apparently did not see a need for privacy.
The following week, Lora sent the following email message to Todd:

hi, todd, it's me, lora. do you know who i am? anyway, the reason i asked you about marriage is because i thought you mentioned kids in [LINC] the other day. i enjoy reading anything from you. talk about a captivating style, boy you've got it. no, i'm not married, but in love, i think. (how do you like all those commas?) i only know you through this damned computer system and what i know, i like. your humor and charm attracts me every time. let's talk again soon. lora.

When Burns called the class to the "center donut" for a short conference right before dismissal, Lora and Todd sat on opposite sides, their eyes downcast or scanning the class as a whole. They didn't make eye contact or make any face-to-face references to their computer conversation.

It wasn't until a week later, almost halfway through the course, that Todd and Lora learned each other's identity for sure. This happened at the "center donut" when Burns had the students go around the circle, announcing and briefly describing their topics for the "Grudin paper."

Lora was first and said, "Pain and the Art of Living." Todd looked up suddenly, apparently startled. Because of the class LINC sessions, he knew that his mystery admirer was writing on *pain*. Now for the first time he knew who Lora was. Similarly, when Todd announced his topic of "Special Places and the Art of Living," Lora realized that Tammy's hunch had been correct.

Todd said he thought it was "neat" that you could talk to someone on the computer for four weeks before finding out who they were. He liked the mystery and the unveiling of identity as the class progressed from week to week. Burns by this time could easily put names to faces. After all, he had seen most of the students in private conferences in his office or after class. But for the students, matching names with faces was more difficult. During the majority of class time, they sat with their backs to each other and got to know each other by name and writing style.

Todd appeared to thrive in this environment for a couple of reasons. He had a strong interest in computers and for this reason had accepted a job working at a local computer firm. He was putting himself through college, and he found that although his knowledge of computers was still rather elementary, he was still able to obtain a job in which this knowledge paid off. Doing simple programming, he was able to make more money than friends of his who accepted minimum wage jobs at grocery stores and fast food restaurants.

Even stronger than Todd's interest in computers was his love of words. He reveled in the chance to be playful with words and to showcase his wit. Despite his hectic schedule of courses and off-campus work, Todd managed to be present at every class. He said he especially looked forward to the days when they used LINC. He also liked the opportunity to choose his own topics for the four required papers.

But did this online class environment work for everyone?

@10

Making_Sense_of_E-text

The t-shirt I was wearing during our adventure was very appropriate as it had a large hot-pink dot which read in very small letters in the center of the shirt, "Blue . . . it's all in the way you look at it."

—Denise, "Storming the Parthenon"

WHEN A STUDENT READS A MESSAGE ON THE COMPUTER NETWORK, THE most elementary task is to find meaning in the words themselves. When this requirement is defeated, a student might ask for definitions, as when Lora wrote, "Please somebody tell me what the heck platitude means." Vocabulary clarification is easier on a network than when reading alone, since there is no need to go through the tedious process of finding and consulting a dictionary. Vocabulary clarification is also easier than in face-to-face conversation because there is no need to "interrupt" the speaker. Side issues can be gracefully and tactfully pursued.

Having arrived at a surface meaning for a message, a reader must next determine to what this message refers. Most messages are heavily context-dependent, yet the exact referent may not be immediately evident. Since several threads of conversation, or topical chains, are woven together in the scroll of messages appearing on the screen, participants often must devote cognitive energy to figuring out what a given message is referring to. This categorizing task is less commonly required in face-to-face conversation.

A similar pattern of utterances might occur when dining out in a restaurant; the conversation, for example, is disrupted when one must communicate with the waiter or discipline one's children. However, in face-to-face conversation, there are other cues to let the listener know in which category the comments belong. On the network, body language, eye contact, tone of voice, and other metalinguistic cues are not possible. Network users learn to supply verbal cues, such as referring to the topic again and addressing comments to particular individuals; but students in Burns's class often omitted such cues. There seem to be two reasons why they omitted these contextualizing cues. First, the students in this class were new to the medium of network "talk" and simply didn't fully realize that their messages would not necessarily appear on the scroll directly after the comment to which they were responding. This appeared to be a novice issue; after more than one semester of experience on the network, students may have begun to use more cues to enhance clarity.

The second reason students may have omitted contextualizing cues is more hypothetical on my part. My examination of network talk, in this class and in others, suggests that online conversants appear to take a somewhat mischievous pleasure in omitting context cues they could so easily provide. I suspect that students are acting on a desire to evoke intimacy in the conversation. Intimacy in conversation is evidenced when conversants share common referents and can simply proceed with the secure and comfortable sense that their meaning will be understood. There is something undeniably satisfying about sending a message which simply says, "Yes!" or "Ain't it the truth." The risk of being misunderstood is apparently worth the pleasure of spontaneous and intimate exchange. However, I have noticed lately on various listservs on the Internet that some members resent a message that says simply, "I agree." Some feel that each message must add significant content so as not to waste anyone's time. The friendly person who says, "I agree" is apt to be flamed by someone who feels the message has wasted time and space. What is overlooked here is that posters generally appreciate this public show of support.

Once a reader has comprehended a message, (s)he must decide whether a reciprocal message is required or expected. Furthermore, the reader must evaluate whether a given message merits a response and whether a worthy response comes to mind. If a message has been addressed to a particular individual, there is pressure to respond in some fashion. However, if the message was simply addressed to the general network audience, then the reader can make a judgment as to whether to respond to that message or continue "shopping."

Martin Steinmann's speech-act theory explores varying intentions of writers. Steinmann states that a "locutionary act" is "an act of intentionally saying something to readers." An "illocutionary act" is "an act of doing such a thing as stating, requesting, promising, greeting, or apologizing."

Finally, a "perlocutionary act" is "an act of producing a certain effect" upon readers (Steinmann 1982, 301–305). Steinmann uses the example of a person who attempts to impress readers by using occasional Latin words or phrases. Although the *intended* perlocutionary effect in this case would be to impress the reader, the *actual* perlocutionary effect might be quite different. For example, the reader might conclude not that the author is knowledgeable, but that the author is pretentious. Certain class members might make numerous references to the textbook with a perlocutionary intent to impress the instructor and might succeed. But this strategy might have the additional perlocutionary effect of causing peers to find these contributions to be ingratiating.

Another speech-act issue in synchronous computer network discussion is the absence of intonation because speakers cannot use it; their sarcastic remarks can easily be taken at face value, resulting in misunderstandings and hard feelings.

In Burns's class, David found it disconcerting not to be able to see his colleagues and concluded at the course's end that for this reason he preferred face-to-face conversation. He felt that he couldn't read *people* by just reading their comments on the network. He added, "I can't tell when people are lying." In his papers, interviews, and online talk, he referred to situations in which he had been the victim of racial prejudice, and this was clearly on his mind. As an African-American student attending a largely white university in Texas, he might have been especially dependent upon a "sixth sense," or "bullshit detector." The "covert" (Hymes 1972, xvii) aspects of communication are generally harder to detect in network conversations than they are in face-to-face ones.

One major difference between network discussion and traditional discussion is that in the former, the acts of reading/listening and writing/speaking are sharply delineated in terms of attention. In a traditional discussion, someone is always talking and thus there is an ongoing task to listen. Any mental efforts at constructing a response must be pursued at the same time as one is listening—or, one must devote energy to screening out the speaking, temporarily losing track of the discussion.

In a computer discussion, one can read the comments at whatever pace is desired; subsequently, if one decides to respond, this can also be done at an individualized pace. In the software used by this class, for example, a student responds by pressing a key which brings up a split screen and a blinking cursor. While composing a response, a student can temporarily ignore the ongoing discussion, devoting all available attention to the act of thinking and writing. This would seem to engender the best possible opportunity for concentrating on the act of composing. A student can compose a response at his or her own pace and even edit it before sending it to the network.

Some students did, indeed, move slowly and methodically through the scroll of messages, considering each one and writing out careful responses. Such students often reread and edited their messages as they wrote, and certainly before clicking on the "send" icon. Others had a totally different style, dashing off cryptic comments with spontaneity, if not abandon. Some students worked at almost a frenetic pace, trying to respond to as many messages as possible and apparently taking pleasure in this pursuit.

Most students found online composing on the network to necessitate the rapid generation of ideas and to be a special kind of "brainstorming." This writing constituted what Peter Elbow calls "helter-skelter writing" (Elbow 1981, 27). Understood as a kind of "talk," it is akin to Barnes's "exploratory talk" (Barnes 1990, 73) and Tom Romano's "freewheeling" talk (Romano 1987, 70). The urgency to read and write quickly seemed to spawn spontaneity and creativity.

Some students commented that long messages were tedious; they admitted that they were more apt to read and respond to shorter messages. A flurry of short messages on a topic seemed to bring about a loose and playful state of mind. Perhaps this is why humor cropped up so often on the network.

When composing a response, students could catch a thought quickly and "jot it down." Before sending a comment to the class, a student could read it and do a quick edit. Or, (s)he could elect *not* to send or "utter" it by simply pressing a key. As Irene wrote in an email message:

> i am less intimidated by writing on a computer . . . its not so final . . . there's always the delete key . . . i am not as afraid to make mistakes anymore . . .

Charles Moran suggests that the screen environment, along with current software, makes online writing more engaging than online reading. He says, "The screen environment, as one composes, makes writing exciting and active." He talks of the cursor as "the lighted moving hot spot where symbols appear and disappear" (Moran 1991, 55). However, since the screen may foster writing more than reading, LINC participants are some-times disappointed to find that their messages are not read with the same enthusiasm with which they were composed. Moran refers to teachers who, after using LINC in their training, frequently reported feeling "lonely" and "unheard" because they received inadequate response and sometimes felt as if they were writing into "thin air" (53).

It could be that those of us who grew up in the age of mere typewriters are accustomed to producing text, not reading text, when we are positioned at a keyboard. The notion of periodically abandoning our own efforts in order to look for words that *others* might have just put on our "page" would have seemed absurd a few years ago and may still feel alien or "off-task" to some. Yet many of today's college students learned to play PacMan, Donkey Kong, and Super Mario before they even learned to read. These games required keen observation of what was happening on the screen and may have conditioned students to be better screen readers than their teachers. Sherry Turkle refers to herself as a "naturalized citizen of the Net, not a native" (McCorduck 1996, 162) because she came to cyberspace as an adult. This distinction becomes ever more significant as new generations of students are, indeed, natives of the Net—meaning this has always been a part of their world.

Burns's students seldom wrote messages of more than seven lines, and thus "monologues" were rare. When they did occur, others often chided the sender in what appeared to be social pressure to keep messages appropriate to screen consumption. Once, for example, David wrote "golly Sharon you sure did write a lot!!!" and Sharon responded: "So I am a little long-winded." Sharon actually tended to remain silent in the brief face-to-face class sessions. Perhaps she found it easier to take up *space* than to take up *time*.

Another difference between traditional whole-class, teacher-moderated discussions and computer discussions is that participants in computer discussions can easily introduce new topics or entertain diversions without thereby terminating ongoing discussions. In Burns's class, students seemed quite tolerant of multiple topical threads within one conversation.

At times, the students also enjoyed the option of participating in concurrent discussions set up on different "channels," so to speak. When concurrent conferences were in process, students had the option of logging-out of a discussion which seemed fruitless or boring and logging-in to one which they found more engaging. Sometimes these "subconferences" were of equal import; at other times, they were spinoffs from the "main" conference. If they were spinoffs, the "main" discussion could proceed, and a particular participant's departure from it was seldom noticed.

If a student mistakenly logged-out of a conversation which turned out to be more salient than anticipated, the student always had the opportunity to rejoin. The text would be sitting there, available for perusal and response by any who were interested. Indeed, since students could respond at their own pace, it was possible to engage in several concurrent discussions—which is what most students did. This propensity to engage in multiple concurrent discussions is one which most students easily developed. Their comfort with this chaotic interplay of topical threads may stem from years of television channel surfing with the remote control. But this is a risky oversimplification. These students have grown up in a postmodern era in which the cultural context as a whole is fragmented. They seemed to be accustomed to fragmentation. Some, like Todd, thrived on it.

Burns occasionally set up concurrent discussions before class began. In this case, there was no main conference, but simply a series of subconferences. In one case, he directed students to create subconferences at which they could brainstorm about topics for their papers. Unfortunately, many students misunderstood the instructions and tried to set up separate conferences for *each and every* student paper. This proved to be problematic because each discussion was associated with a specific student; the ensuing discussions took on aspects of a popularity contest. Noting this pitfall, Burns was careful to structure future concurrent conferences by topical clusters rather than by student.

Multiple threads of conversation in the primary discussion often relate to a similar theme, but raise different aspects of the theme. Furthermore, since the rate of participation is higher than in traditional discussions, there are many more points of view for each participant to consider. Rand J. Spiro and his colleagues (1987), reporting on their research on knowledge acquisition, warn against learning situations in which the learner is limited to a single point of view or a single system of classification because this produces an oversimplified closed system that isn't open to context-dependent variability. They refer to such a scenario as a "conspiracy of convenience" and suggest that knowledge domains instead be conceived of as landscapes across which the learner "criss-crosses" in many directions. (Spiro attributes the crisscrossed landscape metaphor to Wittgenstein). Certainly students using LINC engaged in a great deal of "crisscrossing" of domains. Of course, they built their own domains, as well. Spiro's notion of an *open* system resonates with certain notions of open systems now occurring in the sciences (see, e.g., Prigogine and Stengers 1984).

A student's anticipation of conversation undoubtedly plays a part in shaping his or her thoughts even before arriving at the computer lab. This anticipation may activate a certain kind of "prewriting" or "prespeaking" in the mind of a student. I suspect that this anticipation is qualitatively different from the anticipation that precedes traditional discussion or essay writing. Since the computer "talk" is a hybrid of speech and writing, it would seem that the anticipation would also be a hybrid.

A student reading a text in preparation for an online discussion may indeed read in a different way than (s)he would in preparation for a face-to-face discussion. Furthermore, a student anticipating an online discussion may even think of different kinds of comments (s)he might contribute, when compared with a more traditional academic class. For example, a reticent student who might abhor the thought of reading out loud might eagerly mark a favorite passage in the text, anticipating entering this on the network. A student might come up with a joke, knowing that this can be entered into the conversational scroll without any worry about "timing" or the embarrassment of a negative or lukewarm response. Risk-taking is easier.

When coming across an unknown word in the between-class readings, a student might have an additional incentive to look this word up, anticipating the possible opportunity to impress others by providing the definition online. Another student, however, might choose *not* to look up an unknown word, anticipating the ease of simply requesting a definition from peers during the online discussion.

Canadian educator and communications specialist Marshall McLuhan (1987) talked of cold and hot media; cold media doesn't require immediate response whereas hot media does. These distinctions of "hot" and "cold" can be applied to the cognitive tasks on a computer network. Email and LINC messages are hotter than postal letters (termed "snail mail" by email users), but colder than spoken conversations. And LINC messages are hotter than email.

A spoken conversation, on the other hand, requires instantaneous response. The expectation for response is reinforced by extended gazing and other body language. Long silences between speakers are awkward, sometimes embarrassing. Certainly, a computer conversation is not this hot, since one has the option of reading and writing in a somewhat more leisurely fashion compared to face-to-face conversation. Thus, a student participating in online conversation can take more time to consider a message, think about a response, write it down, play with it if desired, and send it.

Of course, the gestation time one has in answering a snail mail letter is not available in synchronous conversation. One does not have time to sleep on a response but is expected to answer at least within the hour or so of class time. Second thoughts or delayed reactions that occur after class can be sent via email. And, since out-of-sequence response is the network norm, students may feel more comfortable referring to previous discussions than they would in more standard settings.

In discussing cognitive issues affecting computer-facilitated discourse, it should be noted that the dominant technology in a given society can radically shape our popular notions of the thinking process. For example, a recent Smithsonian Institute exhibit pointed out that when the telephone initially came into wide use, people tended to picture the human brain as a switchboard. Now the dominant metaphor for thinking is drawn from our experiences with computers. Anthropologist Sherry Turkle, in *The Second Self: Computers and the Human Spirit*, discusses this tendency to attribute computer characteristics to our minds:

> A computer scientist says, "my next lecture is hardwired," meaning that he can deliver it without thinking, and he refuses to be interrupted during an excited dinner conversation, insisting that he needs "to clear his buffer." Another refers to psychotherapy as "debugging," the technique used to clean out the final errors from almost-working programs and to her "default solutions" for dealing with men. (Turkle 1984, 17)

Turkle refers to overhearing a conversation in a restaurant when a young woman said to her friend, "The hard part is *reprogramming* yourself to live alone" (17). I notice these metaphors in my daily life, too. Recently, as a colleague and I conversed, she prefaced her shift back to an earlier topic by saying, "Going back a few screens . . ."

Not only do people attribute computer characteristics to their minds, but they also attribute human characteristics to their computers. Turkle suggests that frequent computer users begin to think of computers as other *minds*—not surprising in light of the fact that everything we do with a computer is dependent on the computer's *memory* (189). Thus, we hear people say, "The computer's thinking" or, as one of Turkle's young subjects said, "He [the computer] won't take no for an answer" (113).

The students participating in networked conversation in this class faced cognitive tasks that differed significantly from those that they faced in a traditional class. Most students reported that they enjoyed the new challenges, and even the occasional misfires which added excitement and humor to the classroom. Some students, however, expressed a preference for the comfortable familiarity of the traditional classroom.

@11

Yo_Hugh!

An ordinary teacher weighs and bags ideas like potatoes; a skilled teacher makes them open up like buds from a bud.
  —Robert Grudin, *Time and the Art of Living* (1982)

In lots of years talking to teachers about what makes teaching writing work is the faceless masses of lifeless academic prose that *THEY ASSIGN.* Can you believe it: teachers assign crap that they do not want to read when they get it. Unbelievable!!!!!!!! My style is different: you are here to inform me, delight me, surprise me, persuade me, make me feel something important.
  –Burns, LINC

THE FACT THAT STUDENTS ADDRESSED THEIR INSTRUCTOR ONLINE AS "Prof," "Dr. Burns," "H.B.," "Burns," and even "Yo, Hugh" reflects the nonhierarchical class dynamic so common in networked classrooms on college campuses today. Old and rigid roles of "student" and "teacher" simply don't hold up in the networked environment. Burns was aware of this even before the class started, as evidenced by this line in the syllabus: "At the beginning, I'll seem like the teacher and you, the student. But by the end, you should be a teacher too." Despite this invitation to students to become teachers, too, the fact remained that Burns was the wizard behind the screen, the one who orchestrated the class activities and—at regular intervals—assigned grades. Yes, Burns was the chief authority in the class, but his nonauthoritarian persona did seem to foster an informal atmosphere in which students, too, could experiment with various personae.

Toward the conclusion of his career as an Air Force officer, Burns had taken a leave of absence to pursue a doctorate in English instruction. During his graduate studies, he analyzed the English software programs available at that time and noticed they were all closed systems in which the computer always had the correct answer. He set out to design open-ended software in which the computer would "pose questions for which it did not have answers" (Hawisher, LeBlanc, Moran, and Selfe 1996, 43). As a student of James Kinneavy, and immersed in Aristotelian concepts, he drew on Aristotle's *topoi* in designing a program that would focus on invention and topic generation. The result was the heuristic software program, TOPOI, and a dissertation based on student use of the software.

Burns's 1979 dissertation, "Stimulating Rhetorical Invention in English Composition Through Computer-Assisted Instruction," was the first dissertation in the field of computers and composition. (Accordingly, the Computers and Writing Community has named its annual award for best dissertation in the field the "Hugh Burns Dissertation Award.") After obtaining his doctorate, he taught for several years at the Air Force Academy and then joined the faculty of the University of Texas.

Because Burns had always used technology in his teaching, he did not have to overcome a lifetime's habits based on traditional instruction. Since he had been a student himself less than ten years earlier, and now had daughters of college age, Burns could readily relate to students. Perhaps these factors helped him to maintain the flexible stance which stood him in good stead in the new and relatively untamed environment of the networked classroom.

Using his background in rhetoric and computers, Burns also brought a host of life skills to his teaching of "Writing, Thinking, and Learning"— including paternal skills developed in the raising of three daughters, and organizational skills developed during his years in the research and development community of the Air Force.

Burns was willing to join his students in the electronic borderlands and to help them find their respective ways through writer's block and "computer chaos," to use Lora's term. His stance fluctuated from paternal, to official, to fellow-traveler in the world of rhetoric. One moment he was giving fatherly advice; the next moment he was consulting his meticulously maintained daily planner and issuing deadlines as if they were orders from the wing commander. Still later, he was quoting Edward Hoagland: "We spend our lives getting to know ourselves, yet wonders never cease." Regardless of perspective, he maintained consummate good humor.

As mentioned earlier, Burns designed the course around the reading of three books: *Writing to Learn* by William Zinsser, *Time and the Art of*

Living by Robert Grudin, and *Best American Essays, 1989*, edited by Geoffrey Wolff and Robert Atwan. When I later asked Burns, via email, why he selected these particular texts, he responded:

> Text selection is often so personal. Bill Zinsser and I taught together at the Northeastern University Seminars on Writing in 1984. I am a fan of his approach of knowing good, clear writing when you see it and when you write it. I wanted to use cases throughout the course--and z. presents the "writing to learn" heroes field by field--the macro level.--Grudin's theme of time IS a biggie for me to pass on to students--but his cases give us a lot of style work and imitation--the micro level. The *BAE* is the synthesis level--a book I have been buying each year to read the best that America produces in the essay. *BAE* is a very high standard to model!

The class design included two or three LINCs on each book, focusing on a certain aspect of the text—such as style or specific content. The LINCs on *Best American Essays,* for example, focused on Julian Barnes's "Playing Chess with Arthur Koestler" and Annie Dillard's "Schedules" and invited students to explore what elements may have resulted in these essays being chosen as the "best." In addition to discussing these texts, students were to write a paper related to each book, plus a final paper which would be a rewrite or expansion of one of the three previous papers. Burns said this in one of his email messages to his students:

> Do you know what an etude is? A short musical piece which is written to give a musician practice in particular patterns, voices, ranges, paces, etc. These assignments are etudes.

The course was designed along the lines of the classical rhetoric heuristics of Invention, Arrangement, Style, Memory, and Delivery. Burns had moved beyond his heuristic software, TOPOI, and was now intent on exploring classroom uses of email and LINC. He saw network writing as a powerful medium for helping students to move smoothly through the recursive stages of writing; he also wanted them to write for an audience of peers. And finally, he expected them to gain insight into which writing processes—brainstorming, peer talk, drafting, shaping, revising—work best for them at different times.

Burns's responses to students took a variety of forms: 1) launching and participating in LINC sessions, 2) responding to email messages both on an individual and group basis, 3) writing thorough prose critiques of each paper, 4) holding occasional traditional (face-to-face) class sessions at the "center donut" tables, and 5) meeting with each student several times during office hours. This represented an extraordinary amount of individualization, especially with reference to the collegewide undergraduate class norm.

As a personal goal, Burns strove to answer each email message, and he succeeded—though not without some headaches. Like most instructors of computer classes, he struggled with the veritable river of words produced every class day. Nevertheless, Burns felt the time and energy he put into reading and responding paid off. Meanwhile, both online and offline, students voiced appreciation of Burns's response to their writing.

Although the class was strongly based on LINCs, which Burns felt were especially helpful for brainstorming and "invention," he also expected students to garner insights on a twice-a-week basis and to send these to the network, as email, addressed to ALL—forming a sort of rough draft for the upcoming paper. His goals in having students do this were: 1) to engender good working habits and to prevent procrastination, 2) to make each student's evolving paper available to classmates, 3) to give him a chance to follow the thinking of students and to offer help when needed, and 4) to introduce students to the incubation and revision opportunities that are available when a piece is written over time.

To ensure that students would, indeed, post their evolving drafts to the communal network via email, Burns made it clear that students' grades would, in fact, be affected by their *timely* building of a manuscript and their consistency in sharing progressive drafts. He encouraged students to look in on each other's drafts, in e-text, and to respond via email when they had the time and the inclination. Sometimes, if a student was stuck or prematurely "finished," Burns would suggest that this student seek out another to read and comment on the draft. Because the draft had been sent to ALL, any student could easily access it in the class electronic mailbox.

After every class, Burns would stay late, checking the network for any newly revised drafts-in-progress. He would quickly read all of these, composing immediate feedback with his hunt-and-peck typing skills. The purpose of this response was often simply to acknowledge that he had read a draft. If the student was on course, he felt only the briefest of comments was necessary. For example, in responding to Tiffany's draft on the topic of *Chaos*, which she had referred to as "chaoticness," Burns responded:

Chaoticness? I like the part about the "identification in hand."

One of his messages to a student read, simply:

Wow!

Early in the semester, Jake succeeded in sending his paper to the electronic mailbox via modem. To this paper, about a childhood caper with "Drake," Burns responded:

Jake and Drake Inc: Thanks for electronically checking in today. I missed looking over my shoulder and seeing you write though. Your draft is quite good overall. Sounds like the wonder years have also affected your life. Descriptions were excellent. Keep at it. See you Tuesday.

Along with encouragement, Burns nudged students in certain directions from time to time, as in this response to Todd's draft of a paper about the day his grandfather died:

Nice! Kerplunking is just right—might be extended some with sounds of rings or names of ponds visited or . . . Cut the passage down, keeping only the ideas, image, and prose that works hard. Indeed, it must have been a bad day to die. Nice.

Some students were specific about the kind of feedback they wanted. For example, Tiffany sent an extended first draft and asked Burns:

Am I on the right track? How about these entries? Thanks for your previous comments?

And his answer:

right track, yes.

Irene, drafting a paper on "Fun and the Art of Living" apparently wasn't having any fun writing the paper and voiced her frustrations to Burns. He responded, in part, as follows:

Suggestions: This invention, brainstorming, creating, discovering, remembering, stimulating part of writing just causes you so many fits, doesn't it? By the time you read this, 15 days will have passed since you were assigned this "topic." . . . The key word is START. Gosh, you like the agony part of this, and what you should be doing is enjoying the discovery of finding out what you want to write while you are writing. That's where the "fun" is. I am not making light of this "creative" wall; it is the most difficult part of writing: starting.

Indeed, writer's block cropped up in this class as in any other. Tim, for example, was another inveterate slow starter who turned to Burns for help:

I'm blank . . . I should have already had something prepared before class. I'm just too caught up in my thoughts right now about what we discussed. It has taken me 30 minutes just to write this. I thought it was ok to use Zinsser as one of my authors, and I thought you wanted 8-10 computer screens of text as the length of the paper, etc. Sorry about the typos also.

To which Burns responded:

You are absolutely right about being prepared before class too. I hope you can get enough stuff in your portfolio for the next time.

Jake, the technical wizard in the class, chose to attend class from home one day. He had asked Burns to send him an email message with any additional instructions for their upcoming papers. Burns hadn't set the class up with a "distance education" option, but he agreed this one time—in the spirit of experimentation—to send Jake a summary of class. Jake wasn't sure Burns would remember, so he sent this message to Angela:

Hi Angela. I'll be attending class from home today. Unless he makes a mental note of it I don't think he can figure it out. I can get the assignment and send him stuff through [email]. But I'd appreciate it if you'd send me your phone number . . . When it asks about security, hit <P> for private. Thanks!

Students used email to apologize, complain, ask for favors, or simply to ventilate. Thus, when Burns perused his email at the end of class, he could expect to see an assortment of plaintive comments. Such messages could be entered by students between or during classes and, at least, prevented problems from going unaddressed until they were insurmountable.

Apologies

Apologies took such forms as follows:

DAVID | BURNS
I know that my essay is not very good right now. I really did not have a good weekend and did not get to work on this as much as I wanted to. It WILL be better by Thursday.

TIM | BURNS
Dear Burns: This is what I have of my rough draft. It is not really a rough draft. I haven't written any but one real section, and I still need to edit it. . . . Sorry that I'm not delivering what you might want from me. I just keep having to catch up in my other classes. It has been a strange semester so far. I catch up in one class and I get behind in another, and so on . . . Thus, it is not that this class is a problem for me (it is a little different for me because I'm not used to building a paper over time, and I'm having to adjust to this) and that I might not care, because I do. It is just that I didn't budget my time and now I'm paying the price.

TIFFANY | ALL | OOOOPS!
Burns: I'm sorry, I know you said a thousand times label everything xxxtal.xxx so it would be easy for you to find. Well, I just discovered that you meant sending portfolios through the mail as well. So I guess I just now caught on. Thanks-sorry.

TIFFANY | ALL
Well, in case we are suppose to check in . . . here I am. Everything should have been sent to the network. Bye! By the way, remember I forgot to send my portfolios xxxtalxxx-sorry.

Complaints

The following is a typical complaint:

ANGELA | HUGH | BAE PAPER
. . . The printers in this place are really crappy, but oh well. See you on the 27th.

Asking for favors

This from Irene:

> hey i was just wondering, since i wasn't here on the 16th, can i still add a "16th" entry to my portfolio? just wondering. i was forcibly dragged to a lecture that day on scandinavian women artists from the 19th century by my teacher, ursula, so what do you say

Ventings of Frustrations

> LORA | HUGH
> to hugh i imported my file lcstal.016 but it ended up on the computer as lcstal01 what the heck? i'm irritated and going home. oh, also the date is wrong.

And this particularly plaintive one from Angela, regarding FRUSTRATION:

> I just wanted to vent my frustrations for a moment before I continue with my essay. I left WTL in my last class, and, of course, when I went back it was not there. I am not exactly in the right frame of mind right now, so I wanted to write these few lines to get it out of my system. Now on to my essay . . . endeavor to persevere

Venturing into "language space," as he sometimes called it, Burns seemed to follow Dell Hymes's prescription of "starting where the children are," or, to use a phrase Hymes adapted from the ministry, "Speak to their condition" (Hymes 1972, xiv). If the students wrote in slang, Burns often responded in kind. If they experimented with writing conventions, such as dispensing with capitalization, he gave it a try, too. For example, Lora sent the following email message to Burns, inviting his response to her topic for the second paper:

> yo hugh. Pain and the art of living. What do you think? very broad huh? i didn't start a quickstart file. is that going to be detrimental to my grade on this next essay?

Burns responded:

yo lora depends on what happened on your [LINC] cover the positive side of pain too don't be just heavy hearted why am i not punctuating or capitalizing why why why sorry i didn't have your essay finished it was in the first set of turn ins but you gave it a strange name and it took a while for me to find it after reading back through your [email] messages but it will be there for you next time after i finish the boat rocking assessment of how you all wuz robbed okay?

Lora responded:

okay. muchas gracias!

And, on another day, Lora wrote:

yo hugh i have a midterm tomorrow at 4pm. yikes its at the same time as class. oh no whats a girl to do????????????????????

By now, Lora did not hesitate to use all lower case in her communications to Burns just as she did in writing to her peers.

When Burns echoed student expression, he was accepting their way of being and talking. He typically mocked his own awkward use of student conventions, indicating that he was simply joining in their fun with language. During one "center donut" discussion, Burns attempted to use an outdated expression, saying that each of them should write something so powerful that when people read it, it would "roll down their socks." When a confounded student asked, "What's this about socks?!" Todd generously provided the expression Burns was reaching for, i.e., "knock their socks off."

Later, Burns sent the following email message to ALL:

Are you writing more effectively? If so, why? If not, why not? Are the computers helping you to "get the job done?" Are the computers helping you to "roll down socks?" Errrr, knock their socks off, I know, I know, I know.

Answers to the above included Sharon's:

I never seem to have that much trouble with writing when I get started, it is just the starting that scares me. The computer, for some unfathomable reason, has helped me to get over that fear of beginnings.

Casey's:

I think I'm writing more efficiently and effectively because I am writing a little bit all the time instead of waiting till the last minute. Building a paper
gradually helps tons. I've learned to like writing on the computers. Proofing
and editing are so much easier and quicker.

Burns used email to provide positive response to individuals and to the
class as a whole. For example, when Tim wrote in email that he was
"impressed" with one of the class's oral readings, Burns responded:

HUGH | HOW GOES IT
I was impressed too, but I am never surprised by the power of young minds
and young voices. The concentrated skills are there in all of you—if you
manage them and if you are not intimated by your own fears. Saying it
straight out-fast.

Similarly, he wrote this to Holly:

It is a strange combination of the little train who could and Alice's wonder-
land to me.

It should be noted that Burns's acceptance of student topics had its limits. At one point toward the end of the semester, Burns felt he had to guide
students away from topics that were in his opinion, too close to "therapy."
(This will be discussed in chapter 22.)

Michael Joyce notes that in the networked classroom, the teacher becomes
a "learning manager" rather than a transmitter of knowledge. In this role

> She or he knows that margin makes meaning; and she or he attempts to sus-
> tain as many margins, as many fractal edges, as learners can generate.
> Education along these edges is not transmission of knowledge and values but
> rather reforming knowledge and values. The nature of mind must not be
> fixed. It is not a transmission but a conversation we must keep open. (Joyce
> 1992, 11–12)

It seemed to me that, indeed, Burns was sustaining margins or "fractal
edges" within a conversation. Unlike some teachers, even teachers in networked classrooms, Burns did not emphasize closure. Nor did he pepper
the LINCs with probing questions. The students were like jugglers,

throwing apples, oranges, and chainsaws into the air. Burns gave his tacit approval of these acts of imagination.

In this classroom, there seemed to be a continuing sense of tentativeness in which trial balloons were launched, described, and examined. Knowledge was considered contingent, elastic, dynamic. The electronic text generated by the students of this class was one characterized by a disorderly confusion of multiple and shifting perspectives.

Burns sometimes made direct statements to students in which he urged them not to be so dependent on him. For example, he wrote the following to Tim:

> Do you really think it matters what I will say about your writing over the next few years and decades, even unto the year 2011 when I shall retire to the funny farm? I am providing for you an occasion to add to your toolkit many different writing techniques. If I call it an A, great. But you will know the A and B efforts the second you do them—the above average efforts are understood in the great educational cosmos. Write for yourself first, along the lines of the task assigned.

At times, the blurring between teacher and student was evident in Burns's messages, as in these to Casey, Irene, and Sharon; Burns made it clear to the students that he welcomed their suggestions for refining the course.

HUGH | CASEY
Right on, Casey. Starting early helps "tons." I agree that you and your classmates are bright minds. Hey, no surprises for me there. What's interesting to me, though, is that we are not doing a very good job of providing enough confidence-building exercises/lessons/experiences/whatevers into the College Education. I hear more about survival than about learning . . .

HUGH | IRENE
well if i wanted to know the truth, the first two assignments made sense to me—but i don't know if the students always catch on as fast as i would hope. is it the syllabus, the separate class assignments, the models, the something due all the time portfolio?

HUGH | SHARON | R) ABOUT CLASS
Thanks Sharon for your comments . . . Do you have any suggestions about how to make the portfolio "make more sense" when they are first assigned?

This class appeared to be a blending of old and new paradigms. The new paradigm was represented in the electronic communication between and among students and teacher both through email and network discussion. The new paradigm was also represented in the Grudin paper in which paragraphs were self-contained, almost hypertextual, elements which did not progress toward a conclusion. The old paradigm was represented in the writing of the other three papers which for most students did not vary significantly from typical essays written in college composition classes. Papers were due in hard copy, double-spaced, on a certain date, and subject to evaluation and a grade by Burns. Grades on the four essays accounted for 90 percent of the class grades, reflecting Burns's valuing of essays. Burns responded to each student paper with a printed prose critique, as well as a tally of percentage points awarded in the following categories: Performance (20%), Variety and Style (30%), Theme (30%), and Skills (20%).

When I asked Burns if he thought the essay was an expiring genre, he said he didn't think so. He seemed to think of LINCs as heuristics, not as genres in and of themselves. Still, he devoted huge amounts of class time to LINCs and highly valued the writing that occurred in them. At that time there was only the dimmest sense that email or LINCs were evolving into new genres.

Burns had no trouble crossing the borderline and homesteading in the networked classroom. His pedagogy was based on his conviction that students should wean themselves, as much as possible, from dependency on the teacher and should become self-directed learners who, in dialogue with others, construct their own knowledge. He acknowledged his power as the teacher who assigns grades. Nevertheless, he found that the networked classroom could put the concept of constructed knowledge into a virtually tangible form. Perhaps Burns's role in the class was best expressed by Kara in an email message toward the end of the course:

I see now that leadership is guiding the follower, not running the show.

@12

The_First_Paper_Is_Due

You had the availability of everyone's mind for brainstorming.
—Holly

*Stage one: 'BURP' (information ideas); Stage two:
Arrange/Revise, Stage three: Revise/Mechanics.*
—Todd

ON THE DAY THE FIRST PAPER WAS DUE, ABOUT A THIRD OF THE CLASS arrived early. Some students arrived several hours early to actually *do* their papers. Others, who had completed their work on computers at home or elsewhere on campus, came early to make sure they could "send" their papers to the network. They also were required to print up a hard copy to hand in. Sometimes they needed help from the TAs (teaching assistants) who were available across the hall.

The computer classroom was available for open use during the days unless a class was in process. A student coming to the classroom early to work on a paper might find that the computer (s)he usually used was not turned on that day, generally meaning it was not to be used, probably because it was "down"—due to some glitch in the system or in the individual computer. Sometimes a student would discover that a member of another class was occupying his or her customary place. In such cases, the student usually elected to sit at the closest available terminal to this place. When class actually began, there was a tendency to stick with whatever computer one was "on," causing others, as well, to shift from their habitual spots. Students then asked questions of their new neighbors or, in some cases, got out of their chairs to go ask the neighbors with whom they were more familiar.

Class was about to begin and in addition to the usual din, another sound filled the air—the sound of students tearing the perforations off the edges of their accordion-folded computer printouts.

Todd sat three seats down from his usual seat. He was tense, holding a pencil in his mouth like a bone. He tried to wipe the dust off the screen with his hand but was defeated by static electricity which now held the dust in constellations. Abandoning this attempt to deal with visual distraction, Todd turned his efforts to auditory distraction by putting an index finger against each ear, elbows akimbo. He tipped his chair back on two legs and scrutinized the screen. He lowered his chair with a bang and punched a few keys in a quick staccato. The screen flashed from blue to green and Todd sighed with relief. He had succeeded in sending his paper, completed at home and transported via floppy disk, to the network.

Lora had used one of the noisy dot matrix printers to print a hard copy of her paper. She then eagerly tore the perforations from the edges and careened around the room asking, "Does anyone have a stapler? A stapler, anyone?"

Josh, elated about finishing on time, sent the following email message to ALL:

I'm writing just to let everyone know that through hours of agonizing pain and grief, . . . I'M DONE!
Hopefully you have too,
Josh

Steve sat straight at his computer, shoulders hunched. His right knee punctuated the air rhythmically as his heel nervously pumped up and down on the scarred and unbuffed tile. Sometimes his whole foot came off the floor. He gritted his teeth and the bones in his face jumped under his skin. Once his paper was printed, he went to the "center donut" in search of the stapler. To reach it, he tipped his body like a board and slid across one entire table's width like a runaway sled.

Other students like David, Irene, and George sat comfortably. They had completed their assignments well within the deadline and were now printing up DAILY ASSIGNMENT, moving on toward the next computer task.

Lora's paper was an introspective look at her problems with writing, along with an appreciation of three professors who had inspired her to improve. She included the following:

If there's one thing I've done continuously with my writing, it is fail. I was happy when I read Zinsser state that "I've always believed that failure is one of the great teachers, every bit as constructive as success."

Lora had done poorly in an earlier course, and her professor, Kate Frost, in a campus speech had recently alluded to clichés in undergraduate papers. Lora, referring to a tattered copy of the newspaper article about the speech, now bravely quoted it:

> It is very difficult to concentrate on deconstructing D. H. Lawrence or investigating the implications of Shakespeare as a radical Marxist feminist, when you've got fifty undergraduate essays to grade, all of which begin, "Beowulf is definitely a hero." [Kate Frost]

As mentioned earlier, Lora had thought Frost might have been referring to her.

How did Lora's *current* paper begin? With this line: "It was my freshman year of college and was I scared out of my wits."

David had analyzed examples of writing from Charles Darwin, Conrad Lorenz, and Stephen Jay Gould. His paper also explored the concept of jargon, quoting comments two of his classmates had made and adding his own thought:

> Psychology is one of those subjects in which an author, if he or she so chooses, can fill his writing with so much technical "jargonese" that it only takes two or three sentences to become so overwhelmed and confused that you stop learning and instead are taken prisoner by the words.

Irene's paper on three favorite writers, called "What I Missed The First Time," included this passage:

> Like most people, I thought good writing was the kind of stuff you'd see coming only out of "intelligent" words, long comma-ridden sentences, and completely abstract ideas. I ignored what I enjoyed and dismissed it as simple. But there's much more thought (and clear thought at that) that goes into producing something that appears simple when you read it.

Jake had worked on his paper at home and then sent his drafts via a modem. In class today, he wrote this email to explain his preference for working at home:

I just can't get into deep thought in here. It makes sense to me anyway [to work at home]. You always hear about real writers wanting to work in far off secluded places.

Todd's paper chronicled his shifts in major from Architecture to Business to Communication, and he described a favorite writer from each field—Louis Sullivan, Harvey McKay, and Deborah Tannen, respectively. He included the following paragraph on Tannen's (1990) *You Just Don't Understand: Women and Men in Conversation:*

> Tannen never seems pushy in attempts to make herself understood. She speaks through example, and for the most part, that is one of the best ways to teach someone. The subtleties and complexities of human interaction are hard to understand. Changing the way we interact is even harder: "But even if no one changes, understanding genderlect improves relationships."

The popularity of Tannen's book with the general public is one indication that issues of gender and communication were of apparent interest at this time even to nonacademics.

Gender bias was present in the fact that two of the three texts assigned in the syllabus were authored by males. The third text, *Best American Essays (BAE),* included twenty-one essays, of which seventeen were written by males. When asked about gender imbalance in his text selection, Burns pointed out that he had not assigned male authors exclusively; he had included Annie Dillard's "Schedules" as one of the three essays the class was to read from *BAE.* Still, the male bias which has prevailed in literature classes for many years was certainly present in this class. Moreover, most students chose male authors to represent outstanding authors in their respective fields; out of a total of fifty-four authors selected by students in this "scavenger hunt," only eleven were women.

After printing up their papers and depositing them in a stack on one of the "center donut" tables for Burns to read and grade, the students returned to their terminals and read the online assignment for the next paper.

@13

Underlife_and_Identity

Like any other social structure, School needs to be accepted by its participants. It will not survive very long beyond the time when children can no longer be persuaded to accord it a degree of legitimation.
— Seymour Papert, *The Children's Machine: Rethinking School in the Age of the Computer* (1993, 6)

BECAUSE NETWORK DISCUSSION IS NOT MEDIATED BY TEACHERS, STUDENTS need not wait to be recognized or called on by a teacher; they simply "talk" at will. It is not surprising that, given this freedom, students typically broaden the agenda—introducing new topics or bending old topics into new directions. One common pattern which emerged within the computer dialogue was the coexistence of a prescribed mainstream topic along with a variety of sub-topics. Not only did students thereby engage in what teachers refer to as "off-task talk," but they also used modes of expression that were slang-filled and irreverent.

Many of the sub-conversations occurring on the computer network can be understood as an expression of "underlife," a term originally used by anthropologist Erving Goffman (1961) to explain certain behavior of doctors, staff, and patients in mental hospitals. Goffman noted that individuals railed somewhat against the institutional roles assigned to them. Through underlife behaviors, they could carve out unique identities for themselves—identities that went beyond the stereotypes of "doctor," "staff," or "patient."

In the institution of school, it appears that underlife serves a similar function. Robert Brooke looked at underlife as it functioned in a freshman writing class that did not use computers. He had assumed the underlife conversations would pertain to "unrelated subjects like parties and dates," but, to his surprise, he found that most underlife talk consisted of students "developing their own stances towards class activity" (Brooke 1990, 99). Brooke maintains that these underlife conversations result from the desire to step out of, or expand upon, the limited role of student.

As long as there have been classrooms, teachers have been aware of unsanctioned classroom communications that are whispered, mouthed, muttered, written on the bottoms of shoes, discreetly passed on little slips of paper and so forth. Such messages have been typically confined to immediate neighbors or small spatial constellations. Teachers, typically out-of-range, have often assumed that these communications were expressed secretly because of a student-motivated desire for privacy or exclusiveness. While this may be true to some extent, I now see underlife in a different light.

It seems to me that underlife in schools, just as in mental hospitals or other institutions, results not so much from a desire for secrecy as from a desire to expand upon circumscribed roles. I say this because when the students in Burns's class engaged in computer networked discussion, they were all too willing to bring underlife discourse out from under and to express it openly online. Consider, for example, the following off-task discussion which was woven throughout the LINC on Zinsser's *Writing to Learn* which was presented in chapter 5:

19 Todd: all we are is dust in the wind . . .

21 Tammy: Todd: Like sands through the hourglass so are the days of our lives

29 Tim: Todd: you type therefore you are . . .

50 Todd: to tim and tammy: "We're just two lost souls swimming in a fish bowl, year after year, running over the same old ground, what have we found, the same old fears. . . "

51 Josh: Tammy: Are you a DAYS fan?

56 Tammy: Josh: Of course!!! Todd: What drugs are you on? Where do you come up with this stuff?

64 Todd: tammy: don't you listen to p. floyd? You know, "we don't need no educatin, we don't need no thought control" that kind of stuff

67 Josh: In defense of Todd, you can't beat Pink Floyd

72 Tammy: O.K. guys. Whatever you say. I'm not really into p. floyd but I'll take your word for it.

79 Sharon: Todd: You seem to have many philosophical ideas. Have you by any chance seen "Bill and Ted's excellent adventure" and are you an adament folower of Days of Our Lives?"

These ten messages were woven in among the messages between number 19 and number 79, which means there were 60 other messages intervening among these particular threads in the tapestry. Between number 64 and 72, for example, we can see the context in which this underlife discourse was embedded. (Underlife comments appear with asterisks.)

64 Todd: tammy: don't you listen to p. floyd? you know, "we don't need no educatin, we don't need no thought control" that kind of stuff

65 Jake: I did my research on legal writing, and I was able to find a number of books specifically devoted to effective legal writing. The interesting thing was that all of the authors preached strongly against the unnecessary use of legal jargon and archaic lawerly phrases such as: "hitherto the party of the first part . . . " etc . . . Instead, they suggested "plain and direct style."

66 Kara: My other two authors are Roger Brown and Jean Berko Gleason. I want to check on Howard Gradner's work, too. Brown and Gleason both are research informationalists. I enjoy statistics and details, things that can be used as solid proof of the unknown.

67 Josh: In defense of Todd, you can't beat Pink Floyd.

68 Sharon: In my search for authors, I found three that represent good writing in my field. I am aspiring to be an English teacher so I looked for books on how to teach writing. My favorite book is Writing with Style. He has a chapter on people he calls "literary prudes." People who diligently adhere to rules, such as, "never end a sentence with a preposition." A favorite passage of mine is when he describes these people as belonging to a sect and gives their "Articles of Faith" and the rules they abide by. He even calls grammar books their "Sacred Texts." Now, if humurous, well-thought out, easily understood writing is not good writing, I don't know what is.

69 Tiffany: Kara, I agree!! I think computers are great for reinforcement of learning but should never replace the teacher.

70 Angela: What books did you find? Those sound great!

71 Josh: Does anyone know if it is required that you go to law school in Texas, to be able to practice here??

72 Tammy: O.K. guys. Whatever you say. I'm not really into p. floyd but I'll take your word for it.

The ways that time and space figure in a computer networked classroom foster new opportunities for thinking, writing, and learning. In the underlife discourse above, the students did appear to be concerned with issues of identity—just as Goffman would predict. Thus, Todd came across as cynical, irreverent, and not easily sold on the academic agenda. Josh and Tammy appeared to be seeking Todd's approval. All had the opportunity, through this underlife conversation, of making known to the networked community at large that they watch certain television programs and listen to certain music.

Furthermore, this LINC had a literary style quite distinct from the talk generally heard in classrooms. Students were inventing unique discourse. This exchange was obviously not a teacher-pleaser and yet it was openly played out. It was a private conversation, in a sense, and yet it was nonexclusive; anyone could "listen in" and even "join up." Students did not ignore the mainstream topic; in fact, by the nature of the scroll, they couldn't avoid the mainstream topic even if they wanted to.

When underlife conversations are no longer limited by space but can be sent to ALL through the network, the dynamics of dialogue change. Students change the scope of what is being shared, thought about, and written about. Some teachers report that they find the openness and self-revelation refreshing. It helps them see their students as complex individuals, not simply students. Further, it provides a window into the students' true feelings about the curriculum. Burns appreciated these underlife features of student dialogue.

Postmodernism adds another dimension to this notion of identity because with postmodernism has come a recognition that, as Lester Faigley puts it, ". . . the subject is an effect rather than a cause of discourse." The autonomous, rational, stable self is an illusion. Faigley goes on to say that, "What a person does, thinks, says, and writes cannot be interpreted unambiguously because any human action does not rise out of a unified consciousness but rather from a momentary identity that is always multiple and in some ways incoherent" (Faigley 1992, 9). As Goffman pointed out, people create differing personae in different situations and then strive to live up to them (Goffman 1961).

Sherry Turkle, dubbed by some as a "cybershrink," notes that, "In terms of our views of the self, new images of multiplicity, heterogeneity, flexibility, and fragmentation dominate current thinking about human identity" (Turkle 1995, 178). She suggests that "the Internet has become a significant social laboratory for experimenting with the constructions and reconstructions of self that characterize postmodern life. In its virtual reality, we self-fashion and self create" (180). Like Goffman, she considers role-playing to be an inevitable and profound human endeavor. She rejects the common notion that role-playing is something we are merely putting on or faking. Rather, she says, our roles are bona fide aspects of self, aspects to which the healthy person has access:

> You learn to negotiate, to fit them together in some way. Using language of "cycling through" rather than "building a One" is going to be helpful to patients clinically, and help people think about their lives. It's accepting where we are in the culture. (quoted in McCorduck 1996, 164)

Students do indeed try on roles for size in the networked classroom. This construction of self can be as playful or as serious as the block-building activities of young children. And, like block-building, it can result in a desire to topple and start from scratch or to protect with dragon-infested moats. Like block-building, it involves the imagination: one must feel as if (s)he is inhabiting, at least for the moment, the realities one is inventing.

Given the students' investment in this sort of role-playing, the curriculum sometimes is relegated to a back burner or even casually dismissed. Some teachers have been stunned when students openly reject parts of the curriculum they (the teachers) have so carefully crafted. Although it's not unusual to entertain doubts about students' true attitudes toward the curriculum, most teachers have come to expect respectful tolerance. On the network, however, students sometimes bash texts, topics, and assignments with abandon. In this environment, students may readily dispense with the conventional stance of acquiescent and docile student.

Brooke points out, "The point of all these underlife activities is to distance oneself from the demands of the classroom while hopefully remaining successful within it" (Brooke 1990, 103). The student strives to "assert one's fundamental distance from the classroom roles" in order to assert that one "can think independently." Brooke gives the example of one student who wrote a journal entry about how hard it was to write her last paper. Yet, she told a peer that she'd written the paper with no problem the night before. She had written the deceptive journal entry because "that was the sort of thing the teacher wanted" (101).

The recognition that so many students think of school as only a game can be disconcerting to the teacher. Yet, underlife activities are for the most part healthy and productive. For example, when students share their confusions and discontents, they build a sense of community and open up the possibility of drawing on the insights of their peers. One way this occurred was through a category of comments which I call "confessionals." In confessionals, students publicly aired their failure to understand assignments or to fulfill them as expected. In a sense these confessionals blended with the class process of making meaning collaboratively.

Linda (63) said:

Irene, I'm glad to know that I am not the only one who has not completed the reading we were supposed to do.

And Irene (68) responded:

maybe this is kind of like going to confession, Linda.

Sandra shared her anxieties in the following message (83):

Our first paper is to be 8-10 pages long? How are we supposed to write that much? I have trouble coming up with a few lines for [LINC]!

Casey was still in the dark (86):

I'm still confused!! Will someone please help?!?

Irene responded to Casey with the following message (88):

Casey: when you are lost, you are found, my child

Linda admitted that she had not done the reading (89):

—For those of us that have not done the reading, what's a crotchet?

The final "confessional" in this LINC was from Jake who referred to being confused by a math book to such an extent that (95)

After reading it, I was convinced that I had no idea how to subtract ordinary numbers.

Students have always expressed more cynicism for assignments outside the classroom than inside it. Now these expressions are moving into the classroom and the cynicism is more rampant as students become more critical of school in general. To take school at face value is to project a naive persona. Students are sensing, I believe correctly, that school—as it is implemented—does not offer them desired roles. As Brooke says, "The whole call for pedagogical shift is most powerfully a call for a shift in the identity roles offered in the classroom" (105).

To avoid overstating the case, I would like to point out that Brooke found student evaluations of courses were more positive than students would admit to their peers. However, the fact remains that many students apparently experience a disjuncture between the way they are expected to operate in school and the way they think and operate in their lives outside the classroom. I sensed that Burns's students felt a certain urgency about their lives. At the same time, they felt that school was not necessarily helping them to do what they thought they should be doing. Nor did they willingly accept the role of "good student." As mentioned elsewhere, students are often burned out on "doing school."

Computer networks enter both into the cause and the cure of this confusion. They are the cause, to an extent, because they are playing a central role in the restructuring of institutions throughout society. They have rather suddenly provided alternative ways of acquiring information and making meaning. Furthermore, they have provided social links which young people find to be crucial in their finding a niche in society—both in terms of personal life and job opportunities. In schools and elsewhere, computers are causing a lot of ruckus because they are part of change. At the same time, computers may be part of the solution if they can give a voice to those who must now create new ways of doing school. This voice can be heard in underlife.

One sort of irony about underlife is that many teachers, like students, feel that school requires them to play undesired or limited roles. Brooke addresses this situation, as well. He points out that educational institutions may cast teachers in the role of producing "good students" when what they want to produce is "good writers." The distinction, as Brooke sees it, is the difference between writing as a game or writing as a way to "explore, question, and change" elements of their lives (106). He notes, "We would hope they see purposes for writing beyond the single purpose of getting us to give them good grades" (104).

Teachers may be disconcerted not only by the content of underlife, but also by the type of language students use to play it out. If a teacher knows students only in the context of academic discourse, then the typically frank, abrupt, and slang-filled language of students in LINC and email may seem crass and disrespectful. While some language is clearly inappropriate, students benefit from talking in ways that they choose. Slang, for example, is part of youth culture and can be a critical ingredient in the struggle for identity. Role-playing through freedom with language is generally healthy and provides students with an anchor as they grapple with what it means to be a student in an institution with its own pulls on personal identity.

Students who have traversed schools for close to twenty years are all too familiar with what they see as a requirement to produce "cheesy" teacher-pleasing prose. If students are to be, at the very least, respectful to their own processes of constructing self and constructing knowledge, then they must be allowed to choose the language appropriate to the moment. Todd was exercising this kind of freedom when he arrived at the conclusion that "Grudin is a scary dude."

Burns said he did nothing to squelch underlife talk on the network because it helped him to see exactly what was on the students' minds. He conveyed his sanctioning by indulging in off-task discourse himself. For example, he referred to his hunger pangs in an early message and continued to make occasional allusions to off-task topics throughout the semester. Of course, such gestures can go only so far as students are keenly aware that the teacher's primary role is to get them to "play the school game." This fact cannot be disguised.

In dismissing some aspects of school as merely a game, students just may find a space to engage in dialogue of genuine interest. In one sense, it could be argued that everything we do in a classroom is a game of some kind. But if this is indeed the case, then we should at least let students choose and shape the game they play. In doing so through writing, they may find unique opportunities for collaboration, invention, and expression.

Brooke maintains that the sociological term "identity" is closely linked with the rhetorical term "voice" (104). Similarly, Belenky and her colleagues in their study of women's epistemology had this to say about voice:

> We found that women repeatedly used the metaphor of voice to depict their intellectual and ethical development; and that the development of a sense of voice, mind, and self were intricately intertwined. (Belenky et al. 1986, 18)

In a traditional classroom, underlife discourse can distract students from the mainstream discussion—although it can also serve to help students clear up momentary confusions so that they can better follow the discussion. On a computer network, students can participate in underlife discourse without having to lose a single word of the mainstream discussion. Underlife comments occur in their own space and time and are conveniently stored on the scroll. This enables students to move back and forth between underlife and mainstream dialogue with a new ease. Indeed, the distinction between underlife and mainstream dialogue is often blurred.

In this class, I found that LINC was used for a variety of purposes:

1. Expressing emotional response to reading
2. Connecting ideas to one's own past experiences
3. Connecting ideas to one's future plans
4. Expanding upon roles or experimenting with new roles (constructing identities)
5. Criticizing curriculum and texts
6. Defending curriculum and texts
7. Expressing physical discomfort such as sickness, hunger, etc.
8. Policing class, i.e., "Isn't it time to log-off?"
9. Injecting humor, comic relief.
10. Building a community, including support of peers.

Brooke concluded that underlife helps the student begin to see himself or herself as an original thinker. I would add that the original thinking, in this case, is thinking which is put into writing—a probable step toward further thought development.

After using LINC for the semester, students responded to a survey in which they were asked to describe their strengths as writers. Sharon wrote: "I found out that I was good at imagery and using words I normally did not use. I found I could actually sound intellectual." Denise wrote: "I am able to be very descriptive, and sometimes even funny." Tiffany wrote about her "creativeness" and her ability to "think above and beyond." David wrote that his main strength is, "I know what I want to say."

In networked discussion, students seemed to find it easier to move beyond the realm of "teacher pleasers" and to flex their muscles as original thinkers with the courage of their convictions. While we're no longer certain that a person can ever truly think "independently"—given the social parameters within which the thoughts of any individual occur—I still think that at times individuals can think "outside the box" and avoid, to some extent, prescribed roles and hackneyed ideas. Sometimes, it is writing which is the catalyst for this kind of thinking process. This ability to think outside the box is also an essential ingredient in restructuring our educational institutions and bringing them into alignment with changes affecting society as a whole.

A networked classroom can nurture underlife while becoming a curriculum laboratory in which specific topics, ways of talking, and even new words can be tested. As Gail Hawisher and Cynthia Selfe point out, electronic writing classes are sites of "paradox and promise" (Hawisher and Selfe 1991, 64). Teachers can, at worst, be permissive about underlife and then use the self-revelations punitively. At best, however, teachers will recognize the student need to be "more than" and "other than" a student. Teachers can see this as parallel to their own determination to be "more than" and "other than" a teacher.

Burns allowed underlife to go online and was thus able to construct a broader, more complex understanding of his students. Even more important, Burns allowed students to use the network to explore and construct "selves" in the context of the academy. As will be explored in chapter 24, students in this class expressed a desire to play not only with the borders of their own personalities but with the borders of the academy itself.

@14

David

Many individuals in positions have not learned to empathize.
They are still in the infancy of human perspective and are forever
trapped in a closed mind.
　　　　　—David, *"Perspective and the Art of Living"*

TWO CHAIRS OVER FROM LORA SAT DAVID, A SENIOR MAJORING IN PSY-chology. David was a serious student, an African-American who worked in the Texas State Capitol as a legislative assistant. He also worked at a local grocery store. He often spoke of his agenda upon graduation in December; he planned to write a book about race awareness. This book, he emphasized, would be written from an African-American point of view and would pro-mote "mediation instead of hostility."

David happened to sit on the noisy side of the room, dominated by boisterous students such as Lora and Josh. Lora would often talk out loud to her computer, as if the people sending messages to her screen were inside her monitor and able to hear her howls of laughter or her snide retorts.

Next to David sat Josh, a jovial student never without his baseball cap which he wore backwards. Josh maintained almost a continual banter with David. For several classes, the conversation centered on Josh's desire to buy a cellular phone, with Josh chronicling the pros, the cons, the available models, the prices, the uses to which he'd put it. David responded politely with deep-voiced, brief, and friendly remarks. He said in an interview that he appreciated Josh's friendship, but that he found talk, along with the room noise, distracting.

David also reported that he found the class assignments to be confusing, and the time constraints to add to the pressure. "There is so much to do each day," he said, "It's hard." Early in the semester, David sent the following email message to Burns:

> The expectations—
> . . . My goal is to eventually write a book after I have graduated from UT this fall, therefore it will be extremely important to me that I do well in this course. I feel that I already have some pretty good writing skills however, I believe that there is always room for improvement.
> The out of class uses—
> Because one of the jobs that I have is at the Capitol, I want to add new word processing programs to the ones that I already am experienced with. Also this would help with making my eventual goal of writing a book in that this would be helpful in keeping it organized.
> The ultimate goal!!!
> Simple—if I pass this class I graduate, therefore I will pass this class.

Later, when David read the first text for the course, *Writing to Learn*, he found that he didn't like it. Zinsser struck him as a "know-it-all" who was preaching to his reading audience.

In the initial online conference on Zinsser, David was among the first to respond to Burns's prompt. He composed a two-sentence message in his composing screen and then carefully reread it. When he got to the part about "Gustavus Adolphus," he pulled the Zinsser text from his frayed canvas backpack and checked to make sure he had correctly spelled the name of this college to which Zinsser had referred.

> It seems that Zissner's thoughts on the subject of writing reached the University in last couple of years. I say this because of the emphasis placed on writing components just like Gustavus Adolphus did.

Sixteen comments later, David entered the dialogue again:

> I think that the most important point that Zissner makes is that riting can be an enjoyable and vlauble learning experience.

David's priorities were clearly on meaning now, and not on spelling; furthermore, he had noticed that many students made errors and that in synchronous online discussion, the cosmetics of writing were given short shrift. He later said that once he realized that online writing was more like talking, it was easier to participate.

He gradually adjusted his online language to match the informal tone which prevailed:

golly Sharon you sure did write a lot!!! I guess you did enjoy the book.

Sharon had written nineteen lines of print, the average message that day being about five. David knew Sharon; they had been in the same pledge class of a service fraternity, and later their paths had crossed at the Texas State Capitol where Sharon also worked. Four messages later, Sharon responded:

Yes, David, I did enjoy the book. So I am a little long winded. I can't help it, I have a habit of talking too much.

David's only remaining message for the day was to George, concerning the assignment Burns had given them, a "scavenger hunt" to find out which writers they considered good in their respective fields. Since a message from George revealed that his field, too, was psychology, David queried:

George which psychology professors did you talk to? I talked to Dr. Thiessen and Dr. Horn.

The transcript shows that David's question went unanswered. He said that at the time George's failure to respond, "kinda pissed me off," but that he later concluded that computer discussions were so "fast" that you learned to not necessarily expect a response.

Between classes, David asked several of his psychology professors to recommend good writers in the field, and from those suggested, David chose Charles Darwin, Stephen Jay Gould, and Conrad Lorenz. In his paper, before giving examples of what he considered to be good writing by these men, David discussed the issue of good writing itself. He quoted Zinsser, Plato, and Medawar, along with classmates, Todd and Holly. This blending of known experts with classmates was a common occurrence in the papers of Burns's students. Online collaboration seemed to lead to the blurring of lines between established experts and simple colleagues.

When the class moved on to Robert Grudin's *Time and the Art of Living*, David found that he liked Grudin better than Zinsser. In a LINC on Grudin, he again entered the discussion early, announcing his preference for this author over Zinsser—even though many other members of the class were panning Grudin. David's neighbor, Josh, for example wrote:

I don't know about the rest of you, but I really couldn't force myself to read past the first chapter of this new book.

Todd wrote:

Grudin is a scary dude . . .

And Sandra asked:

Are we to abandon everything we were supposed to have learned from Zinsser for this next paper (i.e. writing clearly)?

Irene added:

. . . isn't Grudin the kind of lofty academician type of stuff we were trying to purge ourselves of in the last paper?

David, however, wrote:

I thought that the Grudin book was a lot better than the zisnner book because it allows more freedom in one's thinking.

And, later in the LINC, he wrote:

This writing is clear, you just have to be in the right frame of mind when you read it. Grudin really does make some pretty good points.

This comment by David launched the following online exchange between Josh and David:

Josh: David—I'd have to be stoned to understand this stuff.
David: Josh—I guess you'll have to get stoned then.
Josh: David—It would have to be more important than this for me to get stoned.

This was followed by a batch of messages in which several other students joined in, pondering what drug Grudin might be stoned on. The initial heated exchange between David and Josh, along with the subsequent flurry of off-task talk by others, constituted a mild case of flaming—the impulsive expression of strong feelings.

Later, David said:

> I like what Grudin had to say about how people who view the past, future, and present as the same are usually the ones that have the best grip. Of cours if he's on drugs that would explain how he could view them all at the same time!

With this comment, David stood his ground while at the same time using language playfully in such a way as to appease the students who opposed his position.

As the LINC progressed, the tone of the discussion shifted from being largely negative and flippant to being more serious. Students began to voice the things they *liked* about Grudin. For example, Sharon said:

> Todd, I agree with you, but he does say some things about time that I think we all should think about. . . .

Burns supported David, referring to his earlier comment:

> David—I like the frame of mind idea. A zinsser frame of mind a grudin frame of mind, etc.

Meanwhile, Burns had also sent this brief message:

> Why would I choose such different books?

There were several thoughtful responses to Burns's question. He himself elaborated, saying:

> I use the model technique, don't I? Trading the clarity of Zinsser for the introspection of Grudin. Grudin is writing for himself, don't you think—asking some hard questions. His answers are thoughtful. Do you think you could ever write this deeply on one topic like Time?

Josh remained in a rebellious mood for most of the session, saying at one point:

Time and the art of wasting it—you think?

David, still having fun with his neighbor, responded:

Josh—so what are you saying? That this is Grudin's brain on drugs!!? any questions?

David's writings to Josh could reflect peer pressure to make flippant comments, rather than serious ones, on the network. However, one could also make a case that the network gave David an opportunity to join a specific discourse community which was initially somewhat out of his reach. Moreover, David spoke his opinions and received support from other classmates. As for Josh, if anything was going to induce him to reconsider his opinion of Grudin, it was more likely to be an endorsement of Grudin by peers than any endorsement of this somewhat inaccessible author by a teacher.

At the end of this class, David entered the following email message to ALL:

Yes, the class is making sense to me now!!! AHA!!—David

At the following class, students had another LINC in which they helped each other brainstorm on their proposed topics for the Grudin paper. As mentioned earlier, this paper was to consist of an exercise in imitation of style. Each student was to pick a substitute for the word/concept, "Time" in *Time and the Art of Living*. The respective papers would consist of a series of paragraphs exploring aspects of the chosen topic.

Early in the LINC, David read Holly's comment:

My topic is Knowledge and the Art of Living, and I encourage and welcome any insight into this topic.

David responded:

Have you ever heard the saying that a little knowledge can be a dangerous thing? Also I think that it is interesting how certain leaders in other countries, and probably in our own too, control people by keeping certain information out of their hands. just a thought.

David was gratified when Angela picked up on his message and carried it further:

Holly: This is kind of an aside to David's message about leaders of other countries. That brought to my mind George Orwell's 1984 where they had all knowledge of everyone. Nothing was privacy. There are some things that people shouldn't know. We debated in a gov. class one time about knowledge. Is it always good? For example, would we be better off without the knowledge of the H-bomb? HMMMMM

David had chosen the topic of "Perception and the Art of Living" which he later changed to "Perspective and the Art of Living." In the sixty-seventh message of the day, he ventured to solicit ideas on his initial topic from Todd:

Todd: Do you have anything funny to say about perception?—any quotes?

Todd responded, but not with something funny:

Perception is also conditional . . . on your state of mind, your frame of reference, etc. . . . How could for so long people think of slavery as an acceptable practice . . . anyone with just a little commonsense knows the horror and true cruelty of slavery, but still some "percieved" of it as something that was right . . .

At one point, Angela asked David how he made a certain symbol before each person's name, and he responded:

You have to hold the Alt key down and at the same time press 1 and then 0 on the numeric keypad on the left to make the symbol. Its called ASCII and by entering different numbers you can make different symbols.

Angela asked:

Hey David, that is really cool. How did you know about that?

To which David responded:

By just playing around and reading. Programmming is a hobby of mine.

Thus, by this LINC, David was both soliciting ideas for his own paper and giving advice to others for their papers. Additionally, he was being creative with some visual aspects of keyboarding and receiving praise for this know-how from another student in the class. David thus had a chance to exhibit and explain his growing expertise with computers. All of this is especially significant in light of David's comment in an interview that in most college classes he kept a low profile—reading, listening, and thinking, but not choosing to talk much.

David's completed paper, "Perspective and the Art of Living," consisted of fourteen "Grudin-style" paragraphs on various aspects of perspective. He tied this theme to empathy, racism, and the world of work, three topics of deep interest to him.

The paper included the following comment on empathy:

> From day to day we all encounter different circumstances which require us to change our viewpoint and empathize. If we are to use perception to our best possible advantage, we must be able to discern between what is our perspective and what is that of other individuals. Not only must we be able to tell the difference between them, but we also must apply this knowledge to the situation at hand.

A paragraph on race began like this:

> Racism is one of the evils of our society. It is based in the fear that another is going to get ahead of you . . .

Two reflections on work follow:

> For a moment, imagine that you are an average worker who goes to work day after day, hour after hour, dreading your job because of its monotonous nature. Now imagine yourself as someone who goes to work at the same job and enjoys what he does. What's the difference? The difference stems from the fact that if you love your job, it is likely that you have made things which may ordinarily be boring—exciting. You have taken time [*sic*] the perspective that you can learn something new everyday and have seized the opportunity to do so. If you go to work hating your job, you have probably chosen to be a stagnant robot-like clone of everyone else who is there. All you wait for is the bosses [*sic*] next press of the button or his next "Simon says" command. You are for all practical purposes on remote control.

And:

> Yesterday at work, one of my co-workers asked me "How can you work two jobs and go to school at the same time and how do you deal with all these cus-

tomers in the store?" I replied that "It's because I don't see work and school as work and school but rather as opportunities." The difference between him and myself was that while he was only able to see his job as a necessity while I see it as a necessity that also gives me the opportunity to learn new things and to meet new people. In essence my view was one that took work and school as tools for self-improvement.

David mentioned that he considered what he learned at work to be at least as important as what he learned at school. And, like many others in the class, he sensed the importance of closely watching and analyzing the world of work even during his brief stint as a college student.

Net_Working_in_the
_Workplace_of_the_Future

*Now a new kind of learning must begin. It is slow and scary,
and many workers are timid, not wanting to appear foolish and
incompetent. Hammers and wrenches have been replaced by
numbers and buttons.*
                    —Zuboff, *In the Age of the Smart Machine: The
                    Future of Work and Power* (1988, 72)

ONE TOPIC WHICH EMERGED OFTEN IN THE ONLINE UNDERLIFE TALK WAS
work. Most of the students appeared to have their antennae directed
toward the future and expressed a keen interest in current trends in the job
market. Their comments on the topic of work—whether part-time college
jobs or future career goals—came up frequently and revealed their perspective on their current brief role as students. They expressed a desire to
balance three dimensions of a career—good pay, job satisfaction, and time
for family. In their papers and their online comments, they shared their
concerns about these issues. Often, they shared information about the lack
of one or more of these factors in the work lives of their parents or other
relatives. Angela refers to advice her grandfather had given her:

I worked like a slave all my life. You don't have to do that.

Monica made the following comment in a LINC about Annie Dillard:

[My aunt] used to fund my going to college and was always screaming at
me to take economics and business courses. My grandmother told me to
keep singing and take music courses, and my parents, by this time, just

want me to finish. . . oh, and my mother keeps warning me of the misery of secretarial work, that if i don't finish college, that's where i'll go

Cynthia said in the same LINC:

So is "fear of falling" the fear that if we do not strive we will fail and end up "homelessness"? If so I think that everyone has a certain type of fear of falling. I know that I keep going and strive to graduate because I am scared of what opportunities I may miss out on without higher education. And yes, my parents did tell me over and over again that I have to go to college and I have to be a professional if i wanted to be successful.

It seemed that, in a way, students were under pressure to find satisfying careers for the sake of their parents or other relatives who, in many cases, had not succeeded in this.

Jake, more than any other student in Burns's class, expressed an interest in the newly-shaping technological society. One of his email messages, consisting of topic brainstorming for the third paper, read as follows:

The changing workforce, low skill labor, not a decrease in the total number of jobs but a change in what they demand. Implications? The significance of education in this rapidly changing world. How the U.S. is handling it vs. other countries. Audio/Video communication. Changes in the way we work: teleconferencing, telecommuting. Legal battles i.e. Bell and Cable companies and computer companies. The synthesis of communication and computing. AI, can computers think? What is "to think". How legal and bureaucratic change lags/occasionally impedes technological change. The change in the emphasis of universities from teaching to research. why? what are it's implications? The new relaxation of the anti-trust laws, research consortiums. Increased medical costs due to new complicated, hi-tech procedures. Fringe benefits are becoming one of the greatest costs to employers. This is giving them incentives to lower the total number of workers and to cut these benefits when possible.

As Jake noted, computer technology, especially the technology of computer networking, is radically changing the infrastructure of long-standing institutions. In November, 1994, the *Wall Street Journal* devoted an entire thirty-six-page section to computer networks and the way they are changing corporate America. Staff reporter Jared Sandberg claims, in one article, that the Internet is becoming the "power lunch" of the digital dimension. His report includes the fact that publishers are caught up in the changes, too. For example, London-based Macmillan Publishing Ltd. networked with authors in New Hampshire and editors in New York to produce one series of books (Sandberg 1994, R14).

In the lead article, G. Christian Hill, the *Journal's* San Francisco Bureau Chief, refers to computer networks as "those invisible electronic webs" and claims that "they have redefined the workplace, dispersing employer and employees alike from office hives." Hill's article explores the human cost of this transformation, noting that "some workers resent networks that monitor their every task while managers have bristled at having to share their work over networks with scores of colleagues" (Hill 1994, R1). He claims that networks

> will ultimately propel changes more profound than those wrought by the telephone and the automobile—because they will lessen the barriers of time and distance even more than those earlier inventions. Indeed they promise to change not only the way businesses operate, but the nature of commerce itself. As networks absorb more information and connect with one another, they will create a fully transparent, fiercely competitive marketplace where many goods and services are treated as commodities." (R8)

Hill quotes Matt Kursh, a software executive who thinks of networking as "a revolution" that will "speak to one issue, the compression of space, and therefore time, at a velocity all other things will pale before" (R8).

In still another *Wall Street Journal* article, staff reporter Bill Richards addresses the concept of a company in a box, i.e., a "virtual company" in which all functions are "farmed out" through computer networks, a trend referred to as "radical outsourcing" (Richards 1994, R12). Richards explores the use of networks in enterprises as diverse as film-making and jet design. He reports that film director Steven Spielberg, on location in Poland for the filming of *Schindler's List*, was able to review an animation clip from *Jurassic Park*, then in development, and request the expression on the face of a tyrannosaurus in one scene be changed from "doleful" to "proud" (R10).

Boeing assembled a massive interactive computer network to facilitate designing of its 777 jetliner because the "old fashioned 'paper' way would be too costly and slow." By using graphics and networking technology, engineers have a virtual "plane in a box":

Engineers use the system to call up any of the 777 aircraft's three million parts, modify them, fit them into the surrounding structure, and then put them back into the box so other engineers can make their own adjustments to ensure that no parts clash. (R10)

The *Wall Street Journal* delves, as well, into dissatisfaction with the network revolution. San Francisco Deputy Chief Stephen Yoder states: "The main strength of the networks—giving control to individual workers—is also its greatest weakness" (Yoder 1994, R16).

Other newspapers, as well, often include descriptive and predictive articles similar to those appearing in *The Wall Street Journal*. Meanwhile, the market has been deluged with books detailing changes in management philosophy. These books—on "reengineering," "restructuring," "downsizing," "rightsizing," and "re-inventing"—are read not only by MBA students, but by the general public.

Michael Hammer and James Champy's book on reengineering states that "new ideas will impact today's businesses just as Adam Smith's ideas impacted businesses of the last two centuries" (Hammer and Champy 1993, 6). They state that reengineering requires people to engage in "discontinuous thinking" and to ask not "How can we do what we do faster, better, or at lower cost?" but rather, "Why do we do what we do at all?" (4). When designing corporate structure, they advise entrepreneurs to start from scratch:

> Advanced technologies, the disappearance of boundaries between national markets, and the altered expectations of customers who now have more choices than ever before have combined to make the goals, methods, and basic organizing principles of the classical American corporation sadly obsolete. Renewing their competitive capabilities isn't an issue of getting the people in these companies to work harder, but of learning to work differently. (11)

The effects of reengineering are still being evaluated. However, the ultimate desirability of reengineering is not the issue. The issue, rather, is that the business world is changing quickly and experimenting with new forms of organization—in many cases forms which drastically alter prior hierarchical structures. The press reports on changes in corporate America are infused with hyperbole; yet there is no question that radical change in the structure of business is occurring in many instances.

As various workplace environments become networked, there are indeed contrasting dynamics which, in their extremes, can lead either to a new egalitarianism or to a new totalitarianism. Today's students and teachers need to be aware of these tensions so that they can channel computer applications toward open access and thwart attempts to implement networks for control. For an understanding of both the promise and the threat of a networked workplace, I turn again to the research of historical anthropologist Shoshana Zuboff whose perspective on the computerized workplace has proved invaluable in my own struggle to discover new patterns of interaction, value, and knowledge that are played out in the computerized college writing classroom.

Zuboff believes that the new technological workplace is replacing the old world of industrialism. She sees this as "a historical transformation of immense proportions" (Zuboff 1988, xiii), because technology has the power "to reorder the rules of the game and thus our experience as players" (389). Zuboff points out that "Throughout history, humans have designed mechanisms to reproduce and extend the capacity of the human body as an instrument of work" (8). This effort reached a peak in the industrial age. While some view the computer as just another machine extending human capacity, Zuboff emphasizes that the computer not only extends human agency, but simultaneously produces information.

Zuboff studied a variety of organizations—including pulp mills, a paper mill, a stock and bond transfer office, a telecommunications unit, a dental claims insurance operation, a financial institution, and a pharmaceutical company. She found that in some instances the managers of these organizations focused only on the automating capacity of computers—removing complexity from lower level jobs and channeling information up the hierarchy to managers who became guardians of the organization's knowledge.

However, computer networks afford an opposite flow of knowledge in which managers can render the complex knowledge accessible to workers at all levels. In this new model, complexity can be handled "wherever and whenever it first enters the organization—either during a sale, during delivery or in production." In this new model, enterprises "surrender knowledge to anyone with the skills to access it and understand it" (Zuboff 1995, 204). The knowledge is surrendered through the computer's "voice" which "symbolically renders events, objects, and processes so that they become visible, knowable, and shareable in a new way." Zuboff has coined the word "informating" to describe this unique capacity of information technology to provide "a deeper level of transparency to activities that had been either partially or completely opaque" (Zuboff 1988, 9).

Zuboff claims that while automation *deskills* labor, at the same time the informating aspect of automation *reskills* labor (57). The shift is from skill in manipulating *materials* to skill in manipulating *information:* "Immediate physical responses must be replaced by an abstract thought process in which options are considered, and choices are made and then translated into the terms of the information system" (71). Some of the workers she interviewed were daunted by these changes; others weren't. One said: "With all of this information in front of me, I begin to think about how to do the job better. And, being freed from all that manual activity, you really have time to look at things, to think about them, and to anticipate" (75).

Reskilling in an informated environment consists of developing critical judgment and an ability to deal with symbols and abstract concepts, translating data into information and information into insight (92). One plant manager said, "We are depending on the technology to educate our people in abstract thinking . . . You can no longer make a decision just based on local data" (93).

When an enterprise takes advantage of the informating potential of computers, this leads to more efficient operations, claims Zuboff, and also ends the industrial division of labor which is also a "division of love": "I suspect that the managerial hierarchy drew life not only from considerations of its efficiency but also from the ways in which some members of the organization were valued and others devalued" (Zuboff 1995, 204).

Just as the Boeing engineers, described in the *Wall Street Journal*, were able to bring a more holistic stance to the design of one small part, the mill workers in Zuboff's study also could see their work in a broader perspective. One mill worker said, "To do the job well now you need to understand this part of the mill and how it relates to the rest of the plant. You need a concept of what you are doing. . . . You have to check through the data on the computer to see your effects" (Zuboff 1988, 94). One manager said that, in an informated work environment, workers can "take more of a helicopter view" and "see the whole, not just the part" (202).

In the informated enterprise, knowledge is shared through what Zuboff terms the "electronic text" (172). This electronic text is not authored by a single individual but rather emerges from the input of many people and even from machines (180). The data on the electronic text provides "a public symbolization of organizational experience, much of which was previously private, fragmented, and implicit—lodged in people's heads, in their sensual know-how, in discussions at meetings or over lunch, in file drawers, or on desktops" (393–94).

Zuboff notes that "Individuals take up their relationship toward that text according to their responsibilities and their information needs. In such a scenario, work is, in large measure, the creation of meaning, and the methods of work involve the application of intellective skill to data" (384).

To the extent that organizations become learning communities, egalitarian ideals will be foregrounded. However, this scenario is dependent upon managers who have "a commitment to fundamental change in the landscape of authority" (392). Not all managers recognize and/or endorse the notion of an informed workplace. It is not surprising that some managers are vested in maintaining their own power. They can do this by hoarding information and keeping workers from accessing wide-scale information bases such as that embodied in an electronic text. In such cases, says Zuboff, "The hierarchy will use technology to reproduce itself" (392). But that's not the worst-case scenario. Managers can harness technology to closely monitor workers, thereby robbing them of privacy and autonomy. In other words, managers can use technology to tighten their own control rather than to distribute control throughout an organization. The resulting tyranny through surveillance is referred to by Zuboff as an "information panopticon" (336).

The panopticon is an architectural structure designed by moral philosopher Jeremy Bentham to facilitate total monitoring of those over whom one wishes to exert authority—prisoners, inmates, or workers. The panopticon consists of a twelve-sided polygon of iron and glass in which prisoners are housed. Guards reside in a central tower from which they can easily monitor the prisoners through "universal transparency" (Zuboff 1988, 320). The prisoners cannot view the managers, nor can they detect when they are being watched. French intellectual Michel Foucault used the panopticon as a metaphor for domination by the technologies of power within society's institutions (320). Professionals interested in computer mediated communication (CMC) have expressed concern about the use of computers for surveillance (see, e.g., Hawisher and Selfe, 1991). The centralizing of information afforded by networks can, after all, be readily harnessed by administrators and supervisors to bring about an electronic version of the panopticon—one which controls not through an arrangement of iron and glass but through an arrangement of fiber optic cables and computers. Such an electronic panopticon could conceivably bring about invasion of privacy and ultimate power over subjects connected to it.

Computer networks, by their nature, can facilitate both centralizing and decentralizing of information—and thus of power. The workplace is one place where critical decisions are being made relative to who has access to what. Zuboff appears to take a fundamentally optimistic view of future organizations, sensing that learning will be the new form of labor and that both labor and management will thrive in this scenario. She suggests that the separation of mental and material work, characteristic of the industrial age, is not only outmoded but dysfunctional. As the intellectual content of work increases, distinctions between blue and white collars "collapse" as do distinctions between the manager and the managed (393).

In light of the above work scenarios, what are the implications for teaching? First, if as Zuboff predicts, our industrial institutions are being replaced by learning communities, then we need to carefully consider how schools and workplaces should "interface" in ways that promote values which we in the humanities have historically fostered and promoted. Second, we need to consider the models for associated living which we are creating in our classrooms. Are we re-creating hierarchies in which dutiful students do as told without questioning the reasons? Or are we openly sharing with students our various notions of what universities could be, and also what they are at this point? What would an informated university look like? We are so far from having this that it is almost impossible to imagine.

Zuboff states that managers can use technology to tighten their own control rather than to distribute control throughout an organization. Teachers face the same fundamental choice. Networks allow us to surrender knowledge and control to students, but at the same time networks allow us chilling opportunities to track, record, and report the activities and thoughts of those in our charge.

Our students increasingly recognize that their future careers will be largely defined by how they interact with information and colleagues on computer networks. In Burns's class and others like it, students are having opportunities to experience the excitement and possibility inherent in such concepts as Zuboff's electronic text. It is critical that students become aware of the egalitarian informating potential of technology, as well as of the more ominous panopticon-like applications. As Jake said, "There is an inherent controversy between perfect information and privacy." This tension is played out not only in corporate America, but also in our schools, colleges, and universities.

@16

(Fill-in-the-Blank)_and
_the_Art_of_Living

Isn't it interesting how we seem to form enemies and alliances
with other drivers? We generally feel that everyone who is driving
slower than us is an idiot. Everyone who is driving faster is a jerk.
—David, *"Perspective and the Art of Living"*

THE SECOND PAPER, BASED ON ROBERT GRUDIN'S *Time and the Art of
Living (1982),* was to imitate his style. Grudin's style is indeed unique;
each of his thirteen chapters on "time" is divided into consecutively-num-
bered paragraphs. In his preface, Grudin explains this format:

> Rather than leading readers to preordained conclusions, I wish to make them
> stop and think. Rather than pretending to consistency and connectedness, I
> wish to set off an autonomous interplay of comparisons and contrasts. The
> blank spaces between my writings are as important as the writings themselves.

In Grudin's text, one paragraph might consist of a description of a
dream, another a suggested plot for a movie, a third an insight garnered at
a relative's birthday party. This collection of thoughts has a random quality that fits well with the type of discourse occurring on LINC.
Furthermore, I couldn't help but notice that the pages of the Grudin text
resemble a LINC transcript. That is, the text consists of small blocks of
words, each block expressing a single idea. The blocks relate to an underlying theme yet possess an integrity and independence not found in the
individual paragraphs of the kinds of texts more typically assigned in
English courses. As mentioned earlier, his text is hypertextual, in the sense
that hypertext results in "documents that have multiple points of entry,

multiple exit points, and multiple pathways between points of entry and exit point" (Slatin 1990, 871).

While Grudin does not use the term "paradigm shift," he does devote one paragraph to quantum mechanics, explaining that "modern physics has qualified Aristotle's definition" of time in "important ways." He reviews Aristotle's conclusion that time is a dimension of motion. But, notes Grudin:

> Quantum mechanics has shown that on the subatomic level matter itself has, to some extent, wave nature and therefore motion. Thus time is not only a dimension of motion but also an ingredient of matter . . . The cosmos is not so much a thing in motion as a thing *of* motion, a complex interplay of energies and paces. (21)

Grudin then asserts, "My aim is to project a theory of this sort into the realm of human awareness and will" (21).

While reading such heady stuff, students arrived at themes for their "Grudin" papers in which, as mentioned earlier, they chose a concept of their own to substitute for "time" and developed this concept in a portfolio format similar to Grudin's. Their final portfolios would include their ten best Grudin-style paragraphs, numbered consecutively and leading to no overall conclusions.

Students seemed eager to discuss Grudin, if not to read him. Now about six weeks into the course, they were quite familiar with both LINC and email and displayed a sense of ownership in their use of this talk medium. While they responded to each of Burns's comments, they also showed no hesitation in taking the conversation where they themselves wanted it to go. They also spoke/wrote with obvious candor.

The first LINC on Grudin consisted of a discussion of his style. Burns's prompt read:

> What about Grudin's style? What is style? What makes Grudin different from Zinsser? Why different style for different folks?

The first comment was from Josh, the baseball-cap banterer:

> Different strokes for different folks, I suppose.

While this is hardly a profound response, Josh's comment is significant in several ways. First, it does pick up on the style of Burns's question as posed. Second, it serves to make the transition from teacher to student, i.e., "Okay, we have the ball now." Third, this fast and facile response may well not have been spoken out loud in a traditional class discussion where more formal responses are the norm. Some might say that it would be better left unsaid; but comments like this, at the very least, serve as a warm-up and propel students into an active participatory mode. Initial flippant remarks, like flippant attitudes, are still a form of engagement that can lead, in time, to other more desired forms of engagement. First, however, such remarks must be accepted. The network is accepting, and every comment has its day in the sun.

Short student responses to Burns's question now began popping onto the screen. Steve's message read:

I like Grudin's style but I don't like his writing.

Steve had told me, in halting speech, that because of his stammering he rarely joined in class discussions. It was significant, therefore, that he had jumped right in and even dangled some conversational bait.

Todd's comment, too, was one which would probably not have been articulated in a traditional discussion:

Grudin gives us a shotgun blast of philosophical mumbo-jumbo, while Zinsser used his Uzi, then his nickel-plated .38, followed by a rap from his nightstick. He shot us with his bow and a flaming arrow and finally laid us to rest with a double shot from his homemade rubber-band gun.

Clearly having some stylistic fun of his own, Todd soon followed this with another extended metaphor which captured the hypertextual, non-linear nature of Grudin's text:

Zinsser drove us to San Marcos by way of I-35, Grudin takes us to Paris by way of Pflugerville, left at Albuquerque, thru the Washburn tunnel, over the hills and far away to Madagascar, then North.

Immediately after this, another message from Josh appeared:

I liked the passage where Grudin gets to look at our time from a different perspective; going from a description of what you do during a normal day, then making you ask yourself what would make up a perfect day? It sort of makes you think.

Sharon responded to an idea expressed earlier by Kara:

Kara: I agree that Grudin writes more in spurts, but it really is not choppy. All of his paragraphs in each chapter are related. They form a subtle line of thought even though on the surface the topics appear to be different. And I really do not think that his writing could be considered more intellectual, he just uses different types of words than Zinsser. Unless you mean that by his word choice and sentence structure he sounds more intellectual.

But Kara was busy addressing a comment to Denise. After sending that comment, she later responded to Sharon:

Sharon: Good points! It seems like spurts in that he doesn't seem to form one totally complete thought about the subject. The only thing that seems intellectual is his words. Thanks for the clarification, Sharon!

When two or more students used LINC for a spin-off dialogue on some aspect of the discussion, there was almost always an expression of appreciation, some form of "thanks for listening." When such spin-offs occurred, the participants did not lose out on any of the mainstream conversation. Furthermore, those in the mainstream conversation could follow the spin-offs as well. Even with everyone expressing themselves at once, students were spared the necessity of making hard choices about where to direct their attention. There was opportunity even in the most heated of discussions to take time to consider each and every remark.

Additionally, as noted earlier, students had ample opportunity to compose responses and to enter these into the network. This gave students the chance to enter "wit of the stairway" as described in this passage from Grudin himself: "The French use the term 'esprit de l'escalier' ('wit of the stairway') to describe the brilliant comments that occur to us just after we have left the party or meeting where they would have been appropriate" (Grudin 1982, 33).

Eventually, Steve's bait from the beginning stage of the discussion was picked up by a student, Teresa, who began:

I agree with Steve. I liked Grudin's style but not the content of his writing.

Burns did not try to direct the discussion, nor did he pronounce judgment on the comments of individual students. Rather, he became one more voice, albeit a weighted voice, adding ideas to the conceptual stew. His second entry read:

> What about his word choice? Anyone carrying a dictionary? Here are some of my favorites: ingrained, precious, presence, annoyance, codified, nostalgia, alchemized, resentment, antagonist, traumatic, denial, grievance. And all of these words are just from three entries or so on pp.56-57. This next assignment gives you the chance to stretch your vocabulary—searching for the right words in the right spot.

Evidently, Josh was not impressed:

> Just an informal poll, who's going to Dallas this weekend?

Nor, apparently was Steve. Liberated once more from his speech handicap, Steve included the following observations:

> Grudin uses too many words that need to be looked up in the dictionary. He loses me in his writing because I have a hard time relating to the words he uses. For example, "The habitual act bespeaks a free choice on the part of the agent, because the agent has, in a sense, chosen not to choose, but rather to relax into a graven channel of behavior." OK, sure, I can follow this, but not casually.

And Sandra later supported him.

> Steve: I agree with you. The payoff isn't worth the effort.

Did this constitute open rebellion on the part of students? I think not. Rather, it simply showed that the usual skepticism experienced by some students could be openly aired. It appeared that once disagreements or dissatisfactions were acknowledged, and commiserated over, the path was then clear for ongoing thought. Fortunately, Burns saw himself as a facilitator of open dialogue rather than as a final authority.

Certainly this dialogue involved a lot of "criss-crossing" (Spiro et al. 1987) of the domains. Everyone on the network was induced to consider multiple points of view. Additionally, everyone had the chance to hold up a personal point of view, knowing that there would be ample opportunity to amend, explain, or retract.

By the end of the LINC, Josh of the "different strokes" had read sixty-four student comments relating to style along with four teacher prompts. He had contributed three serious comments of his own. This typified the pattern of response even among those students who began inauspiciously. It was extremely rare for a student to resist the lure of LINC. Meanwhile, Josh received response to his "off-task" question about who was going to Dallas: Several students entered their plans for the weekend. Thus, students harnessed the network to achieve their own needs for expression, group membership, information, or comic relief.

After participating in the LINC session above, students came to the "center donut" for a face-to-face talk with Burns. Burns expressed his awe of the way Grudin took "commonplaces" and turned them into occasions for reflection and insight. The group discussed the idea of "commonplace."

Burns now turned students toward heuristics, so they could begin the process of inventing and developing their own commonplaces in a "Grudin" way. He reminded them that they would again be using email to post their initial thoughts and their progressive drafts to the class. This would make their process visible online to the writing community as a whole. Students were by now comfortable with the network and appeared to appreciate the opportunity to share their writing processes with each other.

Writing academic papers is miserably hard for many students, and misery loves company. Actually, the social context and sense of community mitigated much, though not all, of the misery of paper writing. Students later reported that the posting of their drafts at the end of each class helped them appreciate the way ideas evolve over time. Burns reinforced this concept by frequently referring to the importance of gestation. So, for the kick-off of the "Grudin" paper, he sent his students to the network once again and encouraged them to each come up with and send a "commonplace paragraph" to the network via email. Classmates were to read each other's paragraphs before the next class. Todd, for example, sent the following:

TODD | ALL | ECALPNOMMOC [Commonplace, spelled backwards]
Rooms, on the whole, are very commonplace. But it is what we do in these rooms that make them special places. That is what gives us the distinction between a "house" and a "home". I live in a house. No doubt others have lived there before. This is where I act out the drama that is my life. It is the focal point of all my activity. My days begin and end in this house, and in between I come and go. It is also here that my emotions are kept. Sadness is tucked away neatly in my bedroom. Joy rings triumphantly throughout

when it is overwhelming. Hostilities hide in the closets until we drag them out. To this house I bring "things": food, papers, people, games, laughter, etc. No doubt others have lived there before, but these are the things that make it my "home."

The second LINC on Grudin consisted of brainstorming of topics for the papers the students would be constructing. They all selected topics ranging from "*Trust* and the Art of Living" to "*Challenge* and the Art of Living." During the LINC on topics, students both solicited and contributed ideas.

In the remaining pages of this chapter, and the beginning pages of the next chapter, I will focus on one student, Todd, in order to demonstrate how he benefitted from the response of his classmates.

Todd had decided that his topic would be "Place and the Art of Living." This topic had grown out of the "commonplace" he had written about during the previous class. During the LINC devoted to topic brainstorming, he asked the following question of the class:

My topic is "special places" . . . any ideas on what a special place is or would mean to you . . . what makes a place special?

Holly responded:

Todd: A special place is a place that makes you feel special . . . just kidding. A special place is somewhere you want to go when you feel happy or when you feel sad, somewhere you want to share with someone you care about, a place that takes all of your worries away.

But Todd insisted on a more specific response:

Holly, but what makes you want to go to that place in the first place? How is that place more special than another? Tell me a place that is special to you and why.

Holly responded:

Well, there's this place on the east side of Bergstrom Air Base . . . it's a waterfall in this little woodsy area. The first time I went there was with a guy I had just met (probably not the smartest thing to do, but I trusted him). The moon was full and the night was cool . . . incredibly romantic. It was in this special place that we got to know each other—we talked and talked until about 6 am. Now, I feel like our waterfall knows everything there is to know about our relationship as well as each of us. I feel like the waterfall witnessed our exchange, but it will never tell anyone of all we spoke. Like a special friend, our secret is forever safe with the waterfall.

Angela joined in:

Todd: I know this may sound kind of morbid, but I think of my Grandfather's grave when I think of a special place. It is special in a different sense from what you and Holly have been talking about, but it's special. It's a really unique experience to go there and just sit and talk. It's sad, yet peaceful. My grandfather is the only person who I was close to that has died.

Lora, too, had some thoughts on the matter:

yo todd ever been to san antonio? a special place for me is the chamber of commerce. underneath the west stairway i shared an enchanting moment with my beau, jeff. we were coming home from a party and we didn't quite make it to the car. whoooooooooooooeeeeeeeeee!!!!!!

Denise wrote:

Todd: I think a special place is somewhere that is special to you because of something that has happened to you there. I always remember places like where I was the first time I kissed a boy. . .

Holly joined in again:

Todd: I agree with Denise. A special place evolves from a special memory. I mean, my waterfall may not be so special to me anymore if I would end up breaking up with this guy and marrying someone else.

Like the other students in the class who also received feedback on their topics, Todd had time to read and reread these responses to his topic and his specific questions. As it turned out, the perspective from his peers—as conveyed via the network—had a key role in helping him to refine his thinking about his topic.

This will be explored in the next chapter.

The_Second_Paper_Is_Due

The single most constant thing in my life has been my little old grey-haired grandma. . . . When I was last home, her garden was still in bloom. Her azaleas were spectacular, her dogwoods, both pink and white, were spreading profusely, and everywhere there were loads of garbadaisies and stefanitis. And there was Grandma right out in the middle of it all.
          —Todd, "Special Places and the Art of Living"

As discussed in the previous chapter, Todd solicited feedback from his peers regarding the topic of his second paper, "Place and the Art of Living." After receiving messages from Holly, Angela, Denise, and Lora, he subsequently sent the following email to ALL:

TODD | ALL | PHOTO
I have finally broadened my frame of reference. I know now that there is no size limit that can be placed on calling a place special. I refer here to all of the streets in Austin as a special place. Obviously, some have a greater degree of specialness, for various reasons. I would like to be able to take a large aerial photograph of Austin to illustrate this. The camera would have on it a filter which only shows "Specialness As I View It." This is similar to a thermal photograph, which shows the land temperature in various places. The photograph would have the most special areas in bright red, and as specialness decreased, the colors would become cooler.

Right after this, Todd sent the following email to Burns:

TODD | HUGH | MY PAPER
Dr. Burns . . . As you might have noticed, once again I have moved slower than you might have wished in the process stage. Or have I? Others seem to

have a lot done, especially Sharon! She can write good, Huh? I ain't been able to do that on this time yet. Just kidding. But seriously, I think that, as before, I have finally grasped the concept and am on track . . . Another of my problems was that in the early stages of this assignment on [LINC], I was trying to help others out instead of working on my own stuff . . . a teacher's work is never done, huh? Go Horns. TODD.

After deciding to broaden his frame of reference, Todd added text to his email message of the previous week. This extended "message" illustrates how students used email in this class as a way to build a portfolio while at the same time making their growing drafts public and available to the class as a whole.

TODD | ALL

A momentary special place, as on a trip: Cancun with six friends after high-school graduation . . . embodies carefree thoughts . . . youth . . . not necessarily the +place+, but +who+ I was with . . . and the entire point in my life . . . Not so much physical specialness as mental . . .

I. In search of stability, something which my life has rarely experienced, I look for consistency and security. The single most constant thing in my life has been my little old grey-haired grandma. Her name is Catherine and she is full of just the right balance of sweetness and fire; the most beautifully naive woman in the world. She doesn't like George Bush and I ask her why? "Oh, he's just mean and nasty looking", she says as she piles some more food on my plate. When I am home, we eat on the same table that I have known for twenty-four years. I come through the same door that has been there for four times that long. Her house embodies everything that is warm and gentle and kind and secure and most of all, stable. The security I feel when I am there is like a feeling I have never had, except maybe as a small child in the arms of my parents. In my fast-paced, rushing reality, Grandma's house stands still in time, static and glowing with a love that will last forever.

II. I am your refuge, your protector and I am your healer: When in your life, pain befalls you, and when forces of evil and torment are upon you, come to me. I will hold you and be your refuge. Whenever you are hurt by an insensitive and uncaring world, and when no one else has power to help you, come to me. I will hold you and be your protector. When you lie bleeding from the battle, and your strength is no more, and you gaze up into the black night knowing this will be your last, call for me. I will love you, and I will be your healer

III. Humans are selfish when it comes to questions of perspective. We think that "human scale" is the only scale. As a human,I am able to think on "global terms". Perhaps this is a result of our reasoning ability, but if we can "reason" so well, why do we ignore that the other creatures with which we share this Earth each have a perspective of their own. An ant can lift objects hundreds of times its own weight, and they never seem to be intimidated by enormous heights. I like to think from the feline perspective. My three bedroom house and the neigborhood where i live is an entire world to my cats!

IV. "if you see something that looks like a star, and it's shooting up out of the ground, and your head is spinning . . . from a loud guitar . . ." "if you had just a minute to live, and they granted you one final wish, would you, ask for something . . . like another chance . . ." ". . . and the man in the suit has just bought a new car from the profit he's made off your dreams . . . and today you can swear that the man was shot dead by the gun that didn't make any noise . . . but it wasn't the bullet that laid him to rest . . . was the low spark of high-heeled boys . . ." [from "The Low Spark of High-Heeled Boys" by Steve Winwood]

V. That a place is "special" implies that other places are less special. This takes value away from a place, or better, shows that every day places are taken for granted. Blah, Blah, special, blah, implied dichotomy, blah, blah, inert blah. Contrary . . .

PROCESS: A place is not inherantly special. it was made that way by time and experience. . . . people have shared things at these places . . . when I asked people what there special places were, a common thread emerged. It was not the place they spoke about in detail, but what they had done there. A meadow or a waterfall might be visually beautiful and exciting, therefore people tend to gravitate to these place . . . once there, they do things that are stored in memory. Sometimes a place has proven special to people for so long that they become famous, in the case of national landmarks such as the statue of liberty, or ingrained, like grandmas house. The meaning is in the person, not the place. We yearn to be in these places when we are not.

Simply by it's very nature, special places generate positive emotions and provide security, while unspecial places can bring about fear and negative thoughts. A prison . . . a bad part of town . . . the scene of an accident a year later . . . a former special place after a relationship has ended.

While Todd was expanding his portfolio on "Place and the Art of Living," and being aided by feedback and ideas from his peers, others were having similar experiences with their topics.

On the day that papers were due, students found this CLASS ASSIGN-MENT entered onto the network:

1. Print a copy of this assignment. 2. Print a copy of your paper. 3. Send a copy of your paper to the network (directions included as to correct label). 4. Log off. 5. Go to the 4th floor roof. There we will read some of the selections you have printed out. I will collect your essays at the end of the period.

After everyone had sent their papers to the network, they went upstairs and out onto a roof-top terrace for "Performance." Drawing lawn chairs into a semicircle on the tiles, students nervously scanned the hard copies of their papers for sections to read out loud. This roof-top terrace was adjacent to the Texas Tower, and the bells rang out noisily every fifteen minutes. Construction work created an unfortunate din, so that students had to lean toward each reader and even then could not hear well.

When it was Steve's turn to read, he walked self-consciously toward Burns, held out his paper, and muttered: "Would you read this?" Knowing that Steve had a speech impediment, Burns gladly read his selections for him. Although he had complained during the LINC session that Grudin used "too many big words," so that "It takes intense brain activity to decifer [sic] through his writing," Steve, writing on "Motivation and the Art of Living," actually displayed a surprising talent for writing in Grudin's style:

A bicycle racer, to be a worthy competitor, knows that he must build his endurance. His days of training are like blocks of endurance. He stacks one block upon the other, each day rising to a higher level of performance. He also knows the higher the stack, the more precarious the perch. His blocks tumble faster than he builds if he does not continually reinforce them. What is it then that gets him out of his warm bed on a cold dark morning to suffer first through the chill of the morning air and then through the pain of the ride? Is it his desire to be the best and knowledge of how to do it, or is it his fear of losing what he has worked so hard for?

Lora, writing on "Pain and the Art of Living," nervously twisted her hair and tugged at her shoelaces as she read about a particularly painful childhood memory:

> The two most basic types of pain are emotional and physical. When a parent inflicts both these pains simultaneously on a child, the outcome can be devastating. The most alive memory I have of my father was when I was six years old. My babysitter took some kids and I around the neighborhood to sing Christmas carols. In all the excitement, we didn't realize that we arrived home 5 minutes late. Walking up the street, I saw my father standing in the driveway. His entire body manifested the anger inside of him. As I approached him, my body tensed and my fear intensified. Furiously, he grabbed me, drug me up the driveway, yanked me into the house, and locked us both in the bathroom. He took off his belt and beat me with it until my mother finally broke down the door. I didn't understand what I had done wrong, but I felt a huge amount of guilt. I never saw my father again after that night, which was probably for the best.—those of us who have dealt with pain effectively, swim. Those who have not, drown in their sorrows.

Irene, writing on "Fun and the Art of Living," had experimented with one of Grudin's conventions, a prescriptive list. She had written:

> Exercises for sharpening your sense of fun:
> 1) Ask yourself when was the last time you laughed so hard that a tiny tear started to dribble out of the corner of your eye was
> 2) Try doing something all by yourself, and see if it's enjoyable
> 3) Make a list of synonyms for "fun," starting with enjoyment
> 4) Describe in detail the best time you've ever had in your life
> 5) Describe what you would like to do that you think would be really fun
> 6) Think of what your Mom and Dad think of as fun (this may be fun in itself)
> 7) For the next few weeks, every time you are doing something on "leisure time," write down what it was you did (if it was for pleasure) and why

By way of acknowledging her debt to Lora for the dialoguing they did on their contrasting topics in LINC, Irene closed her reading with these words:

> Pain is opposite of fun. In pain, we are experiencing the opposite end of the spectrum on degrees of fun. Without pain, however, we could not know fun.

When it was Todd's turn to read a paragraph from his paper, "Place and the Art of Living," he chose the passage about his grandmother's garden:

I always hated flowers when I was a kid. My Grandmother loved flowers, but it was me that always had to work in her garden. I soon moved from passivity to literally hating flowers. I would go through her seed catalogues and draw moustaches on pictures of petunias. Being a semi-normal young boy, I naturally wanted to do boy things; as a result, I caught a lot of grief from my playmates. When I was last home, her garden was still in bloom. Her azaleas were spectacular, her dogwoods, both pink and white, were spreading profusely, and everywhere there were loads of garbadaisies and stefanitis. And there was Grandma right out in the middle of it all.

Although the passages were colorful, the performances were dull; the enthusiasm of LINC was noticeably missing. Burns made a comment or two on each reading, but despite his prods, students refrained from commenting on each other's writing. Were the computer relationships too fragile to survive on the roof? Were students too self-conscious to speak when they were visible? Or, were they simply reverting to habits entrenched from years of traditional classroom dynamics? Perhaps a combination of these factors contributed to the near silence.

At the following class session, Burns invited students to send email messages about what they thought of the roof-top reading session. Lora sent the following email message to ALL:

I must admit that I was a bit apprehensive about reading in front of everyone on Thurs. Confidence is not something I've felt about my writing; until now. I'm getting a little more comfortable with my writing but i'm far from being certain of it.

David wrote the following:

It was really enjoyable to sit around and here [sic] what other people think and more importantly how others think. This is an art that has been lost in our age of television. I would really like to do that once again before the class is over. Yes, the class is making sense to me now!!! AHA!!

Holly had been late to the session and began her email message with this message to ALL:

First of all, I would like to apologize about being late to the group reading last Thursday. I fell asleep while I was reading over my paper. I woke up at 3:40, but you all were already gone when I came in to print my paper.

Todd wrote this email message to ALL:

I enjoyed reading our essays upstairs . . . it is refreshing to finally hear them out of the confines of this dungeon, and in an open space. It is as if they were seeds which had come to life in the dark, damp soil . . . because there is where the nutrients of life come from . . . and sprouted into the sunlight . . . full of radiant beauty and color, ready to face the world . . . But seriously, I am feeling an incredible improvement in my writing . . . mostly because I have been doing so much . . . in the process I think I have "re-learned" how to write in the first place . . .

@18

Developing_Community

Sometimes you want to go where everybody knows your name,
and they're always glad you came.
You want to be where you can see troubles are all the same.
You want to go where everybody knows your name.
          —Theme from *Cheers* (TV Program)

On the evening of May 20, 1993, the Ninth Conference on Computers and Writing convened in Ann Arbor, Michigan. After the opening banquet, but before the keynote address, host Wayne Butler came to the podium. Many were hurriedly wolfing down their cake when Butler announced that there was no need for anyone to bolt for their rooms in order to watch the last episode of *Cheers*, airing momentarily. He and the other conference organizers, themselves determined not to miss this historic television event, had anticipated the crowd's dilemma. Butler reassured everyone that he had arranged for someone to tape *Cheers* and that it would be shown during the subsequent two days' cocktail hours. And, indeed, this is what occurred. As Butler later recalled:

> We rolled a VCR and monitor into the hotel ballroom in which we were having the cocktail party, set up the TV in a corner, and set up chairs theater style . . . We sort of set up a *Cheers* setting for the final episode: a "Bar" (Well, a cocktail party in a hotel) where everybody knows your name. (Butler, email, 10/15/94)

A significant group of conference attendees disengaged from animated talk with colleagues in order to watch the final act of this remarkably popular situation comedy. Others had made arrangements for relatives to tape the episode for them. Some, of course, had no interest in this program, but it is noteworthy that many did. Elevator talk during the conference frequently consisted of critiques of this historic program.

To what can we attribute this intense loyalty and interest in the program, *Cheers*? Good writing and good acting are undoubtedly factors. However, I think the *Cheers* bar, "a place where everybody knows your name," appealed to a common longing for community. If the conference attendees, like others in America, did not have such a place themselves, they could at least tune in weekly to a place where the fantasy was enacted.

At a basic level, humans as a species tend to live in collectives—tribes, villages, and most recently cities. It is easy to romanticize the past, positing some golden age of community that existed in frontier or rural America. Such romantic notions are flawed in light of our knowledge that communities have often been mean-spirited, oppressive, or exclusive toward specific individuals or groups. However, the fact remains that many Americans long for a sense of living or working in a community. Most people want a sense of belonging, and many find that this sense is precarious as we approach the new millennium. Comparing our fast-paced urban lives to the slower and perhaps more rural lives of our parents and grandparents, many of us share a certain nostalgia for the idealized—if seldom realized—communities of the past.

In *The Great Good Place: Cafes, Coffee Shops, Community Centers, Beauty Parlors, General Stores, Bars, Hangouts, and How They Get You Through The Day*, Ray Oldenburg explores the importance of the places we live, work, and gather for "conviviality." He suggests that we have become "sorely deficient" (Oldenburg 1991, 13) in informal public life, and he alludes to Dolores Hayden's observation in chapter 2 of *Redesigning the American Dream* that "Americans have substituted the vision of the ideal home for that of the ideal city" (7). Oldenburg asserts that "American lifestyles, for all the material acquisition and seeking after comforts and pleasures, are plagued by boredom, loneliness, alienation, and a high price tag" (13).

What is missing, observes Oldenburg, is the habit of meeting at public places where casual conversation can occur. Oldenburg suggests, therefore, that in addition to a place to work and a place to live, people also need a "third place" where they can freely associate with a diversity of others in a spirit of community:

> Neutral ground provides the place, and leveling sets the stage for the cardinal and sustaining activity of third places everywhere. That activity is conversation.

Nothing more clearly indicates a third place than that the talk there is good; that it is lively, scintillating, colorful, and engaging. (26)

Howard Rheingold, in *The Virtual Community: Homesteading on the Electronic Frontier*, argues that "perhaps cyberspace is one of the informal public places where people can rebuild the aspects of community that were lost when the malt shop became a mall." He quickly counters, "Or perhaps cyberspace is precisely the wrong place to look for the rebirth of community, offering not a tool for conviviality but a life-denying simulacrum of real passion and true commitment to one another. In either case, we need to find out soon" (Rheingold 1993b, 26).

There is much talk lately about the potential of online community-building. For example, journalist Philip Elmer-Dewitt claims that "cyberspace is less about commerce than about community." He adds, "In a world already too divided against itself—rich against poor, producer against consumer—cyberspace offers the nearest thing to a level playing held" (Elmer-Dewitt 1995, 9).

Pamela McCorduck, in an interview of Sherry Turkle, apparently blends her own ideas with Turkle's. She says:

Sherry Turkle sits before a computer screen, both participating in and observing a MUD [multi-user domain]—that theater of text alone. It's the enactment, the very instantiation, of a society built out of language, as hypothesized years before by Jacques Lacan. It is life on the screen, a phrase so pregnant with meaning that you could spend half an hour decoding it. (McCorduck 1996, 162)

Turkle expresses ambivalence about cyberspace communities. She states that an online community can be a "retreat," but

. . . in some cases it is not so much a retreat as a first step in developing strengths that can be brought into "real" life . . . In the best of cases, positive online experiences leave their mark on both the virtual and the real. And they can change the way people see their possibilities; it can affect self-esteem. (*Technology Review* 1996, 43)

Turkle elaborates by saying that to get along socially one must be able to tolerate occasional rejection. In an online environment, one can move on past such occurrences. Furthermore, spending time online can help a person move beyond any tendency to see things in black and white terms. In other words, Turkle claims that people "may come out the other side having had some experience they're able to use to make their lives more fulfilling" (43). Indeed, people with higher self-esteem might well be better members of communities, both on- and offline. Turkle adds that "It would be exciting to see online communities used more to address real-world social crises such as those around the environment, health, drugs, and education" (44). While she is excited about online communities as labs or "social experiments," Turkle is concerned that people might lose a sense of urgency about their real-world problems because they have a virtual alternative.

Some look for a sense of community at the workplace, but this can be achieved only if employees have opportunities to converse. In many cases, computer networks are playing a role in facilitating workplace talk. Shoshana Zuboff, in her study of computers in the workplace, suggests that if managers would allow—in fact provide for—informal talk arenas at the office or factory, that employees would be more productive and loyal. She claims that "The boundaries that delimit dutiful work behavior from social exchange have always tended to be hazy . . . " Noting that the conversation which sustains the oral culture at the coffee break or lunch table is ephemeral, she suggests that when this conversation goes online, the "transient talk" is transformed into a "concrete presence." Referring to a workplace where workers could freely "talk" online, Zuboff notes, "It was as if the ether of sociality that once filled the hallways had suddenly congealed" (Zuboff 1988, 376). One worker said, "It's like being tapped into the grapevine" (367).

Another possible site for the development of community is the college campus, or academia in general. I've heard composition teachers say that they were startled, mid-semester, to discover that students in their classes did not even know each others' names. So accustomed are we to thinking of our classes in dualistic terms of "teacher" and "students" that we may mistakenly assume that *they* all know each other, even though *we* do not. Yet, in a traditional college class, it is often only the teacher who gets to know the students—through papers and conferences. Students may never know even the names of other students in the class. Classes are often large, and universities can be enormous. Students may live in cavernous dorms in which they know only a handful of peers, and they may never encounter these familiar faces during the day's frenetic schedule. In a networked class, such as the one described here, students do develop relationships with peers. They do learn names, and eventually faces. Even more important, they have an opportunity to overcome feelings of isolation and alienation by being in almost constant verbal contact with each other.

Certainly LINC, at its best, can provide a new space for students and teachers to engage in open dialogue. For close to a decade now, teachers and researchers have been actively exploring the potential for community in LINCed classrooms. In *Computers and Community: Teaching Composition in the Twenty-First Century* (Handa 1990a), teachers explore various aspects of community in computer-based classrooms. The authors consider such factors as the architecture, the hardware, the software, feminist pedagogy, and empowerment. Editor Handa notes, "All the contributors believe the computer is a powerful tool that, if used in certain ways, can not only enhance but create a strong sense of community among both the students and their instructors" (xx). While some studies have pointed to positive, community-building aspects of LINC, others (see, e.g., Regan 1993; Romano 1993) have pointed to problems. It seems wise to see LINC as a complex environment in which both desired and undesired kinds of linkings are forged.

I began this chapter by alluding to the *Cheers* bar where "everybody knows your name." Burns's students did indeed express feelings of dissatisfaction with places where no one knew their names. Tiffany, for example, expressed student alienation in her graphic description of class registration—part of her paper on "Chaos":

> With my ID in hand as well as the proof of existence, I approach to retaliate vs. the enemy . . . People fly by as though they were on their last leg, and many wish they were . . . The chaoticness is unbearable. . . .

In an email message, Denise refers to

the disappointment I felt when I went to speak to one of my favorite professors and she didn't know my name.

And Irene alludes to being

clueless, swimming around in my fish bowl, but there are so many fish here that it's getting hard to see.

I think it was a basic need to connect, in the midst of a bureaucratic university, that motivated much of the conversation on the network in Burns's class. The classroom began to take on attributes of a "great good place" as defined by Oldenburg (1991). This is not to say that it was a place without conflict—as will be addressed later in this chapter.

The students in Burns's class met twice a week for an hour and fifteen minutes, and during this time they were in almost constant contact with each other. The potential for the development of community in this networked context is certainly stronger than in a class where students sit silently in rows listening to a lecture and taking notes. Zuboff states that "Visible participation in the meanings and values of one's immediate group helps to build a joint experience base" (Zuboff 1988, 102) and that organizations centered around the electronic text can become "a learning community" (394). Indeed, the students in Burns's class constructed just such a community.

One way that students constructed community was by using email. Email messages, composed for the most part in informal discourse, flowed between students not only *during* class sessions but *between* sessions as well. The initial links occurred in the first week of class when Burns simply invited students to send email greetings to each other:

ANGELA | ALL
GLAD TO BE HERE

TAMMY | ALL
PRAY FOR ME!

HOLLY | ALL | CLASS
Hi! I am a student in this class who is incredibly glad this day is over! Hope you all have a nice three day weekend.

Students reached out to each other in many different ways. For example, George named one of his messages SEX even though it had nothing to do with sex. It elicited this response:

David | R) SEX
Nice attention grabber

Josh tried a different approach:

Josh | ALL | ???????
This class is going to be quite a bit of work, I may drop it. But, then again nothing else is open, so I may not.

And Michelle wrote:

MICHELE | ALL | CLASS
HI. HOW MANY OF YOU ARE READY TO DROP THIS COURSE?!?!?!?!?!?!

Other messages included the following:

DAVID | FIRST DAY
this is a message that I am sending you to let you know I'm alive.

Of course, certain students seemed more intent on making an impression with Burns than with reaching out to their fellow students:

TIM | HUGH | FIRST CLASS
Hey Prof,
This class seems like it would benefit me a great deal, but I'm concerned about the work load. Maybe I'll see you next Tuesday.

LINDA | HUGH | CLASS
Hi, how ya doing. I'm the blonde that was typing while you were talking. Sorry!!!!

Burns felt that a sense of community was important and took steps to foster its development. He sent messages, such as the following, encouraging students to read each others' work:

See what your colleagues are up to. Don't try to second guess the assignment when you can watch and learn from each other. You'll find quite a variety of impressions: reading palms, seeing trees, listening to grandmother on the phone. Meet Nevada-hardened faces at a poker table in California, throw rocks in a pond, meet Mr. Religion, hear about Templeton, and many, many more. Reading [email] is better than . . . well not reading [email]. This is an unpaid pedagogical announcement.

and this:

Many of you are doing a great job remembering some specific memory. You can feel when it is right, can't you? When the meaning of the memory is more than just the memory. Be sure to look at some of the entries in [email].

Which ones do you like? Let your classmates know. For me, I like the turtles, a gambler's face, HEB employment, apples and orchards, self-paced
astronomy, grandmother's rocker, at the zoo, etc.

Perhaps most important, Burns modelled what I call "kind attention."
That is, his reading of student messages was in fact thoughtful listening,
modeling—to use Faigley's words—"spaces to listen" (Faigley 1992, 39).
His responses were always supportive, even when critical. Thus, he did not
blatantly challenge, insult, or in any other way model a confrontational
style of relationship. His very style of support suggested a type of community that might be achieved online.

Students seemed to respond to that modelling by eagerly supporting
each other, as displayed in this series of email messages between Steve and
Josh:

STEVE | JOSH | ECON
Josh, I have a couple of econ writers if you're still looking.

JOSH | STEVE | R) ECON
Steve, I would be grateful if you could lend a few suggestions, Heilbronner
was the only one that I could really come up with. Thanks, Josh

STEVE | JOSH | R) ECON
The only author other than Heilbonner I've found was John Kenneth Galbraith.
My prof said he was a very good econ writer but I haven't found any books
of his as yet. There doesn't seem to be any listed in the library computer nor
in the PCL card catalog. Please let me know if you have any luck.

JOSH | STEVE | R) ECON
I have one book by Galbraith, it's called "Everyone's Guide to Economics." I'll
bring it to class next time, and you can take a look at it. I'm going to ask
another prof. about authors again, and get another.

Other messages of this type include the following:

SHARON | KARA
Kara: Forget what you were taught. Most of those rules do not apply in the
real world. You can use I, me, she,etc. You know which teachers want you
to just repeat what they have said, so for those, do it. Fortunately, most of

them would find it refreshing to read a paper that sounds as if the student is actually talking to them. That is one thing that high school english teachers are being taught to accept now.

IRENE | TERESA
Well put, Teresa . . . Since I haven't done the majority of the reading we were supposed to have done by now, I am going through and systematically commenting on everyone else's comments. I must say, it was an excellent point you make about noise. In other words, it was fabulous.

Sharon and David also exchanged messages in a manner that appeared to support a growing sense of community in the classroom:

DAVID | SHARON | HI
how are you?

SHARON | DAVID | R) HI
i am fine david. i just now saw your message so you won't be getting this until tuesday so, how was your weekend?

SHARON | DAVID | DICTIONARY
well, david, i just want to say thank you for helping me. i really do not know how my paper has turned out, but at least it is finished. i was going to read yours, but you do not seem to have a copy of it in the system. i wanted to critique it and tear it to pieces before anyone else got the chance. just kidding!

Holly sent the following messages of support and empathy:

Kara: I am so glad that I am not the only non-graduating senior in this class! I was beginning to feel so all alone!!

And, with regard to the LINC about Zinsser, the first text studied, she wrote:

Steve: I agree with you about obscurity!! I hate to look up words, and there's nothing worse than an author who forces you to consistently do so!

Students seemed to want to share their relief with each other when they finished a paper. For example, Kara sent this message to all:

KARA | ALL | FIRST ESSAY DONE
I'm glad we're done! I just wanted to finish this topic in my mind by sending a final message. I have completed my first essay on "Writing to Learn" . . . Okay! I feel better now. I feel like this assignment is done and I'm ready to go on!

Linguists shed light on the way that people use language to construct community. For example Deborah Tannen notes that casual conversation often conveys little significant information but simply demonstrates connection and rapport (Tannen 1985, 125). Moreover, when a person is assumed to already know unstated information, often shared background knowledge, this creates a "feeling of involvement" (131).

Written discourse, which typically includes more contextual information than does oral discourse, feels less personal and may not evoke the same feeling of involvement. I think this explains why the students participating in LINC often succumbed to the temptation to send messages such as "Yes," "No way!" or "I agree"; these messages required an implicit shared context and were thus sent in an assumed (or desired) state of involvement.

Many of the LINC messages clearly emphasized interpersonal involvement. However, there was frequently a willingness to share information, as in this message from Sharon:

SHORT CUT
Hey everyone! There is a short cut when you want to transfer to another file. When you have the option to hit the F3 key or list the file name, hit F3 and a list of the files will appear. All you have to do then is highlight the file you want and enter! Presto- just like magic!

The correspondence between Lora and Irene, as mentioned earlier, is an example of an email relationship that grew significantly over time. The following series of messages spanned a period of 49 days.

LORA | IRENE | R) INQUIRY
Hey Irene, I'm lora. We sat next to each other the first day of class. You said you were thinking about dropping, but you didn't. Good for you. Stick out this journey through computer chaos. I'd like for you to read some of my stuff, if and when i get any so-called stuff. Okay? Let me know. I would also like to talk to you about some profs. See you. Bye!!!

IRENE | LORA | PROFS&STUFF

well, lora if i remember correctly you sit in the corner, and i would be glad to read your stuff. but why, praytell, choose me? just curious. anyway i guess you can tell how much i hate using the "change case" key. remember how i told you i was taking a course with Trimble? well it's turning out to be a very personal kind of course, and if you enjoy a class and a teacher that isn't hung up on pretension, bullshit literary theory, and selfrighteousness, you'll like Trimble a lot. how do you feel about this anonymity stuff? i mean, isn't it weird to talk to people through computers? sure you know who the people are, but its almost like telepathy. like you dont even have to be here (modem) for instance.

LORA | IRENE | WHATEVER

HEY YOU, PRAISE THE LORD!!!!!!!! IT'S OVER!!!!!!!!!! I REALLY DID ENJOY YOUR PAPER. wHY THE HELL IS THIS TYPING ALL CAPS?????

LORA | IRENE | CRAP

ok, i don't like grudin. maybe i didn't give him enough of a chance. what did you think?

IRENE | LORA | DUNG

so how did the weekend go? I spent mine working. Not exactly what i'd call memorable. anyway, is everything ok? . . . let me know when you get this.

LORA | IRENE | R) DUNG

irene, i had a lovely weekend. thanks for asking . . . i quit my job this weekend thinking that i had another one waiting in the wings, but . . . . i don't! so, i'm jobless and moneyless. got any suggestions? seriously, if you do know of any places that are hiring, let me know. on a brighter note, I got an a on my first major spanish exam and a b on my math exam. i expected an a on the math exam, but you know how it is when you make stupid mistakes. too bad, uh?

IRENE | LORA | LIFE

if youre looking for a restaurant job, try waterloo on 24th st. they just opened, but i think my friend is quitting, so theyll have an opening.

LORA | IRENE | YOUR ABSENCE

where the hell are you girl? actually, i guess i should say where the hell were you yesterday? i;m here in computer hell land trying to catch up on this paper. i'm leaving you now to get into my pain. . . . lora

LORA | IRENE
yo irene, can you help me out with the no pain no gain entry of my paper?
i know you've got a shitload to do yourself, but i need your help and guid-
ance. pretty please?

IRENE | LORA
ok, but howdo you want to do it? like philosophiclly . . . or relating it to relationships, or physical exercise, or basically growing up in a sheltered environment (out of touch with the ghetto or anything harsh like that)? what do
you want to do, roughly?

Irene said of her email correspondence with Lora:

—It is somewhat like having a penpal, but instead of across the ocean we
are across the floor from each other.

Community grew from the realization among students that many of
them shared the same insecurities about writing. For example, Kara sent
an email message reading:

I enjoyed today's class time. It is encouraging to hear that not everyone is
confident with their writing ability. Also, I enjoy getting feed back from people about my ideas and thinking patterns. . . . How fun it is to hear others
idea, even when I can't understand them or know where they are going.

Similarly, Casey wrote:

It's neat to see what other people are thinking and writing. I enjoy seeing
that my peers have some of the same thoughts I do (that's encouraging).

And Tiffany wrote this:

Hi everybody! So, what does Zinnser mean by "writing to learn?" How
about writing and rewriting and rewriting and rewriting and . . .

Josh expressed satisfaction with the high degree of participation in class
discussions. Since Josh was actually one of the more vocal students in face-
to-face discussion, we can speculate that his comment might well reflect a
desire to hear from others in the class:

The [LINC] system serves as a useful link to get all the people in the class involved in the discussion. I think sometimes people are too hesitant to speak in class and [now] they can talk, and it doesn't have to be out loud.

Students were encouraged to collaborate on the ideas for their papers. This, too, contributed to the writing community, as mentioned by several students. For example, Tiffany said:

It was neat to see how other students' ideas gave information to compile a paper. As I searched through quotes, I was able to select which ones I felt were integratable in my paper. After this I sorted through the quotes as well with my own ideas and organized this paper.

Irene composed a top ten list, mimicking comedian David Letterman:

The top ten things, we the students of this class hate:

10. When people don't listen to what you say. i.e.,"When I ask if they have a select circle card they say paper." (David) [referring to his work as a grocery store bagger]
9. When people interrupt your phone conversations. (Josh)
8. People who hand out flyers during adds and drops. (David)
7. When people lock there bike too close to yours and you have to scratch up your bike to get it out. (Lora and Denise)
6. Dorm food, especially at Kinsolving. (Sandra)
5. People who don't listen and then repeat back to you what you just said.
4. Poodles. (Irene)
3. Snakes and when people smack. (Casey)
2. People who hang up on your answering machine. (Tiffany)
1. The pilsbury dough boy doing anything, i.e., his birthday party, rapping, playing violin, break dancing, swinging from a rope. Whatever happened to just pushing in his stomach? (David)

A successful community is one in which diversity of perspectives is tolerated, if not celebrated. Interestingly, the idea of perspective came up frequently among these students. As already discussed, David wrote an entire paper on "Perspective and the Art of Living." Others simply commented on perspective. Denise wrote, "We should constantly challenge ourselves by imagining what we would do if we were in someone else's situation." Todd's essay included this comment: "Humans are selfish when it comes to questions of perspective. . . . Perhaps this is a result of our reasoning ability, but if we can reason well, why are we always so ignorant of differing perspectives?" Indeed, differing perspectives were showcased on this network, perhaps providing a catalyst for students to elaborate on their thoughts and opinions.

In LINCs, students frequently referred to each other by name; they also included numerous supportive comments such as "I agree" and "Good point." Such comments from peers are quite rare in traditional classes that I have observed. In non-computer classes, sentiments of support are commonly expressed in body language, such as nodding in agreement. Much is made over the value of such body language. However, it appeared to me that students were especially grateful, when online, to see support actually spelled out on their screens. In this manner, the suggestion of support became a fact of support—as in the recent MCI television commercial which responded to AT&T's challenge to "Put it in writing." And, the recording of such sentiments in writing also made them a more public and official endorsement.

Of course, there is a down side to computer communication, as well. The sense of freedom experienced by participants on a network can result in a lessening of inhibitions normally present in classroom discourse. The term *flaming* has been adopted to refer to this phenomenon, and in recent years, flaming has received increased attention at conferences in which computer networks are discussed. During the question-and-answer sessions that follow presentations and forums on aspects of networks and community, the discussion often bogs down over the dilemma of flaming.

Part of the dilemma over "what to do about flaming" stems from the fact that flaming on the network means different things to different people. The term *flame*, as applied to electronic communication, was originally coined by computer hackers and defined in the first edition of *The Hacker's Dictionary* (1983) as a verb meaning, "to speak incessantly and/or rabidly on some relatively uninteresting subject with a patently ridiculous attitude." A "flame session" was defined as "a meeting in which everyone flames; a 'bull session.'"

By 1993, *The New Hacker's Dictionary* provided a somewhat different take on the verb *flame*. The first definition read: "To post an email message intended to insult and provoke." The first definition of the previous edition was now demoted to the second definition. Similarly, the definition of *flamer* had evolved from a user who is a "fanatic" to one who is "obnoxious." The term "flame war" had been added and was defined as "an acrimonious dispute, especially when conducted on a public electronic forum such as USENET."

The Jargon Watch section of *Wired Magazine* (1.4) captured the coinage "NLB," i.e., "nonlinear behavior (from Chaos Theory), used to describe emotional or irrational flaming on the Net." The example given is "That gun-control topic is overwhelmed by NLB."

Michael Heim defined flaming as "the tendency to write messages on the computer so directly that the usual norms of civility and politeness fall away" (Heim 1987, 209). The problem is that what is considered civil by some may be considered bland by others; and what is considered polite by some, may be considered "holding back" by others. Thus flaming appears to be in the eye of the beholder and is a relative term indeed. Detailed and thoughtful elaboration by a network user could even be considered flaming if it was viewed by another as tedious, unnecessary, or unimportant.

Insults are certainly construed as absence of politeness by many; yet the notion of insult is problematic. For example, Tannen found that males often use verbal aggression to "start interaction and create involvement" (Tannen 1990, 163). Many men, according to Tannen, seek, embrace, and enjoy conflict (150). What may appear to some as a hostile comment may actually be intended as an invitation to friendship. This no doubt also occurs occasionally in the conversation of women.

Lee Sproull and Sara Kiesler found that "People behaved irresponsibly more often on EMS (Electronic Mail Systems) than they did in face-to-face conversations" (Sproull and Kiesler 1986, 1509). It is not clear, however, exactly what they consider to be "irresponsible." Candid comments, especially those which offend some, may be construed as irresponsible. But is it any more responsible to camouflage one's true opinions in order to gain the approval of one's instructor or peers? Jerome Bump reports that several of his students welcomed flaming as a form of "emotional honesty" (Bump 1990, p. 57).

In recent years, however, flaming seems to have become more of a problem. What started out as flickering flames has erupted into full-fledged forest fires at times, and reports of such fires are increasingly aired at conferences and in academic journals. In the very room where Burns's class met, other classes have had outbursts of flames in which students have made hostile comments based on race, ethnicity, gender, and sexual orientation. Individual students, or groups of students have used the network to voice their prejudices and hatreds—sometimes even targeting members of the class (Regan 1993; Romano 1993).

Some believe that the college classroom is the ideal place for prejudices to be aired. Here, it is argued, students can become aware of their biases; in dialogue and debate, they can engage in reflection and learn to separate rational beliefs and opinions from irrational ones. However, positive outcomes cannot be guaranteed. Furthermore, instructors are rightfully concerned about the emotional and physical safety of students in their charge.

In corporate settings, flaming can also be a problem. Zuboff says, "Oral communication tends to be more highly charged, emotional, and potentially conflictful. When communication must be face-to-face, interpersonal attractions and antagonisms are kept high" (Zuboff 1988, 177). Zuboff acknowledges that network conversation can include this aspect of spoken conversation. She says, "People tend to be less reflective when they are immersed in the present-tense dynamism of utterance and action" (178).

Rheingold notes that the incidence of flaming is jeopardizing the Internet. He says that when one flames online, the ultimate punishment is to be ignored. Referring to overt racism that has occurred online, he says that such breaches of civility threaten the continuation of free online communication; if rules and sanctions become necessary, conviviality will be sacrificed. His hope is that respectful norms will develop (Rheingold 1993a). Another problem with some network environments is that the contributions of some participants are given short shrift because of the same prejudices that affect communication in more traditional settings. Students who felt silenced in more traditional settings may now voice themselves freely only to find their comments routinely ignored (Takayoshi 1994).

In Burns's class, flaming consisted more of brash spontaneity than of open hostility or the airing of prejudices. Nevertheless, the spontaneity was welcomed more by some students than by others. Irene was offended by an off-color comment by Todd. Others found Lora's comments annoying at times, citing her way of demanding attention, sometimes over something as trivial as how to get her computer to stop typing in all capitals.

In general, however, students in Burns's class did not find flaming to be a problem. From what I observed, the conflict was relatively benign and did not require intervention by the instructor. I don't know why dangerous flaming didn't occur in Burns's class. Perhaps, at this early stage, students were still quite conscious of the teacher as authority figure and assigner of grades, or perhaps they were awed by the technology. It could be that the texts and content did not happen to lead the class into controversial areas.

Perhaps the face-to-face time at the "center donut" was important in reminding students that the online voices belonged to real people with real feelings. Or, the intense and early online interaction may have created a sense of camaraderie which mitigated against any impulses to be offensive. It is unlikely that this was an unusually enlightened and kind group of students, but perhaps Burns's civility and expectation of mutual respect somehow permeated and shaped the class culture. Although I don't know why flaming wasn't a problem in this particular class, I do know that flaming, in general, is a valid concern which merits further dialogue among teachers and students.

Rheingold explores the concepts of conflict and community in the context of the WELL, a Bay-area online community:

> Whatever community is, it is not necessarily a conflict-free environment. There has always been a lot of conflict on the WELL, breaking out into regular flamefests of interpersonal attacks from time to time. Factionalism. Gossip. Envy. Jealousy. Feuds. Brawls. Hard feelings that carry over from one discussion to another . . . A core of people must flat-out believe in the possibility of community and keep coming back to that amid the emotional storms in order for the whole loosely coupled group to hold together at all. (Rheingold 1993b, 53)

My own thinking about community has been complicated by what I saw on networks both during the semester of Burns's class and afterwards. After observing this class, I joined the discussion list, Megabyte University and, myself, became part of an online community. I noticed that discussion lists, like one-semester classes, are transitory. Megabyte University is still a thriving listserv, but as an open system, the participants who comprise it vary from day to day and week to week. It is problematic to frame such a freeform collective as a community. My overall stance, however, is an optimistic one. I feel that the online communities that emerge and disperse on discussion lists, chat lines, or one-semester classes do influence people in primarily positive ways. I think that online communities have the potential to develop within the participants an aesthetic of community—a sense of what it feels like to be "in community" with others, especially with others from diverse walks of life.

I feel that online experiences can lead to a sharper appreciation of what enhances or jeopardizes community among people. I suspect that this aesthetic, these experiences, carry over into settings where more enduring communities can develop. Or, perhaps, in this postmodern age, enduring communities are a thing of the past, and we will have to satisfy our yearning for community within the brief, but meaningful, groups which we encounter or deliberately select. In either case, a new aesthetic will serve us. I will talk more about this in the final chapter.

@19

Academic_Discourse _Communities

One of the things that ticks me off the most is the "decorum" that pervades English departments that keeps people talking like pompous philosophy professors. All of us, tenured and graduate, have some real problems that need to be talked about honestly.
—Fred Kemp, MBU message, March 3, 1995

Begin with where they are as language animals, endowed with the form-finding and form-creating powers of mind and language.
—Ann E. Berthoff, *The Making of Meaning* (1981, 9)

As discussed in chapter 6, students in this class unanimously denounced obscure writing, writing that is intended to "impress," and writing that includes field-specific jargon. Their rejection of this kind of writing was spurred by the opinions William Zinsser expressed about such "pompous" writing. Students were all too ready to jump on Zinsser's bandwagon, seemingly taking his ideas one step further into a rejection of virtually all academic prose. This topic was aired again during the second LINC on Zinsser's book. The discussion included many criticisms of obscure prose which students often equated with academic prose. Holly was first with this comment:

> Although Zinsser seemed to have a lot of crotchets and convictions, I think the majority of them were peeves of many of us. I mean, who likes to read a sentence so long that you forget what it's about before you finish reading it?

Then, Angela added her opinion:

Since my major is Sociology/Pre-Law, I am faced with this stuff all the time, and it really gets frustrating.

And George agreed:

It seems there is a misconception in society that we, in order to write intelligently, must use such eloquent language that the reader has to spend hours interpreting what we have just said. I think we learn this from our high school English teachers and from studying too much poetry.

Irene referred to this as "ulto wordiness."
Sandra, too, logged in against obscure writing:

I don't like writing that uses "big words" that don't mean anything to the common folk. It sounds impressive but doesn't communicate the author's ideas and makes the reader feel stupid for not understanding what the words mean.

And Sharon wrote:

I also don't like people who use a thesaurus to try to find BIG words to stick in their paper in order to sound intelligent. Most of the time the words are misused and it is usually obvious that the person doesn't really know what the word means.

Todd took this theme even further with a long satirical comment on verbosity:

I wish to reveal an aspect of literary style which is at first, believed to be a logical and knowledgable enunciation of relevant facts pertaining to a field which undoubtedly is of great interest to the party or parties involved in collecting, assembling and presenting such information. In the broad sense, they might attempt to expound on the virtues of a particularly interesting or challenging field whereby the facts are presented to a group of constituents who have a vested interest in becoming knowledgable in that area through intensive study, collaboration of ideas, and dissemination of facts through a logical process known as thinking. In presenting a set of findings, this group attempts to dissuade the layman from encountering and interpreting verbosity within the collection of data that has been presented for approval, and or study. Profundity within a document submitted is viewed characteristically as an inclination towards attempts to obscure, or veil the true and correct set of ideas. When digestion of facts from those presented is desired, then the juxtaposition of key elements is fueled. First by a need to question the methodology and coalesce the imbibing transmogrifications. Further more, anti-volumescence creates an imbalance to frutify significant strategic minutions. As a result, a multi-dimensional rift flanges the derivations of color, sound, the earth, air and sky. Also relevant for consideration are the facilitational support factors which can boost, if not control, regular flux movements in and around the system. For this reason I feel that only through symbolic behavior responses we can correct the representational elements affecting our challenge. Thank you.

Burns added his comment to the scroll:

Todd, what a message you have left for us. I too am facilitationally fluxed in most symbolic behaviorial response systems in which representational elements affect our challenges.

Todd continued in a mocking vein, recasting the woodchuck tongue twister in academic prose:

What amount of wood fiber could be consumed and digested by a small rodent with a name that is also characteristic of said fiber if this rodent had the capacity to accomplish this action?

Lora commented on the use of the passive voice in such prose:

Also, I agree with zinsser when he said that active writing is much more effective than passive writing. I don't know how many times i've found myself asleep on top of a passive, ramble-on-forever kind of book.

Sandra commented:

I agree with Zinsser when he says that in an English class, students "reach for a 'literary' style that they think the teacher wants and that they assume is 'good English.' But this style is no part of who they are." [Quoting Zinsser 1988, 13-14]

In composition theory, the notion of an academic discourse community has received much attention in recent years. Patricia Bizzell, in her landmark essay, "Cognition, Convention, and Certainty: What We Need to Know about Writing," pointed out that individual writers are not purely autonomous but rather negotiate meanings within differing discourse communities. In contrast to cognitive theorists who analyze writing in terms of mental processing, Bizzell pointed out that minds do not operate in isolation but as part of "discourse communities." Within such communities, people accommodate not only language but systems of belief and value. Accordingly, she noted that writing difficulties "should be understood as difficulties with joining an unfamiliar discourse community" (Bizzell 1982, 227).

Bizzell suggested that when students join an academic discourse community, they acquire perspectives which enable them to analyze and change their social positions. She is to be credited with drawing attention to the fact that many students find academic discourse to be an alien discourse. However, others have since pointed out that a student entering academia does not simply master academic discourse, join the academic discourse community, and live happily ever after. For example, Carol Cohn (1987) demonstrated that specific professional discourse communities, academic or otherwise, do not simply open up new areas for thought but effectively shut down other areas. While attending a seminar with experts on nuclear diplomacy, Cohn found that she could no longer refer to peace. If she used the word "peace," she was laughed at for being soft-headed. The closest referent she could find in the "new" discourse was "strategic stability."

Another problem is that students acquiring academic "ways with words" (to borrow Shirley Brice Heath's 1983 expression) fear losing their former language and along with it their membership in neighborhood and family communities. At the 1996 Conference on College Composition and Communication, Caroline Pari noted that the books she acquired during her schooling—and stored in tall bookcases—were "building blocks of her academic life," but also bricks "in the physical, emotional, and intellectual walls" between her and her family. Says Pari:

> The wall began to be built when I learned that academic words were dangerous to use at home in my Italian-American family . . . My emerging academic voice threw my father into a rage far worse than any rage I had seen when I made the mistake of cursing at home. I will never forget one day when my father yelled

at me for using "big college words." Maybe I used the word "objectivity" or asked for "justification." All I remember is his booming voice and red face, "Don't you talk that way here!" (Pari 1996)

Pari found that her education did provide her with the tools to break her allegiance to patriarchy and custom. Indeed, she was able, in Bizzell's words to "analyze and change her social position"—just as Bizzell hoped students would be able to do. At the same time, Pari experienced shame over her concurrent "non-elite discourse." She was fearful of inadvertently lapsing into her neighborhood language while at school, an event that caused classmates to tell her she sounded "dumb."

As a teacher now, Pari wants her students to understand the ways that class and language intersect, but not at the cost of silencing students. She says that she now wants her students to learn that their languages are of value in academic discourse. Similarly, Mike Rose (1989), Ira Shor (1986), and others have noted the way that academic communities erect unnecessary hurdles for minority and/or working class students. While some of this may be inadvertent, or unconscious, it serves to perpetuate existing hegemonies. Lillian Bridwell-Bowles puts it well when she says, "Writing classes often serve as a gatekeeper, protecting the academy from the infelicities of 'errors' generated by differences among dialects that derive from social, racial, and ethnic difference." She suggests that standard written English (not to mention academic discourse) "does not allow our class roots to show" (Bridwell-Bowles 1992, 359).

Mary Belenky and her colleagues (1986) found that gender differences caused road blocks as well, causing women with nonacademic ways of talking and constructing knowledge to feel unworthy of membership in academic communities.

Mikhail Bakhtin (1981), Lev Vygotsky (1962) and others have contributed to the growing awareness that language consists not of neutral tools used for thinking and expressing, but rather carries with it enormous cultural baggage.

Still another problem with the notion of an academic discourse which defines and upholds an alleged academic discourse community is that close scrutiny reveals that academic discourse is not a single unified language. Conventions of such discourse vary from nation to nation and from discipline to discipline; even within a discipline, the discourse found in journals and heard at academic conferences is not necessarily reflective of how academicians use language in their offices, hallways, and classrooms—the very sites where a sense of community might be most keenly experienced or missed. In these places, tenured professors may indulge in informal discourse which would not be sanctioned for mere novices. Even in published articles, seasoned academicians are at liberty to use language which might raise eyebrows were it to come from a newcomer.

As described in chapter 24, new genres are making inroads in the academy. Bridwell-Bowles talks of the need for flexibility, for "diverse discourse" to be allowed—if not promoted—within the academy. Again, I refer to Sherry Turkle's "liminal moment" in which "things are betwixt and between, when old structures have broken down and new ones have not yet been created" (quoted in McCorduck 1996, 105).

Min-zhan Lu suggests that "We could also encourage [students] to see themselves as responsible for forming or transforming as well as preserving the discourse they are learning" (Lu 1987, 447). Because community is created primarily through language, and because the language of academia is so fraught with political implications, no one seems quite sure how, or even if, students can truly become part of the academic community—especially if it continues to be construed as a discourse community using some sort of stable academic vocabulary and conventions.

While the notion of induction into such an academic community may have a certain limited validity for those preparing for careers in academia, it is altogether suspect for those (i.e., most students) preparing for careers in other fields. I find myself aligned with those favoring a relaxing of emphasis on academic discourse. For example, Joseph Harris says, "Instead of presenting academic discourse as coherent and well-defined, we might be better off viewing it as polyglot, as a sort of space in which competing beliefs and practices intersect with and confront one another" (Harris 1989, 20). He also quotes a recent comment of Bizzell's: "Healthy discourse communities, like healthy human beings, are also masses of contradictions . . . We should accustom ourselves to dealing with contradictions, instead of seeking a theory that appears to abrogate them" (quoted in Harris 1989, 20).

Discourse communities enacted by scholars who publish in academic journals have developed conventions of which students should at least become aware. For example, they should understand the ethical and practical importance of citations, and they should understand that field-specific jargon generally derives not from a motive to cloud an issue but to clarify it. However, as I see it, the major goal of undergraduates is not to master the discourse style of scholars, but to grapple with ideas. If this grappling, as it were, leads students deeper into scholarly prose, that's a good thing. At the same time students need the space to use their own language, and to express their frustration with other languages that appear to them to deliberately thwart understanding and/or democratic participation in the conversation at hand.

At the close of his book, *Fragments of Rationality*, Lester Faigley calls ethics (among other things) " . . . a pausing to reflect on the limits of understanding. It is respect for diversity and unassimilated otherness. It is finding the spaces to listen" (Faigley 1992, 239). What universities should become are places, or indeed spaces, where students from diverse backgrounds can come together—bringing to these spaces, without shame, their own ways with words.

@20

E-text_Comes_of_Age

We are still bemused by the three hundred years of Newtonian simplification that made "rhetoric" a dirty word, but we are beginning to outgrow it.
        —Richard Lanham (1993, 51)

ELECTRONIC TEXT, OR *e-text*, IS OFTEN REFERRED TO AS A HYBRID, reflecting features of both spoken and written language (Faigley 1992, 168). It is a hybrid, but it is more than *just* a hybrid. In describing e-text, theorists often use terms and analogies which have not typically been used to describe either talk or writing in the past. Moreover, descriptions often include the very same words or concepts used by scientists and others to allude to the shift from Newtonian constructs to quantum constructs. For example, in chapter 8, I alluded to the frequency with which e-text is described in terms of water—"fluid," "turbulent," "flowing," etc. In this chapter, I will examine other concepts used to describe e-text, including observations that it is "unpredictable," "temporal," "chaotic," "emergent," "visual," "brief," "synergistic," "associative," and "multi-authored."

First, let's consider the unpredictability and temporality of e-text. Richard Lanham (1993), for example, notes the dynamic nature of e-text, stating that "the digital text becomes unfixed and interactive" (32). Certainly e-text is not contained in the way that traditional text is contained in a finite and stable book. Walter Ong's contrast between book literacy and orality is relevant. He says, "Print encourages a sense of closure, a sense that what is found in a text has been finalized, has reached a state of completion" (Ong 1982, 132).

The e-text that we find on computer screens, although based on print, returns us to certain elements of oral culture in that it is not trapped between the covers of a book. Not only does e-text not look the same on everyone's screen (as does printed text in a published book), but it appears, disappears, and continually evolves. This temporal quality of e-text may also foster temporal notions of meaning, just as book literacy has, over the years, fostered relatively stable notions of meaning.

Myron Tuman also calls attention to the temporal quality of e-text and suggests that e-text confronts us with the notion of literacy based on a "virtual text":

> The longer and the more intensely involved we become with a virtual text— the more familiar we become with its inherent flexibility—the less satisfied we are likely to be producing what can only be a mere snapshot of what in its electronic form seems to have a richly multidimensional life of its own. (Tuman 1992, 58)

This contrast between the "snapshot" of the text and the fluid, moving text brings to mind the coordinating quantum concepts of particle and wave.

The snapshot notion emerges repeatedly on the WWW. Eric Crump, for example, states that "Snapshots may be what essays have to become to survive in cyberspace." On his *RhetNet* Interactive Historiography page (<http://www.missouri.edu/~rhetnet/ih>), Crump introduces the *RhetNet* series of "snapshots" saying, "The point is to capture an idea. Ideas are slippery . . . The texts collected here are attempts to seize a moment. They may be pithy, sometimes witty, sometimes infuriatingly incomplete, but if they are provocative we'll consider them successful at what they are intended to do" (Crump 1996).

After each "snapshot" (short text), a series of reader responses are made available through hypertext links. Additionally, the reader is asked, "What's your take on this stuff?" and provided with a window to add still another response. The "snapshot" is clearly considered one brief take within an ongoing dialogue. In the home page of *RhetNet*, one finds a collection of editor Eric Crump's favorite quotes, including this one: "Photos used to be a way of freezing reality. Now they're a way of thawing imagination" (quoting Jaron Lanier, Olympus advertisement, *Wired*, 4.10). This self-consciousness about the duality between the static and the fluid seems intrinsic to the sensibilities of the time.

Cynthia Selfe also refers to the essential differences between the "static" and "immutable" nature of printed pages versus the "fluid" and "dynamic" nature of pixelated text on screen (Selfe 1989, 7). Although she does not mention Newton, I see features of the Newtonian to quantum shift in her description. She suggests what might be considered Newtonian predictability in her apt description of the printed page; and she suggests what might be considered quantum unpredictability and fluidity in her description of the computer screen.

Lanham repeatedly refers to the "oscillation" between looking at texts and through texts. When a reader looks *at* a text, he or she is noting features of the writing itself, whereas when a reader looks *through* a text, he or she is not conscious of surface features but only of the meaning "behind" the words. This at/through dichotomy also seems to resonate with the particle/wave dichotomy in quantum physics. Indeed, Lanham refers to paradigm issues in such passages as this:

> The textual surface has become permanently bi-stable. We are always looking first AT it and then THROUGH it, and this oscillation creates a different implied ideal of decorum, both stylistic and behavioral. Look THROUGH a text and you are in the familiar world of the Newtonian interlude, where facts were facts, the world was really "out there," folks had sincere central selves, and the best writing style dropped from the writer as "simply and directly as a stone falls to the ground," precisely as Thoreau counseled. Look AT a text, however, and we have deconstructed the Newtonian world into Pirandello's and yearn to "act naturally." (Lanham 1990, 5)

I agree with Lanham's notion of oscillation, but as mentioned in chapter 3, my use of at/through differs significantly from his. I see the *at* to reference the stable Newtonian page and the *through* to reference the myriad complexity inherent in linking to other minds—as *through* a screen into the network. My view conjures up images of Alice going through the looking glass and into a strange and unpredictable realm. In a way, my view is opposite of Lanham's because he finds the *through* to be the stable Newtonian world. Of course, he is apparently exploring the distinction between words and what people assume these words reference, whereas I am exploring the distinction between words that one personally enters on a stand-alone screen and words that come to the screen via a mysterious and infinite web of links. Given oscillation, I can see the validity of Lanham's point, but it is a different point than the one I am making.

One way to look at this is in terms of equilibrium and disequilibrium. While Newtonian physics focused on equilibrium, Nobel Prize-winning physics professor Ilya Prigogine helped turn our gaze toward disequilibrium which he claims is a more common occurrence (Prigogine 1984, 128).

Educator William Doll draws on Prigogine's work in discussing the way an "open system . . . needs fluxes, perturbations, anomalies, errors: these are the triggers which set off reorganization" (Doll 1987, 8). He further alludes to "complex" situations in which "A small perturbation, acting among many intertwined elements, can have a multiplying, even exponential, effect." He goes on to say that some of these effects are "transformative" (12). LINCs and other e-text arenas are indeed characterized by disequilibrium; they are open systems in which one *small perturbation among intertwining elements* can have disproportionate and unpredictable effects.

The concept of "emergence" also frequently enters discussions of e-text—a kind of text which always seems to be in a stage of becoming. This is not the same as "a text in need of revision" which, as Fred Kemp points out, has been narrowly viewed as "damaged goods seeking repair" (Kemp 1995, 183). Rather, it is an open-endedness which is increasingly valued by those who are comfortably adapting to the new world view and the conventions and genres that are evolving as a part of this view. As Kemp says, a computer-based conversation has "no controlling thesis, no disciplined pattern of exposition" (185). He continues: "The 'thought' that the written conversation engenders is purely a product of the conversation itself, not a pale, reconstituted (always imperfectly) copy transmitted from one brain to another" (186).

John E. Goodwin notes that "The medium seems to invite statements that 'this section is under construction.'" Goodwin, who himself uses the conventions he proposes, calls this "the 'cathedral model' of text production . . . the product itself is never really finished." Goodwin adds that the text results from both a "top down" process and a "bottom-up one in which sections are created piecemeal and tacked together as ideas emerge" (Goodwin 1993, Section 2.3). He notes that unlike print medium which locks texts into published editions, e-text makes it possible for documents to be *never* final, but "continuously revised" (Section 1.3).

The emergence of *ideas* in e-text environments has also been noted. WEB-surfing, email, and electronic conferencing seem, at times, to have a special synergistic power in fostering invention and the creation of ideas. Journalist Philip Elmer-Dewitt notes that "Some of the most successful netwriting is produced in computer conferences, where writers compose in a kind of collaborative heat, knocking ideas against one another until they spark" (Elmer-Dewitt 1995, 67). Jerome Bump notes the "synergistic" effect of computer conversation, and many of his students commented on this in questionnaires completed after a semester online. One said that network discussion was "where I get most of my ideas," and another said, "It helps you to get your ideas to surface" (Bump 1990, 57). Seymour Papert, the MIT mathematician who invented the programming language LOGO, believes that computers in themselves "have catalyzed the emergence of ideas" (Papert 1980, 26).

Joseph Valacich, Alan Dennis, and Terry Connolly compared idea generation between face-to-face group sharing and "electronic brainstorming (EBS)." When the people in their study worked alone and then pooled their ideas in face-to-face sessions, they had to focus on remembering their ideas, listening to others, or trying to contrive an opportunity to speak rather than on generating new ideas" (Valacich et al. 1994, 451). But in EBS sessions, they eliminated production blocking—the blocking of input due to waiting for an opportunity to contribute—and produced "more unique ideas" than did equivalent face-to-face groups (463).

Just as the emergent nature of *thought* is foregrounded in LINC and other e-text forums, so too is the emergent nature of *language* itself foregrounded. Students must struggle to find a fit between the words they use and the meanings they are striving to create or to communicate. The "talk," as opposed to "writing," nature of electronic writing seems to foster this kind of open stance toward language. In analyzing the differences between spoken and written discourse, Wallace Chafe suggests that talk can serve as a sort of "growth tip" of language usage. He goes on to say that "Written language [is] the repository of more stabilized linguistic traits, traits that spoken language is freer to replace through normal processes of change" and that spoken language "seems to be the locus of ongoing language change," allowing "new senses" to develop for old words (Chafe 1985, 114–116). The seemingly fluid and experimental use of language common in spoken conversation may in itself foster an exploratory state of mind.

Linguists and others have thus found that oral language is not an inferior kind of language but, in fact, has certain advantages over written language. Indeed, Deborah Tannen suggests that literary language simply "builds on and intensifies features that are spontaneous and commonplace in ordinary conversation" (Tannen 1985, 153). E-text captures the vitality and elasticity of oral expression and puts this language literally before our eyes so that we can appreciate it, mock it, or celebrate it as the situation warrants. Shoshana Zuboff observes that this new written form is "more immediate and raw than, for example, written reports that are heavily edited and otherwise shaped to conform to local standards" (Zuboff 1988, 180).

The affective quality of much of network "talk" has been evident in the transcripts presented in these pages. Other teachers in network classrooms have commented on the frequency with which students discuss their feelings. For example, Bump studied network use in two undergraduate English courses and one graduate course and noted that many students mentioned the relative ease with which they could express feelings (Bump 1990, 57). Comparing network discourse to traditional classroom discourse, Wayne Butler and James Kinneavy (1991) found that network responses contained more "candor" and "depth."

The increased academic interest in "talk" comes at a time when the general public is showing a parallel interest in conversation and how it affects our lives. Deborah Tannen has found a receptive audience for linguistic analysis outside of academia as witnessed by the fact that her recent books[1] have been bestsellers. Ray Oldenburg's book, *The Great Good Place (1991)*, has also received much attention, possibly because it has struck a chord with people who indeed do miss public places where they can converse.

Among my friends, colleagues, and relatives, I see various conversations occurring on networks which simply would not occur otherwise and which seem to be enhancing lives. For example, the high school students who participated in my dissertation study are now dispersed in colleges across the country, but they stay in contact through email. They also occasionally converse with their parents by email, sharing information which would probably not make it into a letter or a phone call. Email simply provides people with many opportunities to "talk" that they might not otherwise enjoy.

We return now to the "writerly" side of the hybrid. E-text as a *written* form has been evolving its own unique conventions. Selfe explores what she calls the "multilayered grammars" of the screen, based on the fact that screens are "temporal windows on a virtual text." The virtual texts of the computer, moreover, "exist only in the memories of the computer, the reader, or the writer." Whereas the printed page is a "structural unit" the screen is a "temporal unit" (Selfe 1989, 7). In computer-networked writing centers, Selfe posits, students and teachers have opportunities not only to learn the conventions and grammars of this new kind of text but also to invent grammars appropriate to it.

Selfe found that students who composed texts to be read on computer screens "invented and exploited a new set of literacy skills that their teachers never imagined" (13). For example, when students composed texts to be read on screen, they used color as an indicator of logical structure, and they broke their text into "screen-sized chunks" (12). Thus,

> Using different fonts, font sizes, symbols, highlighting, and graphic elements, they have not only adjusted their writing to the conventions of the screen and the computers, but have also reconceptualized the content of their assignments in terms of these conventions. It seems possible that the grammar of the computers, the word-processing package, or the computer itself changed the way in which writers think and express thought. (13)

This fluid text, with its variety of fonts and other visual features, can render electronic texts virtual "paintings" (Lanham 1993, 37). Along these lines, Burns informally referred to computers as "electronic easels."

Goodwin, convinced that writers must become more sensitive to the needs of audiences reading from screens, has collected and systematized conventions which take advantage of e-text's strengths and alleviate its shortcomings. He refers to problems in "navigating" through e-text and suggests that writers of such text provide paragraph headings and dispersed tables of contents to facilitate such navigation.

He also advises, "Think less in terms of traditional categories like 'Table of Contents' or 'Index' and more in terms of data structure" (Goodwin 1993, Section 2.1, Trick 5).

Goodwin notes that a screen can show about twenty-four lines of print, but that readers will want to see at least one break within these twenty-four lines: "If I see a paragraph that fills the whole screen, I tend to want to scroll down and skip ahead" (Rule 4.9). He notes, as well, that "In E-text, the paragraph, not the page, is the fundamental frame of reference for the reader" (Section 2.5) and that e-text is "logically a scroll," not a page (Section 2.1). Indeed, Goodwin's document does not contain page numbers and that is why I cite him by sections. He claims that "The most marked characteristic of E-text style is brevity" which he applies not only to paragraphs but to the "overall work" (Section 2.2).

The emphasis on brevity has spawned acronyms that are substituted for common expressions. A Cornell mailing list (COPYEDITING-L) included a batch of these that were later included in the "Nothing But 'Net'" monthly feature of *Sky Magazine* (May 1996), an in-flight magazine. Some of the common acronyms included were LOL (laughing out loud), ROFL (rolling on the floor laughing) and ILSHIBAMF (I laughed so hard I broke all my furniture) as well as IANAL (I am not a lawyer) and TPTB (the powers that be). Conventions such as these add to the novelty and appeal of e-text.

Like Goodwin, Fred Kemp notes the importance of brevity in e-text conversations, claiming that "long and carefully prepared comments are often ignored" because they are too much, too late and are seen as "irrelevant or too taxing to be responded to" (Kemp 1995, 187). The emphasis on brevity brings to mind the "depthlessness of postmodernity" (Faigley 1992, 165). The brevity requirement is disturbing to some who fear that in discounting long messages, people are turning their backs on reflection and depth of analysis. With time, the quality we associate with "depth" will possibly evolve into an equally worthy quality that might be termed, if you will, "breadth."

We may come to value the holistic complexity of breadth as highly as we currently—in our Newtonian mindsets—value "depth." It is possible, however, that the brevity requirement is resulting in a new elitism that disenfranchises the comments of some who do not yet find brevity comfortable or productive. The hypertextual "chunking" of text is bothersome to some. Michael Kinsley in his Webzine, *Slate*, elects to group hyperlinks at the ends of articles rather than in the text with the hope that "even on the Web, some people will want to read articles in the traditional linear fashion—i.e., from beginning to end—rather than darting constantly from site to site" (Kinsley 1996). Kinsley frequently expresses his ambivalence about the new conventions of e-text.

Journalist Walter Mossberg (1995) is also ambivalent, but makes the point that when the *Wall Street Journal* is published in hard copy on "dead trees," much information is left "on the cutting room floor" due to the space constraints of the day. In an online version, information does not have to be left out but can be made accessible through links. Thus, while "surfing the Net" may suggest gliding over the surface of information, the links provide a remarkable potential for what we traditionally think of as depth.

Some see the flourishing of email to represent a sort of renaissance of written language. In a *Time Magazine* article, Elmer-Dewitt talks of the "startling" rebirth, in everyday life, of writing—a medium which, he notes, was demoted after the invention of the telephone. He observes that letter writing is experiencing the "greatest boom" since the 18th century," and he quotes Jon Carroll, of the *San Francisco Chronicle* who writes, "It is my overwhelming belief that Email and computer conferencing is teaching an entire generation about the flexibility and utility of prose" (Elmer-Dewitt 1994, 66). The article refers to nationwide online political, technical, or artistic discussion groups which have become so crowded that one must write well to be noticed: "Good writing on the Net tends to be clear, vigorous, witty and above all brief" (67).

Another characteristic of e-text is its "polyvocality"—its combining of many voices. Along these lines, it is moving away from the primacy of the autonomous author. In the workplaces she studied, Zuboff noted:

> Finally, the electronic text does not have an author in the conventional sense. It may be produced from many individual acts of "authorship" (for example, account officers enter their own data, managers send messages, customers provide data through automated teller machines), or it may result from impersonal and autonomous processes (for example, microprocessors register data from the production process, optical scanners read and input data). (Zuboff 1988, 180)

Kemp makes a related point: "Electronic texts, and especially extended email conversations, tend to diminish the authority of the writer in favor of the authority of the writing itself, and thereby reduce the competition between the conceptual freight and the medium of transmission" (Kemp 1995, 183).

Tuman sees this as part of a move from "critical" thinking to "associative" thinking (Tuman 1992, 66), with the latter fostered by online composition. He notes, "All forms of computer-based writing seem to be returning us to a world of multiple notions of authorship, based on multiple notions of texts" (64). Moreover, networking puts writers in immediate touch with peers:

> The new networking technology is important, not in providing us with greater power in composing individual texts, but in providing us with the opportunity to communicate through reading and writing immediately with other people in situations similar to ours, or in providing students with the opportunity to communicate in real-time with each other, rather than with their teachers. (84)

Carolyn Handa points out that the computer's arrival at this time is not mere coincidence, but rather "a tool reflecting the politics and ideology" of the times. She says that "Emerging at a particular period in time, in a particular social context, the computer is a tool reflecting the ideology of both" (Handa 1990b, 161). She notes that Karen LeFevre and others refer to the idealization of the solitary author as being a reflection of the capitalism and individualism that characterized the industrial age.

Students at times seem to push against e-text's restraints, as if the alphabet as a symbol system is no longer sufficient in and of itself. One example of this is the use of emoticons—sideways smiley faces and so forth which are created from letters and other symbols on the keyboard. In one LINC session, David used the auxiliary numeric keyboard to create an icon which he attached to every message, a kind of signature. When Sharon asked him how he did this, he explained, and within seconds several students were experimenting with the graphics possible through using the CTRL (control) key and the numeric keyboard:

Sandra: ᵃᵃ ᵃᵃₐêîôûåÅæÆæÅûåîôâê»«ᵃᵃᵃ_(2<FPZi¿«»
David: ‚}ñoäà#%ëçêè_
Sharon: ᵒᵒðèàìùÄÜÖÿÿÉÜÄìèàòìÄùÜÖÉÿ_

Jake quickly composed, out of Xs and Os, a spectacular full-screen version of an alien standing in front of his spaceship. This brought the following response from Angela:

Jake: You graphic stud.

Here is the message which won Jake such high acclaim:

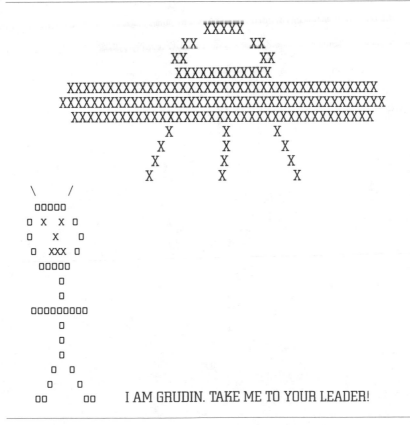

Note

1. Deborah Tannen's best-selling books are *That's Not What I Meant!: How Conversational Style Makes or Breaks Your Relations With Others* (1986), *You Just Don't Understand: Women and Men in Conversation* (1990), and *Talking Nine to Five: Women and Men in the Workplace: Language, Sex, and Power* (1994).

@21

Answers_in_the_Winds _of_Change

Where classical science used to emphasize permanence, we now find change and evolution; we no longer see in the skies the trajectories that filled Kant's heart with the same admiration as the moral law residing in him. We now see strange objects: quasars, pulsars, galaxies exploding and being torn apart, stars that, we are told, collapse into "black holes" irreversibly devouring everything they manage to ensnare.
—Prigogine and Stengers, *Order Out of Chaos: Man's New Dialogue with Nature* (1984, 214–15)

IN CHAPTER 8, I REFERRED TO MAXINE HAIRSTON'S HISTORIC ARTICLE, "The Winds of Change" (1982). I suggested that in the fifteen years since Hairston's observations, we can see changes not only in the winds, but in the waters. It is no accident that we turn to metaphors of wind and water to describe this shift—whether we call it a "paradigm" shift or not. As literary theorist N. Katherine Hayles points out, the waterfall has become the icon for chaos theory just as the clock was the icon for Newtonian mechanics. Says Hayles:

> The clock is ordered, predictable, regular, and mechanically precise; the waterfall is turbulent, unpredictable, irregular, and infinitely varying in form. The change is not in how the world actually is—neither clocks nor waterfalls are anything new—but in how it is seen. (Hayles 1991, 8)

In this chapter, we briefly peer through the lenses of scientists, considering in particular the shift away from a Newtonian world view toward a new emphasis on quantum mechanics and chaos theory. As mentioned in chapter one, physicists and writers share the common goal of describing and interpreting experiences and observations. Throughout this chapter I will make frequent references to the insights of Danah Zohar and Ian Marshall—philosopher and psychiatrist respectively. They suggest that modern physics provides a *model* for new ways of thinking while, at the same time, it *reflects* new ways of thinking—calling forth the concept of "feedback loops." They state that "Physics is not some separate and remote field of learning. Like everything else conceived by the human mind, physics is a product of consciousness and a product of the evolution of consciousness" (Zohar and Marshall 1994, 36).

Indeed, scholars in the "hard" sciences, the "soft" sciences, and the humanities are questioning the rigid lines that have traditionally been drawn between the paradigms and procedures used within differing disciplines. For example, Ilya Prigogine a Nobel Prize-winning physical chemistry professor whose office is only a short walk from the University of Texas English department, spoke recently about new ideas replacing an "old view":

> For me, the interest of complex systems theory is that it shows that only a small part of nature is ruled by deterministic laws . . . The old view was that the "hard sciences" are deterministic, while the "soft sciences" such as sociology, were not. . . . We now can see a narrative element emerging on all levels of our description of nature. Thus, the recent progress achieved in this field contributes to a reunification of human culture. (Prigogine 1996, 7)

Earlier, Prigogine, along with Isabelle Stengers (philosopher, chemist, and historian of science) stated that quantum mechanics has taught us that science is not based on objective "reality," but is dependent upon "conceptualization" just as is literature (Prigogine and Stengers 1984, 226). They stated that the "wealth of reality . . . overflows any single language, any single logical structure" and that each language—including music—can express only part of reality (225).

Meanwhile, Hayles has explored links between science and literature in some depth. While she is interested in intersections of quantum physics and literature, she is even more interested in intersections between chaos theory and literature. She points out that the word "chaos" has been sensationalized to the point that some consider anyone using it to be a dilettante (Hayles 1991, 2). Moreover, she admits that studies in literature and science should be challenged: "What do the parallels signify? How do you explain their existence? What mechanism do you postulate to account for them? What keeps the selection of some theoretical features and some literary texts from being capricious?" (19).

In spite of these valid concerns, Hayles defends her explorations by asserting that she wants to "arrive at a deeper understanding of the connections between literature and science (and hence implicitly of the underlying cultural dynamics)" (19–20). She adds that the term *chaos* "serves as a crossroads, a juncture where various strata and trends within the culture come together" (2).

At risk of being considered a dilettante, I am suggesting that composition theorists might find food for thought in dipping occasionally into the literature about quantum mechanics, chaos theory, complexity theory, fractal geometry, and so forth. Since these areas of inquiry are of our time, they are inevitably part of the cultural matrix within which our sensibilities are shaped. Students who are immersed in popular culture absorb these radical new ideas as one part of postmodernism. At the very least, new models in physics and math provide us all with compelling metaphors.

What I suggest in this chapter is that to the extent that we can understand and at least partially accept the new physics, our pedagogy will resonate with newly-evolving world views and with the sensibilities of today's students. I have chosen to use the word *paradigm* only for describing this basic shift from a world view based on Newtonian physics to a world view based on quantum mechanics.

First, let's revisit the broad issue of paradigm. The world views of civilizations go through stages, many of which persist for centuries. While at no time is there absolute consensus, there is a reigning "paradigm," to use Thomas Kuhn's (1970) term, which largely shapes the thinking of people within a given culture. For hundreds of years, people believed that the sun rotated around the earth, but later came to accept an entirely different explanation of the universe. This new paradigm was not just a scholarly issue for astronomers, but was deeply implicated in people's concepts about their place in the universe, the nature of truth, the origins of life, and so forth.

As Kuhn and others have pointed out, there is a long time span between the introduction of a new paradigm and its acceptance and internalization by the general public. Even those who can accept a new paradigm intellectually may be unable to fully integrate it into their world view. They may understand that the categories they use for thinking are invalid, yet they persist in using them. As I mentioned earlier, most of us still refer to the sun's daily appearance as a "rising."

Newton presented his *Principia* to the Royal Society of London in 1686. This described fundamental concepts of mass, acceleration, inertia, gravitation, and so forth. These concepts have played a key role in shaping science for over 300 years. Newton, certainly a genius, described some aspects of the natural world with stunning accuracy. The Newtonian paradigm, shaping a mechanistic world view, laid the groundwork for the scientific and industrial revolutions.

Early in these revolutions, Newton's concepts moved beyond the realm of physics and shaped thinking in virtually every discipline that existed at the time. Zohar and Marshall observe:

> The sheer power and simplicity of Newton's three mechanical laws of motion, and the apparent force of the new empirical method, drew nearly every influential social, political, and economic thinker of the seventeenth, eighteenth, and nineteenth centuries to use them as a model. (Zohar and Marshall 1994, 24)

Zohar and Marshall describe how influential theorists in economics, philosophy, sociology, and psychology used Newtonian metaphors to shape the thinking in these fields. In philosophy, for example, Locke "once described himself as a 'mere underlabourer' to the 'incomparable Mr. Newton'" (25). Adam Smith, they note, drew on the new mechanistic science in articulating his free-market economics and the division of labor. Assembly line factories made people work as if they, themselves, were part of the machinery. Auguste Comte, who coined the word sociology, called his new science "social physics" (25). Zohar and Marshall quote Vernard Foley:

> The basic building blocks of Newton's physical world were so many isolated and impenetrable atoms that bounce around in space and collide with one another like tiny billiard balls. . . . Political thinkers of the time compared these colliding atoms and their interacting forces to the behavior and interactions of individuals in society as they confront each other in pursuit of their self-interest. (25)

Mechanistic physics shaped Western civilization and led to impressive accomplishments.

Within Newton's world view, people saw the physical world largely in terms of "resources" which could be manipulated, through science and technology, in infinite ways. As Astronaut Buzz Aldrin said on the twenty-fifth anniversary of the Apollo 11 Moon landing: "We were privileged to be the eyes and hands for all humanity—a species with the audacity to dig a hole in the ground, recombine the materials and fly to the moon"

(Aldrin 1994, 49). This is impressive, to be sure—an accomplishment that would have been impossible without Newtonian physics.

As Prigogine and Stengers put it, Newton's ambition was to present a view of nature that would "escape the clutches of time." Similarly, Einstein and others sought an underlying simplicity in nature. But now the theories of, "thermodynamics, relativity, and quantum mechanics have all demonstrated the limits of classical physics" (Prigogine and Stengers 1984, 217).

Even as physicists are finding limits to Newtonian physics, people in a variety of fields are voicing problems with the Newtonian world view that radically influenced Western culture for centuries. Bureaucratic institutions based on such mechanistic metaphors as the "wheels of government" and the "machinery of state" have led many to feel alienated from their work and from the natural world. Perhaps this partially explains the alienation and cynicism of "Generation X."

The behavioristic theories in psychology, which tended to reduce behavior to the simple mechanism of stimulus and response, are now widely regarded as oversimplified and inaccurate descriptions of human behavior. The mechanistic nature of our schools has also come under fire. Many criticize the "assembly line" nature of these institutions in which it is common for elementary and high school students to sit in rows, take orders (follow directions), and move to another room only when a bell sounds. The classrooms are typically arranged in a linear fashion, with students progressing through the years—as if on a conveyer belt—from one "grade" to the next.

Some feel that the Newtonian emphasis on the mechanical precluded our ability to see other faces of reality—with unfortunate or even tragic outcomes for life on our small planet. For example, shortly after the twenty-fifth anniversary of the moon walk, columnist Ellen Goodman noted:

> In retrospect, the landing on the moon doesn't seem like the beginning of a new age. It seems like the end of an era—at least in our relationship to nature. By 1969, we had completed the centuries-long transition from a species in awe of nature, to a species that believed in the conquest of nature—even space . . . To many, the idea that humans should strive for dominion over nature seems as quaint now as planting a "waving" American flag on the windless surface of the moon. (Goodman 1994, A-11)

This new critical take on the mining of the earth is echoed in Myron Tuman's critique of print literacy. Tuman refers to the "transformative power" of the "new industrial technology" as "a force that literally ripped open the earth and re-made the physical landscape" (Tuman 1992, 29). Tuman asserts that now our attention is "turning away from the prospects of miraculous discoveries . . . and in the direction of altering our own behaviors" (43). He adds:

> . . . We are all becoming more aware of the need for conserving energy, for changing our lifestyles, and especially for finding more cooperative patterns of existence. Developers and entrepreneurs of all sorts, all proponents of industrial culture, are right to see in the moral fervor of environmentalists a direct challenge to the foundation of industrial culture. (43)

Tuman goes on to say that if print literacy is based on industrial culture, then it, too, "stands ready to topple" (43).

Even Buzz Aldrin concedes, "Ironically, the view of Earth from space has confirmed for many the notion that man should make his pilgrimage not to the stars but to the needs of a suffering humanity. But a whole people must have the humility to nurture the Earth *and* the pride to go to Mars" (Aldrin 1994, 49). Goodman, Tuman, and Aldrin might agree that Newton's paradigm has entered what Kuhn would term a crisis. At the very least, they all point to problems in continuing our single-minded dedication to what technology can do. The industrial revolution, once considered to be the pinnacle of progress, has failed in many ways to bring people the satisfactions promised.

The planet Earth, under the Newtonian paradigm considered to be a source of infinite "resources," has begun to show signs of breaking under the strain of humankind's "progress." Meanwhile, new "tools of thought" including new metaphors, can be found in the narratives which describe the shift from mechanistic Newtonian physics to quantum physics. This is a shift away from the simple and toward "the multiple, the temporal, and the complex" (Prigogine and Stengers 1984, 2). For example there is a new understanding of light. For years, scientists debated whether light was made up of particles or waves. Physicists discovered that they could design experiments in which light manifested as a series of waves and other experiments in which it manifested as a stream of particles. While getting a clear reading of its wave "reality," the particle reality was "fuzzy." While getting a clear reading of its particle "reality," the wave reality was "fuzzy."

The impossibility of measuring both the position and momentum of light at the same time is called the Heisenberg Uncertainty Principle. In quantum physics, the question "wave or particle" has been answered: It is both *at the same time*. Nonfiction writer Gary Zukav states that "Whatever it [light] is, it is *not* the 'moving particle' we thought it was, because 'moving particles' have both position and momentum" (Zukav 1979, 113–114).

For modern humankind, steeped in Cartesian either/or thinking patterns, the Uncertainty Principle is almost impossible to comprehend. It may be that the human mind is incapable of grasping this reality. Indeed, physicist Niels Bohr said that the significance of quantum mechanics made him dizzy (Prigogine and Stengers, 225). While we cannot readily think in "quantum" terms, new generations may find it difficult to think otherwise. Successive generations will grow up in different cultural contexts and their thinking will increasingly support a different way of perceiving reality. The changing paradigm is bound to bring a shift in sensibilities such that a linear deterministic world view will eventually become antiquated.

Quantum physics is, among other things, a new way of looking at relationship. In Newtonian physics, reality was reducible to separate and impenetrable atoms bouncing against each other in fairly predictable ways. In quantum physics, the emphasis is on quantum *systems* which overlap and combine to form an "emergent reality." Zohar and Marshall explain: "Just as solid, Newtonian particles that meet must clash and go their separate ways, wave fronts that come together tend to overlap and combine. The reality of each is taken up and woven into the other" (54).

Another concept in quantum physics has to do with potential. An atom may become unstable, and its electrons may move into different energy orbits. There is apparently no way to predict which orbits a given electron will "choose." What the electron does is try out different paths at the same time as though it is "smeared out all over space and time and is everywhere at once":

> In much the same way that we play with multiple possibilities in our imaginations, or launch "trial balloons" to see how something might work out, the electron puts out "feelers" toward its own future to see which path ultimately suits it best. . . . In the language of quantum physics, these feelers are known as virtual transitions—they are the possible journeys the electron makes before something actual (something measurable) happens. (49)

When the electron finds a new orbit, this is termed a "real transition," but as physicist David Bohm points out, even the virtual transitions have real effects (quoted in Zohar and Marshall 1994, 49).

In our daily lives, most of us have no need to understand how particles behave at the subatomic level. However, an understanding of physics—of the relationship, for example, between particles and waves—provides metaphors, or "tools of thought" (Selfe 1989, 6), which we can apply to observable aspects of our lives. In chapter 20, I discussed how the particle and wave dichotomy figures in metaphors used by several composition theorists (Tuman, Selfe, Crump). For example, the electronic text is wave-like, while the printed text is particle-like.

Another important element in the new paradigm is the connection between systems. Increasingly, systems are viewed as parts of "ecologies." The concept of a "web of connection" is shifting the focus in many disciplines. In the discipline of psychology, for example, there is a move toward analyzing the individual within a social context—in other words, in his/her web of connection. Whereas older models of analysis featured a single therapist and a single patient, newer therapeutic models may feature a team of therapists working with entire families—and close friends—all searching for insights in terms of webs of relationships.

In other disciplines, we see a similar emphasis on context. Evolution, once understood by the general public as a simple matter of "survival of the fittest" is now seen as co-evolution in which the survival of species depends on the relationship of that species to other co-existing species. Botany, which in my schooling was portrayed in terms of the way individual plants worked, now is more apt to be seen in terms both of evolution and ecology—thus again looking at webs in terms of the dynamics of time and space.

The business world, once based on the hierarchy of production, and marketing within relatively static systems, is now seen as part of an evolving matrix of international connections. The current view is that businesses thrive to the extent that they can be in immediate touch with consumers, modifying their products as soon as the shifting needs and desires of fickle consumers can be detected, intuited, or manipulated.

In current educational models, the new paradigm is leading to ungraded classrooms with students of differing ages and skill levels. Students of varying abilities are being "mainstreamed," and curriculum designers search for ways to teach "across the curriculum," erasing the lines formerly drawn between discrete, self-contained disciplines and units.

The field of medicine is also aligning itself with this new paradigm. Like the above fields, medicine for many years relied on specialization. Doctors were trained—in a Newton-like mind set—to examine only one part of the body—the heart, the skin, the bones, the kidneys. This isolating of body parts has proved to be problematic; if a patient goes to the wrong specialist, his or her diagnosis might be missed. The specialty of Family Practice was created, providing training across the curriculum of medicine, and preparing doctors to look at the whole patient before considering treatment of specific parts. This was a return to the more holistic approach of the general practitioner, but with the addition of residency training. Other more holistic approaches to medicine are gaining respect as well. Bill Moyers's book, *Healing and the Mind*, was a bestseller. Thus, in both mainstream and alternative medicine, practitioners and patients increasingly acknowledge connection rather than isolation.

When students write on a network, they are putting their voices, their views, into a web of connection. Within this web, they can see themselves as unique, yet also part of an interconnected whole. When they write messages and then delete them before sending them, they are—if you will—putting out feelers toward the future, similar to the quantum concept of potential. Even if these messages are not sent, they have an effect in that they have affected the path of the individual writer's thinking. Another way that *potential* figures into a computer discussion is that students play with identity, using words to enact various facets or constructs of self and then seeing—indeed, *experiencing*—how these experiments go over with the community at large.

As our culture moves away from the certainty and predictability of Newtonian physics, and toward the uncertainty of quantum physics, there seems to be more appreciation of intuition along with a growing recognition that logic is not as objective and reliable as once supposed. There is much talk about nonhierarchical and nonlinear systems, and people are experimenting with restructuring institutions accordingly.

Finally, the concept of "emergence" seems itself to be emerging from metaphors of thought implicit in quantum physics. This new valuing and recognition of the way our concepts evolve over time, and, in context, is in opposition to a prior mind set in which we assumed our perceptions and concepts captured a static "reality." Older constructs still *serve* our thinking but no longer *dominate* it.

While quantum mechanics is reshaping the discipline of physics, chaos theory is reshaping the discipline of math. As mentioned earlier, the implications of chaos have been of special interest to literary theorist Hayles. She notes that in Western civilization chaos has been viewed negatively as the opposite of order. However, in Taoist tradition, chaos is "the necessary other . . . Not-order is also a possibility, distinct from and valued differently than anti-order" (Hayles 1991, 3). Mathematical chaos theory has helped Western society to view chaos in more positive terms because in mathematics chaos can result in order of two kinds. First, it can result in order through self-organizing or emerging system. Second, it can reveal a deep structure of order that appeared chaotic only on the surface or to the untrained eye.

Certainly these two notions of chaos—either as the turbulence from which new ideas emerge or as a phenomenon in which deep structure is present—figure in the humanities. Some writers refer to the turbulent confusion which precedes a sense of direction; or, they may refer to the recognition of a pattern where, at first sight, none was apparent. Using chaos theory as an organizing construct, Paul Taylor (1993) performed analysis of word repetitions in LINC transcripts and found evidence of order emerging from complexity.

Students in Burns's class frequently evoked the term "chaos" to describe their experiences in the networked classroom. Remember, for example, Lora's plaintive email message, "Wow, am I confused. Should I continue this adventure in computer chaos?" Yet, ultimately, the network provided her with a sounding board and a mirror which facilitated her writing. Tiffany even wrote a paper on "Chaos" and later had the courage to dig deeply into the mystery of her unconscious behaviors as a sleep-walker. From a sea of confusion, she sought meaning—as will be seen in chapter 23. It was writing on a network which helped her to do this.

Underlife can also be viewed as a kind of chaos. In this class, underlife consisted of a seemingly random batch of ideas which students brought into the classroom. Yet both kinds of order arose from underlife: students were sensitive to the ideas which emerged from this soup as self-organizing systems. And the potential was there for Burns and me and others to see deep structure in the underlife. For example, the underlife constituted a class culture with its own conventions and implied values. From the disorder of underlife, students forged relationships and broadened the scope of collaboration.

Niels Bohr was able to accept the precepts of quantum mechanics, but commented, "Anyone who is not shocked by quantum theory doesn't understand it" (quoted in Stephen T. DeBerry 1993, 27). As radical or "shocking" as quantum physics may be, it is now widely accepted within the scientific community. In Kuhn's terms, we could say that physicists and other scientists are now involved in "normal" science—working out the particulars of a quantum world view. In the social sciences and the humanities, the shift from a Newtonian world view to a quantum world view is harder to define; many are understandably skeptical of claims that such a shift really means much to nonscientists. Still, those in the humanities who choose to think in terms of quantum mechanics and chaos theory do so largely because of "aesthetic appeal"—again borrowing from Kuhn's terminology. Some are finding metaphors drawn from quantum physics to be useful in capturing evolving sensibilities which include elements of postmodernism.

The paradigm shift away from a Newtonian world view and toward a quantum view has vast implications for student writing—both in terms of process and product. As Richard Lanham (1990, xv) says, "To teach writing through electronic text is to put our students deeply in tune with the central tonality of their time."

Making_Meaning
_from_Memories

*They always want a blonde shooter. I guess they think blondes are
good luck and, at the craps table, luck is the name of the game.
When a blonde gets her hands on the dice they start throwing the
money on the table. There's a high noise level in casinos, but when
there is a hot shooter at the craps table that level doubles, triples
and even quadruples. Suddenly, everybody wants in the game; or
at the very least, to watch.*
          —Linda, "They Always Want a Blonde Shooter"

ON A DAY IN NOVEMBER, IRENE WALKED ACROSS CAMPUS, PONDERING WHAT
her next paper for "Writing, Thinking, and Learning" should be about. She
thought about the class and remembered how at semester's beginning she
had found it so high tech and stressful. Now it seemed a comfortable place
to take stock of her life, to sit back and reflect. The computer screen was so
accepting. She found the other students accepting, too. She had developed
a feeling of trust. She was thinking that in her next paper she would like to
write about her yearning to travel, perhaps to live abroad.

    Sandra also headed toward class. She passed the pond where the turtle
had earlier sat on the rock and provided the epiphany now etched in her
memory and recorded in her Grudin paper, "Happiness and the Art of
Living":

> One day I was running from one end of campus to the other, not because I was
> going to be late for class but because I was frustrated from my busy schedule.
> As I was passing a pond, I spied a turtle in it and stopped to watch him. He
> was attempting to climb onto a rock upon which two other turtles already sat.
> He placed his front flippers onto the rock and gradually pulled himself up the

side of the rock about half an inch at a time. But when he was about halfway to the top, he slid back into the water. Again he placed those flippers back onto the rock and pulled, and again he slid back into the water. On the third attempt, however, he made it to the top.

Writing about the turtle had transformed the passing moment into a signifier of something, she didn't know what.

Josh had tried to access email from the library where he was working on the computer. He had sent the following message:

Are the dates all screwed up or what???

David, bagging groceries at his part-time job, asked each customer, "paper or plastic?" and then reached for the kind of bag the customer had selected. Bored with the repetition and mindlessness of his job, he turned his thoughts to figuring out the politics of employment at the super market. Recognizing that it was, indeed, politics, he couldn't help contrasting this with the politics he observed at his other job, working at the state capitol. During one such reverie, David decided that he would write his next paper about these two jobs.

As the holidays approached, Lora found herself thinking a lot about her mother. Should she go home for Thanksgiving or not? A sense of duty pulled her home, and it would be nice to see her brother; but lately her relationship with her mother seemed to be painful. She noticed in herself the very attributes which annoyed her so much in her mother. This sense of annoyance tugged for her attention, and she decided to give in and explore these feelings. It was the dependence of her mother which seemed to be her mother's downfall. And she saw dependence in her own life, as well. She thought that she would like to write about this in her next paper.

Linda had enjoyed the essay in *Best American Essays*, 1989, called "Confessions of a Low Roller" by Joseph Epstein. It had evoked memories of her own days in Las Vegas as a "blonde shooter." She decided this would be the topic of her next paper.

Sherry Turkle noted that the computer serves as a mirror to some, and can even become a "second self" (Turkle 1984). Burns frequently referred to the computer as an "electronic mirror." While computers have been considered by some—usually people who don't use them—as impersonal, it seemed that in this class, students engaged in various kinds of self-reflection, and self-construction, while writing to the network.

By the time students began their third papers, they were well aware that their drafts would be readily available, through the network, to all their classmates. It would not be surprising, under these circumstances, for students to retreat to safe and impersonal topics. In fact, just the opposite occurred. For their third papers, many students chose topics which required them to take risks. For example, in the next chapter, we will see how Tiffany gazed unflinchingly at her dreams and nightmares.

The third paper was to be inspired by, or imitative of, one of the essays read in the third text, *Best American Essays*. Burns had assigned three essays from this collection, and students were to choose two additional ones. The three assigned essays were "Playing Chess with Arthur Koestler" by Julian Barnes, "Schedules" by Annie Dillard, and "Heaven and Nature" by Edward Hoagland. Students were free to plumb remembered experiences, shape them, and share them with an audience of peers. This enterprise appeared to take them into sorting out past relationships with grandparents, parents, and friends.

Students began announcing their topics to the network. David, for example, sent the following email:

I have decided to write my paper about my experiences at working at the Capitol and at HEB. I plan to talk about what my initial expectations of those jobs were and how they differed. In addition I intend to discuss how childhood and in some cases adult experiences have been useful in the workplace . . . it was during this time which i feel that i really started applying lessons from things that I have learned and really started listening to what my parents and adults have told me all my life. Some of the more special experiences include: seeing session for the first time. Facing people in the professional world. Coming to grips with the fact that in some cases ability is not as important as who one knows. Also, the genesis of understanding how to change ones situation and begin grow in what sometimes seems to be an infertile environment.

Linda began brainstorming online about her experiences as a blond in Las Vegas:

Well here is my [email] message—the one I was supposed to send. These are the things I am going to talk about and how they all relate to being a blonde in Vegas—and the things that I have learned out there—pretty interesting stuff—by the way I loved the Wolfe [Joseph Epstein] piece on Las

Vegas . . . Las Vegas: Casinos: New–New: THe Excalibur (Name Contest the Summer before and trying to pick a name for the hotel)–The Mirage–Lions and tigers and bears–oh my. What a jungle–Volcano that goes off every thirty minutes . . . MGM is back–New theme park built on the Trop golf course.–Old man–For some reason I am an old man magnet. Some girls are nerd magnets, well I'm an old man magnet.–The tables–poker pit–blackjack–counting cards–the guy who got caught, nonsmoking pits, red dog, Shanghai poker, when its hot its hot when its not move–craps: Blonde shooters, pass/don't pass, come/don't come, stickman, one for the boys–the strip: Old (The brightest Street in the US)–Dirty, some cool hotels, the Golden Nugget (U2 VIDEO) All white and gold, the man with the cig in his moth in form of the ? Fremont HotelNe–w: Trop, Excaliber, Dunes, Stardust, Caesars, The Mirage, Circus Circus, Sands, Hilton, Ballys, Aladdin–When it used to be Sand (Dad)–All day all night–the town that never shuts down, McDonalds even has a lighted sign on the strip–pit bosses–they run the show, different shift, their word is final–the one in the non-smoking pit that kept hitting on me–Mom–Blackjack at the pool, swim up blackjack tables at the Trop–Don't leave you alone anywhere–Eunis–the blackjack dealer.

And Jake wrote:

I'm going to work on this at home, and I will fill this in with what I do there tonight. I just can't get into deep thought in here. It makes sense to me anyway; you always here about real writers wanting to work in far off secluded places.

Despite his interest in high tech, Jake chose to write a piece about his experiences with a childhood friend when he was thirteen and living in rural America. Rather than brainstorming a list of "ingredients," he started his first few paragraphs:

Jake and Drake Inc. When Drake Jones caught me pulling weeds in Mr. Martinez's vacant lot, I thought I'd die of shame. I had hoped to finish the job early and get out before any of my friends saw that I had sunk to performing such a loathsome chore. But the late June sun had beaded my brow, and the rough hickory handle of the old hoe had raised and broken blisters on my palms, which were still soft from nine months of seventh grade.
The discomfort of the blisters and the sweat under my wide-brimmed straw hat had combined with the alluring knowledge that Drake and all my

other thirteen-year-old buddies were taking their ease swimming down at the river, and that made me thirsty. I was having a drink at the faucet behind the Martinez Brothers' Machine Shop when Drake apprehended me. Drake had a frog gig in one hand and a stringer of enormous bull frogs in the other.

Lora had this to say:

well hugh, it looks like this essay couldn't have approached me at a better time in my life. this past weekend has forced me to look at my relationships and realize that dependency is playing a major role within them. you hear many people say that dependency is hereditary. i've always had a problem believing this, but now, it's becoming a reality. i guess i should say i've been somewhat ignoring my dependencies trying to pretend that they don't exist. something is knocking on my reality door and wanting me to open up and let it all hang out, so to speak. and i think it's time for me to come full circle in admitting my dependencies and trying my damndest to delve into my solitude. this paper, for me, is going to be therapy. bear with me.

(Incidentally, it is interesting that twelve students read this message of Lora's and she, herself, read it four times—two times at each of two classes.) Coincidentally, Todd announced a similar subject to the network:

I have decided to undertake the task of relating my experience as the only child of a broken-home and an alcoholic mother. I have wrestled for several years with thoughts about my childhood, and blamed many things on it. I am not sure I understand what it means to "come to terms" with something, or if I even need to. Maybe by forcing myself to analyze and then express these thoughts and feelings in an organized manner, I might better understand what it all was about . . . why I am who I am: I am fiercely independant. I have a temper. I am quick to judge and quick to react. Maybe I can find some answers to these things . . . maybe not . . . but, like Kriegel, "When the day comes, I want to be able to fall into my death as nakedly as I once had to fall into life." What do you think?

By now, people had come to expect interesting messages from Todd, and the email footer revealed that many students read this post. Todd read his own post twice, and I read it once:

(LINDA 11/04 17:35) _ (DAVID 11/04 17:37) _ (JOSH 11/04 17:35) _ (DAVID 11/04 17:40) _ (LORA 11/06 17:47)–Reply _ (CASEY 11/06 17:47) _ (HOLLY 11/06 17:50) _ (ANGELA 11/06 17:53) _ (HUGH 11/06 19:32) _ (SHARON 11/07 16:29) _ (TODD 11/08 16:41) _ (DENISE 11/06 17:13) _ (TODD 11/08 17:32) _ (ANGELA 11/08 17:44) _ (JOAN 11/15 17:51)

As indicated above, Lora responded to Todd's message:

yo todd sounds like you and i have a lot in common. our papers seem to have a similar beginning. i'm sort of trying to come full circle with many things in my life, mainly my relationships with my mother, my lover, and most importantly, myself. i just thought i'd blab this to you.
(ANGELA 11/06 17:52) _ (LINDA 11/04 17:54) _ (JOSH 11/04 17:53) _ (HUGH 11/06 19:28) _ (TODD 11/08 16:40) _ (LORA 11/06 17:11) _ (JOAN 11/08 17.22)

To which Todd replied:

LORA, i'm not even really sure i feel like taking the time to attempt to do this one . . . especially with so much else going on . . . I bet you never thought you'd do this in a ++class++i#$^&^*&^(^&%whoaaa..../??????) . . . i can't wait to read some of your thoughts . . . funny how I didn't say "hear" huh?_
(LORA 11/06 17:11) _ (KARA 11/06 17:14) _ (JOAN 11/08 17:23) _ (JOSH 11/06 17:45) _ (ANGELA 11/08 17:45) _ (HUGH 11/08 19:04)

Burns was pleased that students seemed to be settling into topics with more ease than had been the case in the earlier papers. But he had problems with some of the proposed topics. He had wanted them to engage in memory work, but not to get into heavy psychological stuff—"therapy" as he called it. At a "center donut" meeting, he told the students that this essay was supposed to be personal and to involve memories, but not to be therapy. He trusted that students would know where to draw that line. But they didn't. Lora, Todd, and Tiffany all checked with him after class about the appropriateness of their topics. We will see in the next chapter how Tiffany handled the situation. Burns advised Lora and Todd not to write about the alcoholism of their parents.

Todd readily dropped his topic of alcoholism and came up with the more benign topic of learning to play the guitar. Now fully accustomed to growing his ideas in a network incubator, he immediately began posting his thoughts on his new topic.

TODD | GWEETAR
topic change: the experience of guitar, and it's impact on my life.
I. lessons that I hated
II. My Father who turned me on to rock and roll
III. My love of music
IV. What made me finally do it:
A. J.P. had one, so I got one
B. Beck . . . so good, made me want to be good
C. After the initial experimentation, I began to unlock and explore the possibilities it offered, and the invitation to seek a discipline which sets good players apart from great players . . .
V. "Practice, practice, practice . . . until you get a guitar whelt on your chest" I read this quote from Ted Nugent almost two years ago, and it has become my own mantra . . .
II. Another appeal to me is the camaraderie that musicians share, especially those of the same instrument.
III. I have found that my knowledge goes in steps and plateaus.
IV. The sound, however, is but small compensation compared to the inner satisfaction . . . Becoming one with the guitar; knowing it as you know yourself.
V. I have a white Fender Stratocaster named Georgeanna.
VI. I consider myself still a beginner
VII. When I was about eight, I got a small-version acoustic Yamaha for Christmas. I began taking lessons from my elementary school music teacher . . .
I still have that 3/4 scale guitar. It hangs on the wall to serve as reminder of my lost years and a kick-in-the-pants to "practice, practice, practice".

Lora was bitterly disappointed at Burns's not approving her topic. She complained to Tammy about this but eventually picked the safe topic of vegetarianism.

Linda knew her topic was all right because Burns had included a reference to it in a message to ALL in which he celebrated the "variety of impressions" already appearing in their online drafts and brainstorming. She immediately began drafting her paper:

LINDA | ALL | LLBBAE
THEY ALWAYS WANT A BLONDE SHOOTER . . . They always want a
blonde shooter. I guess they think blondes are good luck, and at the craps
table, luck is the name of the game. When a blonde gets her hands on the
dice they start throwing the money on the table. There's a high noise level
in casinos, but when there is a hot shooter at the craps table that level doubles, triples and even quadruples. Suddenly, everybody wants in, or at the
very least to watch.

I was talking to this old man at a table in the Holiday Casino. He said he
once saw a guy pass for fourty-five minutes straight. If you know anything
about craps you know fourty-five minutes is a long time to go without crap-
ping out. If you know nothing about craps, except that you throw the dice, let
me fill you in a little. First of all, if you throw a seven or eleven on your first
roll (or in casino talk, coming out) you win, if you throw snake-eyes, three
or twelve you "crap out", if you throw anything else, that number is your
point. You continue rolling until you make your point or you throw a seven
or eleven. If you "crap out" you lose the dice and a new shooter comes out.
The odds of keeping the dice for fourty-five minutes without "craping out" is
astronomical.

At first I was a little intimidated because there were so many people
crowded around the table and the game went so fast. When I figured it out,
it really wasn't that hard. There are four men who run the table, the stick
man, two men who keep track of the bets and one man that changes chips.
The men who run this table are the most arrogant, self-centered, egotistical,
horses-rears that you have ever met. My father has often wondered where
they get these people. I've decided that there's a school they go to, and I'm
not talking about dealers school (it's the same one that they sent DPS officers to, prick school).

Irene wrote about a relationship that had ended badly:

Ron's fit of jealousy and our fight in the street of Chicago . . . rain, cold, holes
in my shoes, strange people, a general feeling of malaise the accusation—
flashing back to the scene, how it looked and how it could have looked—the
fight a."i know what i see" b."this has happened before" . . . my rage

Tim who had missed the previous class and explained that he was working at home, had nothing to show for his time away from class and sent only
this message:

This entry only contains today's work because I forgot my disk! oops!

One rather intriguing development in the class was the emergence of "grandparents" as a popular topic. This had begun with the Grudin paper in which two students, Angela and Todd, had written about grandparents.

Angela had written of her grandmother's continuing grief over the death of her husband:

ANGELA | ALL | COMMON 2
My grandmother rocks silently in the old, familiar easy chair in the living room. The chair sits in the back of the room, unobtrusive yet comforting, much like its owner. Its worn wood and faded fabric belies of the kids and grandkids rocked to sleep. Waking from the trance of the creaking rocker, she ponders what to make for supper. Tears well up in her eyes as she realizes that it really doesn't matter, not since my grandfather passed away. The ringing of the phone suddenly pierces the deafening quiet. The incessant ringing that used to frazzle her nerves is now a welcome sound. Upon answering the phone she enters the well-known world of who-said-whats and who-did-whats. But her oblivion is suddenly shattered when the friendly voice on the other end grows sullen and relates that "Betty's husband passed last night." She is thrust back into her world of sleepless nights and companionless days. Trembling, she hangs up the phone, and realizes it's going to be another long evening
My grandfather thought his purpose was to make a living to provide for his wife and three kids. We worked all his life at the electric company—a job he hated because it kept food on the table etc. I dont think it ever occurred to him that he could do whatever he wanted. I remember him telling me one Sunday evening the summer before I went to college, we always went over there for sunday dinner, to go to college and do the best I could. He said, "I worked like a slave all my life. You don't have to do that." It had never dawned on me before that he was unhappy with his job all those years. (since then I've talked to my parents a lot about that) I wish he could have lived to see me become a lawyer.

And, as seen in chapter 17, Todd had written about his grandmother. He also wrote about his grandfather:

TODD | ALL | GRUDZIN
It was a cold October day when I got the phone call from my Father that his Father, my Grand father, had passed away. We talked only briefly, as he was

busy making arrangements, and he told me that I should not drive down yet. When we hung up, I put on my big red and black checked coat and sat on my balcony with the doors open. This jacket is incredibly warm, and it was more so since the heat from the inside had warmed it up. I remember looking out over the hills on this cold, grey day. I was warm in my jacket, and comfortable. It was cold outside and warm inside. I was suspended between the two feeling helpless. My mind was racing, speeding through memories which were dusty and old. I thought of other cold days that my Grandfather and I had spent throwing rocks in the water. We called it "Kerplunking." I wondered where he was and tried hard to imagine what he felt the instant before he passed. This to me is as elusive an undertaking as wanting to walk on the sun. But the sun didn't shine that day, and even though I was warm there on my balcony in my big jacket, I felt cold inside. It was a sad day to die.

In drafting paragraphs for her third paper, Sandra wrote this about her grandmother:

As a child she had to work to help support her family. She never got more than a fifth grade education. At sixteen she married my grandfather, just back from World War I, and started her own family. She worked in a laundromat. I have a picture of her and her co-workers lined-up in front of the laundromat smiling with big baskets full of clothes in their arms. The picture is packed away.
She bore a boy and a girl. She struggled through the Great Depression, trying to help support her family, living off rations (seems like she always had). She saw her son go to war in World War II. Over the next twenty years she raised five more children in a drafty, wooden-framed house in Goliad, Texas. But what was her life really like before I knew her?
Back in Goliad, Texas, Granna and Grandpa would sit out on the front porch in the evening with the kids lying on a blanket at their feet, and Granna would read Tom Sawyer and tell ghost stories. While the kids listened, the parents periodically spit their snuff out into the yard. The kids would get splattered in the process, and when they complained, Granna would say, "Well, get out of the way! It's good for the rose bushes!"

Apparently, many students were only one generation removed from a rural lifestyle. Sandra's essay continued:

Granna had a great fear of lightning and thunder. Whenever a rainstorm approached, she would unplug all of the electrical appliances so that they wouldn't "burn out." Then after everyone was a asleep, she would walk around the house with her flashlight, shining it in their faces asking, "Are you asleep?" Granna enjoyed being around children, and children liked her because of the colorful way she talked. Because of her lack of education, she communicated with them more easily and wasn't always trying to correct them. Everyone could count on Granna to take care of her neighbors and their animals. One neighbor, a Mrs. Stevens, had cataracts and couldn't see well. She raised chickens and rabbits and had a dog. Granna would help look after her animals and would send food over to her every now and then.

Teresa wrote about a visit to her grandmother and aunt, including this passage:

It is a sad fact to admit or accept, but things do not always go as planned; that as human beings we must constantly adapt ourselves to change, for better or for worse. In the 1950's my grandmother got pregnant, then got married. I think she wanted to say "I'm not ready yet," but realized it was too late. Her schedule, her plans, from that moment on were changed, and like so many of us, rather than waiting around for a sturdy anchor before taking the plunge, she fell in, though with much hesitation. I think she never got over it, or if she did, she had no one strong enough to hold her firmly in place while the world around her changed. And now that she is older she faces the challenge of reconciling herself and her ambitions with her regrets.

Holly wrote of the way memories of her grandmother help her deal with the "chaos" of her life.

A DIFFERENT KIND OF HEIRLOOM   My sister and I crouched onto the edge of our seats as the familiar sight of my grandmother's house came into view.

As my mother turned into the driveway, we could see the slouching, elderly figure in the screen door, awaiting our arrival. Nearing the house, I recognized the white-gray hair flowing softly around the wrinkled face. Although Grandma had lived a full, hard life, her hazel eyes still danced with mischief, and she always seemed ready to laugh. . . . At five o'clock, my uncle would get home from work, my grandfather would come home from the field, and we would eat supper. Then, at the end of the day, my grandmother would flop down in her chair and declare, "I am so tired. I didn't do no'ding all day 'cept cook!"

One day my sister and I decided to change the monotony of the system. We begged my grandmother to play Monopoly with us after lunch. At first, she gave excuses, but finally she relented. When we began playing, my sister and I assumed one of us would win since my grandmother was older and a bit out of touch with the game playing world, or so we thought. As the game wore on, my grandmother not only acquired the cheap properties, but she proceeded to capture Boardwalk as well as all the railroads and the utility companies. This was a different side of my grandmother. This was my grandmother, the real estate queen! . . . Every time I become really depressed or overwhelmed with stress and there seems no way out, I think of my grandmother's voice and try to hear her tell me what to do. Although I know she isn't really talking to me, just remembering her voice brings a certain calmness and serenity to the chaos I am trying to quiet.

Kara was brainstorming about her topic on diet for her third paper and included this reference to her grandfather:

Why our bodies can't flush out all the cholesterol we take in, my grandfather just had a heart attack.

Angela included this passage in an email message:

When you were talking about the technique of flashback, I was thinking about a time when I found a baby bird that had fallen out of its nest in my grandmother's backyard. I remember crying and begging my grandmother to save it, and there I was crouched underneath a tree trying to shoot birds as they came in to get a drink.

At the following class, she added new information to her idea:

flashback to bird in GM's backyard that fell out of tree—the one we tried to save GM said that if baby birds are touched by human hands that the mama bird will reject it and it will die. Does this tie in?

And at the class after that, she developed the idea still further:

When I was a little girl my grandmother and I found a baby bird in the back yard that had fallen from its nest. I cried and pleaded with my grandmother to "fix it," but she couldn't. When it died I was heartbroken. She told me that even if it had lived its mother would have rejected it because mama birds will not raise a baby bird that has been touched by human hands. "Why Grandmother?" Do birds have a keen insight about humans? Can they sense the danger and evil that we can do even though we often do not realize it ourselves?

I wondered if writing about grandparents was a way the students worked at reconciling their "postmodern" on-campus lives with the more tranquil lives so many of them had experienced or witnessed in the small towns where they grew up. Perhaps this focus on relatives left behind is a normal concern of students who have left home for the first time. Or, could it be that the high tech environment spurred a kind of nostalgia?

Meanwhile, even as they struggled to make meaning from memories, they struggled with the imperfections of technology. David had tried to transport his paper from another word processing program. It came out in an indecipherable form, a fact which he explained in his email:

> This is my final paper. It looks like this because it was done on another processor and I have been unable to provide a compatible copy.
> GOOD WRITING IN PSYCHOLOGY? . . . Ge_ ß Life!ì
> Th_ sig_ o ß learne_ individua_ i_ hi_ o_ he_ abilit• t_ stat_ ì thei_ idea_ i_ ß clea_ an_ consisten_ manner« Bu_ th_ sig_ o ß ì successfulô learne_ perso_ i_ th_ abilit• t_ conve• these idea_ i_ ß ì stimulatin_ an_ intellectu- all• interestin_ manne_ i_ additio_ át_ ì hi_ ábein_ áclea_ áan_ áconsis- tent« á Writin_ áals_ áafford_ áth_ ì opportunit• át_ learn« Writin_ assis_s u_ i_ takin_ ávagu_ áidea_ ì tha_ áexis_ onl• i_ ou_ head_ an_ makin_ the_ mor_ áconcret_ áan_ ì complex« Wha_ i Einstein/Socrates/o_ Darwi_ ha_ neve_ writte_ ì anythin_ down+ I thi_

Jake was having better luck in coordinating technology. He had now fully mastered his modem, and Burns wrote to him:

> Jake and Drake Inc: Thanks for electronically checking in today. I missed looking over my shoulder and seeing you write though. Your draft is quite good overall. Sounds like the wonder years have also affected your life. Descriptions were excellent. Keep at it. See you Tuesday.

@23

The_Growth_of
_a_Student_Paper

*You know, I really don't like this freshman bit either—topic sen-
tence paragraph, three main bodies, and a conclusion. Why don't
we just teach them something similar to portfolios? It seems more
expressive, creative, as well as encouraging.*

—Tiffany, email

WHEN COMPUTERS BECAME LINKED, OR NETWORKED, THE PRIVATE COM-
posing screen suddenly had the potential to be a public space for sharing
texts. Although collaboration and peer response was not new, it now could
be pursued with relative ease. Papers which had been stored in class files or
sent as email did not have to be printed up, but could simply be "opened"
on anyone's screen.

We have already seen how Todd's paper evolved with input from his
peers. In this chapter we will look at Tiffany's process of writing "Chaos
and the Art of Living" and then at her process of writing "Dreamage." In
both cases, her choice of topic emerged in the context of online class discussions, and her ideas took shape in an intuitive process which was nur-
tured in dialogue with teachers and peers.

Tiffany's topic of "chaos" emerged in the context of an online class discussion about a text which she initially found elusive. Her first message
about Grudin's *Time and the Art of Living* read as follows:

This book was really far out. In the beginning I was lost and not sure what
I was reading; however, I eventually found it interesting. I am still not sure
what I am reading. All I know thus far is that each segment focuses on an
idea. Each idea flows with elaborate meaning, which for some I haven't

discovered. This is a completely different book from Zinsser—what a change.

A couple of messages later, she added:

Although i have never been hypnotized, it reminds [me] of something that would be said while undergoing hypnosis. It seemed to be something you would read to relax and just really explore the "unexplored."

Tiffany was especially interested in this message from Irene:

mr. burns; i think you chose this book so we couldn't get stuck in a zinsser mode. Just like they do in a philosophy class: just when you think you've got it all figured out, they spring a whole new philosopher on you, who defies everything you once believed to be true.

To which Tiffany responded:

Irene: Agreed!

Still later, she added:

It really makes you stop and think. It is [a] different style, which in some instances it makes you read on to find out how it all fits together. Really unusual. I think his audience goal is to try and reach everyone and get them to explore ideas that you really don't think about.

Later still, Tiffany comments:

I don't know about the book itself, but it sure did make for an interesting [LINC].

And later,

The following excerpt was powerful: "One of the most mysterious operations of time is the way in which things silently divorce themselves from us and slip into the past." That is really scary isn't it?

In writing her paper, "Chaos and the Art of Living," Tiffany attempted to make sense of things which are not easily categorized. She included a paragraph on a modern abstract painting which puzzled her, a mirror slipping from her hands and shattering before her, her own birth experience, an angry encounter at a football game, an ant war she had watched helplessly, and the pain of looking through old photograph albums.

As described in chapter 22, students modeled their third papers after one or more essays from *Best American Essays*. Burns encouraged students to "research" their own lives, to select remembered experiences, and to shape them into essays just as the authors in *BAE* had done. Tiffany didn't take an easy path, but instead decided to explore her sleepwalking and her dreams. In discussing the purpose of her intended essay, she wrote:

> the reader who reads it should have to think. It should force them to think about their own dreams, how dreams relate to their life, and why dreams exist.

Her brainstorming process consisted of composing a long list of images, followed by four rough paragraphs:

TIFFANY | HUGH | TMDBAE
Gambling of Life
schoolhouse fire; helpless, race against time
(greenery, charcoal)
taking pictures down
being able to mobilize around the house in the dark
my parents/TV
fear of my brother scaring me.
standing in line cafeteria food
dream about those things in life which you had dream(nightmare) about
bad things in life which you don't want to occur
don't ever fully remember(recall) dreams; usually told by a spectator; once told then its as if you remember it all over again(remember bits and pieces)
feel like you've been there before—dreamed it
if stressed tend to dreamabout bad things—release?
gamble to see what could possibly happen if this actually occurred
explore the unexplored with out injuring yourself—take risks
another life with a hidden replica
trying to forget those unpleasant thoughts

difficulty to separate real from imaginary—Did that really happen or was I dreaming?

what are dreams all about?

DREAMAGE   A collage is a collection of unifying pieces of materials varying in texture and color created to from a picture. After dreaming the night away, our memory recollects only fragments of the dream. Ironically, these fragments of bits and pieces vary in their own texture and color. Some dreams are nightmares while others are fantasy; comparitively, some are dark and hidden amidst our fears, while others are bright and bold shining with sheer proudness. Collectively, these dreams form their own picture—a "dreamage," which in one way or another affects our lives.

As far back into the depth of life, I envisioned a childhood trauma: Among the greenery and barroned land sat a little red schoolhouse with an outer pure white trimming. I was standing in the lower level of the little schoolhouse, when as fast as my eyes could flicker, people were running past me and screaming. I could not understand what aroused these individuals. Eventually, I realized the warmth and the brightness of the deadly fire. How was I to escape its encompassing arms?

My only other recollection of this dream is a visual image of me outside escaping the traumatic fire. The greenery has now turned to charcoal.

One night my parents said they heard this—"dum thump, dum thump, dum thump, dum thump," escaping from my bedroom. As curiosity had arisen, they stumbled into my darkened room where they saw me perched on a stationary bicycle. My hands grasped the handle bars, while my feet vigorously turned the objects of movement. With a question of sanity in their voice, they asked, "What are you doing—its night time!" I replied with a trip and a mumble as I slowly crawled back into bed.

Tiffany's writing process was nonlinear, as she seemed to be considering images which presented themselves as fragmented memories. These images had a fractal quality. *Fractal* is an adjective coined by Benoirt Mandelbrot to describe geometric dimensions which are affected by scale levels. The classic example is the problem of measuring a shore line. While we may assign a length to a given piece of shore, a more precise ruler would measure every indentation until the shore line would be infinitely long. N. Katherine Hayles says of fractal forms that they "possess additional fractions of dimensions, with the fractionality corresponding to the degree of roughness or irregularity in the figure" (Hayles 1990, 13).

Kara soon responded, unsolicited, to Tiffany's draft:

KARA | TIFFANY | R) TMDBAE
My sister used to sleep walk a lot. One night a lady saw her walking down the street in a long white night gown. With her blonde hair blowing in the wind, she looked like a ghost. She went to a neighbor's house and knocked on the door. When they opened it, she said her parents had been murdered and she needed a place to sleep. The neighbors were scared to death, they called and my parents were asleep still. They came and got her! I thought this might interest you.

Tiffany immediately responded:

TIFFANY | KARA | DREAM
Hey, thanks a whole bunch! You made my day. I was so down because Hugh said my topic is not adequate for this essay. I was so frustrated. Thanks for sharing your dream—I might use it as an example in my paperOOOK???

Hugh, having read Tiffany's email to Kara, responded:

HUGH | TIFFANY | R) DREAM
I did not say that, did I? Think "learning" theme.

and:

HUGH | TIFFANY | R) PORT
I have to see how much you have written as I review the portfolios thus far. ALL I am saying is to focus and to address the theme of learning. So I now would like to give you this tiny insy ounce of encouragement. But I have decided to give you a ton of encouragement. Be careful to focus, but do not change topics now since you are experiencing the learning to love it stress. Besides, you have a week to go before the paper is due. Isn't this stress better than the night before stress? Good luck.

And so, Tiffany began adding to her draft, inserting information here and there, in a nonlinear manner. For example, at the next class, midway through her notes, she added Kara's story by simply cutting and pasting Kara's email. She made word changes here and there, such as changing the word "picture" to "collage." Additionally, she added the following details to the passage about the fire:

I raced for the fence as I was fighting for life. Apparently, everyone but I had escaped the treacherous blaze. I was on the side of the fence with the fire, while everyone else was secure on the other side. The last vision I have of this is the attempts of me trying to climb the fence with my mother on the other side (upset) guiding escape.As a child, the realization that this was a dream never occurred. I believed that this traumic event had taken place, until I was about eleven years old when I asked my mom if I had attempted to escape a fire. The assumption was made that I must have dreamed it as a child. Is there a significance of why a child would dream such a traumatic event which never occurred? Maybe this occurs because people want to explore the unexplored. If this occurred, what would I do type of thing.

She added a sleepwalking story told her by her brother:

My brother once told me a story of a guy who was sleeping over at this girls dorm room. The girl's roommate heard a noise in the middle of the night. She saw the guy crawl out of his girlfriend's bed and walked over to the sink. As he gazed at the sink for awhile, he slowly stubled his way over towards the closet. He walked into the closet and then snuggled into bed. The next few days the two girls smelled a horific odor coming from their closet. Not only was the putrid odor on her clothing, but there were yellow stains as well on the clothing. Needless to say, she had to wash all of her clothes.

And she adds two other memories:

My last few years in college, I relocated to a new apartment. My walls were rather bare, so I hung a photograph of a rose above my red and black covered bed. The picture was attached to the wall by means of a wire, which forced the picture to rest at an angle. Occasionally in the mornings when I had awakened, the picture was laying on the floor. At first I could not understand how this would happen. As I thought about it, I could vaguely remember removing the picture from the wall in the middle of the night; however, I could not recollect as to why. Did I think the picture was going to fall down? Maybe the angle of the picture had an effect.
One night as my parents were sleeping they heard an alarming noise in our living room. In response to the sound, my father jumped out of bed to discover what was going on. As he walked into the room, I was standing next to the piano. "Tiffany, it's time to go to bed now," said my father. "No, I am

standing in the cafeteria line." Confused, my father took my hand and led me to my bedroom.

Meanwhile, she heard from Kara again:

KARA | TIFFANY | R) DREAM
You can use the dream if you would like. I can give you more visual descriptions and details if you want them. Good luck! Just keep your mind on your topic and you can think of a learning experience to focus the paper on. If you would like any input, let me know.

Tiffany continued adding to her draft at each class. At the next class, she changed the opening phrase, "gambling of life" to read: "Dreams are like gambling with life." There were more word changes, such as the word "traumatic" for "bad." In one place, she added the sentence, "If we dream about trauma, does it relieve fears along with stress?" Now, she para phrased Kara's anecdote:

Kara, a classmate, shared a breathtaking experience of her sister. With sleepwalking as a common occurrence, Kara's sister was walking down the street one evening in a long white night gown. She looked as if she were a ghost with her long blonde hair blowing in the wind. As she approached a neighbor's house, she knocked on the door. When they opened the door, she claimed her parents had been murdered and she needed a place to sleep. Frightened, the neighbors phoned her parents, who had been sleeping, and they took her home. Why would someone dream a nightmare as terrifying as this one? Was her sister worried about her parents for some unknown reason? Could it be that deep down inside she has a fear?

She added a long section exploring dreams and their possible meanings:

With no control over these actions, my overiding fear was that I would sleepwalk outside. What prevents this from occuring or does anything? Maybe a fascination with houses confines me indoors. Amazement sur rounds my curiosity of how people are able to mysteriously tour their house while dreaming without bumping into walls or injuring themselves.

Tiffany continues the process of dividing her text into chunks, perhaps a return to "Grudin" style or perhaps an accommodation to writing online:

Have you ever dreamed of falling off a cliff or something to the like? I can always remember those nights I dreamt of falling. The event of falling was superimposed with a slanted bed while I felt a lost of balance. As i continued to fall in my dream, I slowly tumbled out of bed. As my body hit the hardened, wooden floor, the realization of dreaming was determined. Maybe the golden caution sign securely buried beneath the solid ground: "Watch for falling rocks," should be altered . . . "BEWARE OF FALLING BODIES."

They say as you grow older, sleepwalking becomes less prevalent. I remember as a freshman in college at UT my roommate Stacey experienced many of my active nights. I would wake up in the morning and she owuld say, "Do you remember what you did last night?" Hesitating, I replied, "No . . . what?" Once she said I was semi-awake after sleeping heavily while she was studying on her bed. As I popped up from my bed I said in a maddening, sharp voice, "What are you drinking?" She replied, "Water . . . ?" as her eyebrows scrunched towards her forehead. "No you're not!" I said with a tone of disbelief and anger. Stacey said in agreement, "Okay, then I'm not." After gazing for a few minutes, she watched me as I swiftly bent over to look under my bed. Stacey asked, "What are you doing?" With my eyes peering under the bed I answered, "there's a cat under here." Within a few minutes I supposedly returned to a lying position and fell asleep.

She adds still another anecdote provided, via email, by a classmate who had read her previous draft:

Sandra dreamed she was Batman and Robin was her companion. As they flew through some curtains, they entered a timewarp. Here, they met "carpet people," who were composed of a darkcolored carpet square. Depending on which way the carpet was turned determined the appearance of a head. The heads looked as if they were brown-colored balloons; however, they had no distinctive facial features. When the carpet people's head disappeared, the carpet people had control. Batman and Robin's main objective was to take away the power from the carpet people, which they accomplished by removing the carpet. Conquered, the carpet people were given heads and lost all control. As Batman and Robin went back through the curtains, Sandra saw Alice from the Brady Bunch cleaning her kitchen.

On a day when they were supposed to send their finished papers, Tiffany sent the following message to Burns:

This is not my finshed product, I'll send that to you later through the network. I wanted you to know that what happened yesterday. Apparently, I saved it under tmdbae.n15 as well as tmdbae.n19. When I pulled tmdbae.n15 up my almost completed paper that I had done on the 19th was saved under tmdbae.n15 also. I don't know why it only saved to paragraphs under tmdbae.n19, but I was relieved to find out I still had my paper. So, here is the one I was going to send you yesterday. The final is coming through the network.

And then came this:

TIFFANY | HUGH | TMDNAE
GREAT!!!! My disk did not save my paper and I lost it all but the first two paragraphs. I was going to send it to you today, but unfortunately, I will have to come back tomorrow and retype my entire paper. Just thought I'd let you know. Thankfully, I printed a copy of it

Five days later, Tiffany modified her draft by adding more details. To her description of the fire dream, she added the "outpouring emotional support" of her mother. She added the following section as well:

While it was only an assumption, we concluded that I must have dreamt it as a child. Is there a significance in why a child would believe a dream was an actual occurrence in life? While I have never been trapped in a fire, it is possible that I was curious to experience the detriments of a fire without facing the reality . . . Similar to a representation of gambling with life, dreams allow for creative experiences and thoughts centered around the individual. The limits of a dream are infinite since the risk level in dreams are so low. Normally, we do not like to contemplate on the subject of death, because we fear it might come true . . . Dreams seem to be an outlet for an emotional pyramid; however, on the other hand, what about those which frighten reality . . .

She adds her latest thoughts on Kara's sister's dream, as well:

As I reflected on this dream, images raced through my mind. My God, I thought, what instigated a nightmare as terrifying as this one? Could it have been that she was worried about her parent's life or a fear of abandonment?

After "experiencing" her dream, my body felt a rush of eerie chills, which inspired me to ponder over my own.
While my dreams primarily consisted of escapades around the house, my over-riding fear was that I would sleepwalk outside. What prevents this from occurring or does anything? I have often wondered how a sleep-walker chooses his/her destination.

She invites the audience into the topic with this addition:

Imagine yourself being told that you urinated in a closet, or even that you dreamt your parents had been murdered . . . It is just as if we have another life or a hidden replica. Have you ever had that uneasy feeling . . . ?

She now adds this right before her description of the sleepwalking event in which she had removed a picture from the wall and put it on the floor:

It is difficult to separate real from imaginary. We ask ourselves—Did this really happen, or was I dreaming?

She now prefaces Sandra's dream with the following statement: "Many times our influences on dreams originate from insignificant surroundings in reality."
And summarizes with this:

Although this was a rather comical dream, it demonstrates a typical effect which our surroundings have on our dreams. Sandra's dream probably developed from childhood television viewing. In retrospect, I remember when my parents would not allow me to watch "scary" movies at night as a child. That seemed to puzzle me as a child.

Finally, she provides a conclusion:

As we build our collage of dreams, each piece signifies its own unique experience. While we explore the unexplored, we determine the boundaries of cause and effect. As we explore, create, and diversify, our dreams seem to form a unity centered around ourselves. Continuing to add each cre-ation, we collectively form our own picture—a dreamage.

Tiffany had enjoyed the process of writing this paper in portfolio style. She had definitely "pushed the envelope" in her choice of topic. Yet this had enabled her to write about a topic which intrigued her. She had remained engaged in this topic and was satisfied with her final product. She wrote the following about her process:

TIFFANY | BURNS | PORTFOLIOS

So, what do I think of all the portfolios? I was really able to relate to them because I am the type of person who prefers to work on rough drafts through computer rather than paper. In fact, since I have learned to use computers so well, it is almost impossible for me to write rough drafts on paper. I really enjoyed working with the portfolios. They gave me a chance to organize my paper, as well as see how my writing developed throughout. In addition, there were times when I was so confused and frustrated [but] by the time I completed the portfolio there was this paper—it seemed to naturally develop. What have I disliked about them? All the trauma they have put me through. The pressure to do well, the messed up disks, and unreliable computer memory forced me to go practically "NUTS." I am still in one piece—how? I don't know!

I definitely believe that I learned to write by writing.

The process of writing an essay typically involves the re-searching of remembered past events through the filter of one's current frame of mind or point of view. As such, essays involve a writer in bringing together disparate elements into a new pattern. Tiffany stretched this process in a new direction, concentrating on consciousness itself. Perhaps this had something to do with writing on computers for the first time; unlike typewriters, computers also have a "subconscious" and a "conscious" mind, the subconscious being the memory which is invisible until "opened" on the screen.

Students_Battle_the_System
_(and_the_Genres?)

*Daily I struggle with falling into the UT system. It seems as if
everyone runs around here just following the patterns set for
years. . . . As I begin my senior year, I feel myself fitting the mold
I have been so dead set against.*
                                        —Kara, email message to ALL

STUDENTS IN COLLEGE DO STRUGGLE WITH ISSUES OF "FITTING THE MOLD."
They negotiate the issue of fitting the mold in choosing their clothing,
choosing their leisure time activities, choosing what professions to prepare
for, and so forth. This negotiation also affects how they conform to the
role of "student," as elaborated in chapter 13 ("Underlife and Identity").
In writing classes, the issue of fitting the mold comes up with regard to
assignments. Students must decide to what extent they will go along with
the terms of assignments and to what extent they will negotiate these
assignments according to their own styles, interests, and abilities to get
things done.

Students are often cynical about assignments, finding many of them to
be distant from their own true interests and engagements. They may find
that the persona they have to step into to write a traditional paper does not
resonate with their current constructs of self. This adds to a feeling of playing a game—which in turn can feed resentment toward school in general.
Students are increasingly resistant to "paying their dues" to an academic
world which at times seems out of step with the *real* world in which they
plan to spend most of their years.

On the other hand, students know how school is played, and they are
resigned to play the game for a few more years. Because of this, they

appreciate a syllabus which provides explicit formulas for the products (usually papers) upon which they will be graded and eventually given a ticket to participate, with privilege, in the *real* world. It's as if they're saying, "If I have to play this game, at least give me a clear rule book."

Until recently, the mold of standard academic writing could, at least, be taken for granted. Students and teachers were, for example, familiar with research papers and essays and no one questioned the academy's emphasis on these genres. With the advent of computer networks, and recently the WWW and hypertext, students are devoting greater and greater proportions of their reading and writing time to dialogues, "polylogues"[1], and hypertextual linking. Even before these radical changes in literacy, students were beginning to express a jaundiced attitude toward academic prose, as seen in chapters 5 and 6. David, in one LINC session, commented that he wished that more of the writing he was asked to do in college related to writing he would be doing in his career.

In terms of the paradigm shift model described by Thomas Kuhn (1970), we might say that certain genres are entering a stage of crisis because of a cultural or epistemological misfit. Various accommodations are being made to render academic genres acceptable to those who must write and consume them; however, these accommodations may eventually cease to suffice, and whole new models may emerge. Whether these will be considered academic discourse remains to be seen.

The traditional academic research paper appears to be one of the at-risk forms. Because the processes of research are constructed so differently now, so too will the products begin to be constructed differently. Two generations ago, students gathered data for research papers by painstakingly writing out notes on 3x5 index cards and then attempting to blend this information through paraphrase and judiciously placed quotes. One generation ago, students gathered data by Xeroxing articles and highlighting pertinent data with fluorescent markers. Again, they were to use paraphrase, judicious quotes, and logical organization to construct a cohesive, well-organized essay that makes a certain "point" or "argument."

Now an even bigger shift has occurred as students can readily surf the World Wide Web, "download" data to their "hard drives," and print verbatim transcripts from far-flung sources within moments. The data they access on networks may be in essay or research-paper form, but increasingly it is not. Instead, data may come in the form of conversations and linked "packets" of information. In presenting one's findings, the task in composing is to blend not only quotes, but graphics, video segments, and sound. The very term "research" is quickly evolving in this new online environment as is the concept "paper."

The less often that students actually read academic research papers or essays, the less readily will they consent to write them. They simply won't see this as relevant to acquiring, constructing, and sharing information and knowledge. Even before the technology explosion that brought hypertext, CD-ROM, and Net surfing to our desktops, students were resisting standard academic genres. For example, consider the following LINC composed by Angela, Sharon, and Lora after Burns referred to the importance of "research" as an element in the third paper assigned. Note, incidentally, how Josh and Tim apparently chose to ignore the very topic of research. [The asterisks denote intervening messages which have been omitted for the sake of clarity.]

Angela: Hugh: Does our essay need to show signs of research?

Sharon: Hugh: does this mean we have to research something? I thought this was like a personal essay, not like a research paper?

Hugh: Absolutely—research. Recovery and discovery of information. But there are lots of different kinds of research.

Sharon: Hugh, from your last statement, we seem to only need research something in order to get the facts straight (well, that was a pretty obvious conclusion) So you do not mean heavy duty research, just factual research, right?

Josh: I wonder what time Alex Trebek gets up in the morning?

Tim: I liked this passage: [Referring to Annie Dillard's essay, "Schedules,"] "My working the graveyard shift in Virginia affected the book. It was a nature book full of sunsets; it wholly lacked dawns, and even mornings."

Lora: ARE YOU TALKING ABOUT A SPRING CLEANING OF OUR BRAINS/ IS THAT THE KIND OF RESEARCH YOU'RE TALKING ABOUT

Sandra: What did that quote mean?

Hugh: What is heavy duty research, Sharon?

Angela: Hugh: Do our papers need the Grudinlike quality of having an underlying meaning to which we can all relate?

Sharon: Hugh, heavy duty research is going to the library, looking up lots of books on a particular subject, taking notes, and then trying to fit all those notes into a cohesive whole.

Granted, in the above case students were confused about whether they were to be writing a personal essay or a research paper. Nevertheless, I detect a subtle mocking of the whole enterprise of writing research papers. We can rail all we want about the bad attitude of kids these days, but it is the thesis of this book that students these days are developing an attitude or stance that is actually adaptive to the paradigm shift in which we are enmeshed. An expression in common parlance is "been there, done that." It is this dismissive attitude that students often display toward traditional academic genres.

In the second LINC on Zinsser's book and the "Zinsser paper," students engaged in the following discussion about the assignment:

Teresa asked:

Does anyone know "what in the heck" we are supposed to be doing now?

To which Sandra responded:

No, I have no idea what the first assignment will be about.

Similarly, Irene said:

At this point, I have no ideas what I'll be writing about.

Later Irene asked Sharon:

What's the crazy assignment about?

To which Sharon replied:

—I think that the assignment is to write what you think good writing is and use examples of writing from the authors you chose. The trick is to get 8–10 pages. My suggestion would be to use lots of long quotes.

Kara also responded:

We are suppose to use our author's pieces like Zinsser has. We will comment on their "writing to learn" process, and if they really write well. Just think of one piece you have read or paragraph of one, and try to evaluate and dissect it. Then write your ideas and opinions like Zinsser by using quotes from your pieces to support or use as an example. Good luck!

It is interesting that students didn't seem to care if Burns read these almost mutinous comments. Students may no longer be as invested in pleasing the teacher as in times past. In this class, at any rate, the desire for rapport with peers was apparently more compelling than any desire for approval by the teacher. Although students could simply have asked Burns for clarification on the assignment, they apparently preferred to clarify the assignment among themselves.

I think there are at least two reasons that students engaged in this dialogue about assignments. First, they were making meaning together, collaborating on their evolving sense of what the assignment was. Second, they knew—as do students everywhere—that there is power in numbers. As long as they all responded to the assignment in approximately the same way, they knew that the professor would be relatively powerless to insist that they *all* should have done otherwise. They could shift the burden of blame onto the teacher. This is nothing new, but I think that when students are in the midst of a misfit between school requirements and their own sense of what is appropriate, this group meaning-making and group defining of assignments becomes increasingly prominent.

Lillian Bridwell-Bowles suggests that students be invited to critique "the rhetorical conventions that they are expected to employ within the academy" (Bridwell-Bowles 1992, 349). She quotes Adrienne Rich who says, "As long as our language is inadequate, our vision remains formless, our thinking and feeling are still running in the old cycles, our process may be 'revolutionary,' but not transformative" (349). Bridwell-Bowles notes that she has been experimenting with new forms that reflect her increasingly cross-disciplinary scholarship, and she refers to this as a personal paradigm shift:

> I have sought alternatives—a more personal voice, an expanded use of metaphor, a less rigid methodological framework, a writing process that allows me to combine hypothesizing with reporting data, to use patterns of writing that allow for multiple truths, what Dale Spender has called a "multidimensional reality," rather than a single thesis, and so on. (350)

Bridwell-Bowles acknowledges that argumentation and standard academic discourse have a role, but that "students may need new options for writing if they, too, are struggling with expressing concepts, attitudes, and beliefs that do not fit into traditional academic forms" (350). She uses the term "diverse discourse" to describe "attempts to write outside the dominant discourse" and to do "something 'with' and not 'to' the reader" (353).

One of her students, reflecting on a piece written in diverse discourse, commented that it was "a peaceful cacophony" (365). The term "cacophony" might well apply to LINCs and other forms of electronic communication, as well.

The electronic text makes what we do in schools visible in a new way, just as it made the organizations Shoshana Zuboff studied visible in a new way (Zuboff 1988, 179). The electronic text indeed lays before us, in glowing letters but not necessarily glowing terms, the processes that comprise school practice. Even as the electronic text gives us pause to question our tried and true practices, it also causes us to question our tried and true products—our genres.

Myron Tuman states, "It is usually a mistake to assume that a new technology will be used to extend, rather than transform an existing practice" (Tuman 1992, 5). He posits that, "Essays have been at the center of school-based literacy this century in large measure because as miniature books they reflect the commitment of print culture to the task of generating and comprehending such focused texts" (4–5). He goes on to predict that books and essays will not disappear entirely but will become "marginal to the central project of literacy education" (5). Further, he paraphrases Lanham's (1990) belief that today's students "do not possess, nor should they, the capacity for silence and reverence before the printed page (akin to the quiet of a concert hall or museum)." Rather, they possess "skills honed by a new electronic technology" (16). Tuman cites Lanham's list of e-text attributes: "volatility, interactivity, easy scaling changes, a self-conscious typography, collage techniques of invention and arrangement, a new kind of self-consciousness about the 'publication' and the 'publicity' that lies at the end of expression" (Lanham 1990, xiv-xv).

Some educators, recognizing student resistance to such tasks as reading the "classics," writing standard research papers and essays, and using academic prose, fear that literacy is in danger. Tuman argues that indeed literacy, as we know it, is on the wane. However, he points out that this will not be the first time in history that the commonly held notion of literacy underwent transformation. In much of the pre-industrial world

> reading . . . was defined largely in terms of the ability to recite socially important, often religious or nationalist texts, and writing, when it was taught at all, was defined in terms of the ability to transcribe texts (hence the emphasis on penmanship and spelling). It is only with the great tide of industrialism that the now pervasive notions of reading and writing as the ability to comprehend and to create new material were established. (Tuman 1992, 1)

Tuman notes that paradigmatic shifts in literacy have, throughout history, evoked anxiety from those who cherished the status quo. For example, he points out that Socrates was concerned with what would become of the art of memorizing once writing was possible (3).

Tuman ponders what genres will emerge when the "paradigmatic text" in composition classes becomes something other than the essay. He explores new options for "text," noting that it could be a newsletter:

> Or what if the paradigmatic text moves in an entirely different direction, becoming, for example, a research report generated from a carefully structured search of the new electronic storehouse of collected wisdom (and information), a modern electronic database? Or moves in a third direction, where the paradigmatic text is no longer a text at all but an electronic conversation in which different parties read and respond to each other instantly (in real-time) and informally over a computer network? (4)

Seymour Papert believes literacy is not just a matter of reading written words, but reading the world, and reading media. He criticizes the tendency to associate literacy exclusively with the reading of written words. He has coined the word "letteracy" to refer to this narrower concept of literacy, and reclaimed the word "literacy" to have a broader meaning. He sees a move, now, "from letteracy to media-based knowledges acquisition" and suggests that " . . . The movement from letteracy to media-based knowledge acquisition may be even more important than the movement from preletterate to letterate culture" (Papert 1992, 12).

As mentioned in chapter 20, Cynthia Selfe (1989) described the ways her students were using color, a variety of fonts, and other new rhetorical devices in their academic papers. A few years after Selfe's chapter on this "multilayered grammar" was published, *College English* published Gail Hawisher and Charles Moran's "Electronic Mail and the Writing Instructor," urging composition theorists to give more attention to email since "at many work-sites and within some academic communities it is fast becoming our principal form of organized communication" (Hawisher and Moran 1993, 627).

Recently, a few scholars have begun to publish in new forms which capture some of the qualities of email and online conversations. In 1994, for example, *College Composition and Communication* featured a book review by Nedra Reynolds et al. of Lester Faigley's *Fragments of Rationality*. This review consisted for the most part of a LINC transcript, featuring comments by Reynolds, her students (who had used *Fragments of Rationality* as a class text) and Faigley (who was logged-on remotely).

In February, 1995, *College Composition and Communication* published a series of responses to the "debate" between Peter Elbow and David Bartholomae, including one by Wendy Bishop which she titled, "If Winston Weathers Would Just Write to Me on E-Mail." Her review is significant both in terms of form and content. It consists of a numbered list of paragraphs, including excerpts from her students' writings, personal musings, and even a poem *about* email. She claims at one point that what she is doing is "blurring my genres publicly as they are blurred internally, experientially." She also states that "Much of my (academic) world is constructed on the Internet these days" (Bishop 1995, 101).

One of her paragraphs reads, in part: "The biggest master narrative I encountered as a woman in schools was that of academic discourse: certainty, logic, war, linearity, Grammar A, unitary, authoritative, author-saturated" (98). Through both the content and form of her review, she proposes an alternative to the "master narrative."

Pushing the envelope ever further, Michael Spooner and Kathleen Yancey's "Postings on a Genre of Email" appeared in *College Composition and Communication* (May, 1996). This article consisted entirely of email messages—including unattributed messages between Spooner and Yancey, but also including attributed messages lifted from online discussion lists such as Megabyte University and Cybermind. Multiple reviews of this article prepared by Deborah Holdstein, Carolyn Miller, and James J. Sosnoski were also included.

Holdstein claimed that Spooner and Yancey evoked "in a single essay many of the most salient issues involved in technology and composition studies in a scholarly and innovative merging of form and content reminiscent of Pope" (Holdstein 1996, 280). Miller noted:

> Continued attention to genre can serve to problematize what it is that students write and why and how it is related to what they will write as adults . . . Email may help us finally understand students as rhetors, communicators for whom genres are not academic forms but effective social instruments. (Miller 1996, 288)

Sosnoski commented that the most important aspect of email "is that it gets writing virtually out of the classroom" (Sosnoski 1996, 292).

Meanwhile, scholarship is moving virtually out of academic journals and online. As mentioned in chapter 20, the *RhetNet* home page features, for example, a link to *RhetNet* Snapshots. At this writing, there are seven "snapshots" or brief academic essays listed here and accessible with a hypertext "click" of the mouse. One, indeed, was entitled "Evolving past the Essay-a-saurus: Introducing nimbler forms into writing classes" by Beth Baldwin (1996). Critics are quick to note that Baldwin's snapshot argument against essays is itself a kind of essay. However, her essay—if indeed it is an essay—consists of only three or four screens and includes usage such as "cool metaphor." Most intriguing is the fact that Baldwin reports that she no longer requires essays, but instead invites her students to write "conversational (dialogical or multilogical) pieces."

When even academic journals are publishing such multivoiced and multilogical pieces, and when online journals—both refereed and unrefereed— are becoming a major source of scholarly exchange, we must certainly pause and take stock. One of the speakers in Spooner and Yancey's voice collage quotes Rob Wittig who predicts, "The period we are entering . . . will see the ascendance of a new aesthetic animated by the vision of the cultural world as composed of mobile 'interchangeable' fragments—common property—messages constantly in motion, ready to be linked into new constellations" (quoted in Spooner and Yancey 1996, 273).

In an address at the Computers and Writing Conference in Logan, Utah, Yancey spoke about genre—asking if email montages could be considered essays. If so, she went on to ask, what would we value in such essays? What would we teach our students about such essays? She went on to say that this new kind of essay would have

> a text whose logic is intuitive, associative, emergent, dialogic, multiple; which admits narrative and exposition as patterns; to borrow from Susan Miller, it allows for differentiation without exclusion, such that it resists becoming unified in a community of shared final ends. It is an essay of radically different identity, politics, of radically different mentality. It is an essay I hope we will all learn to read and to write. (Yancey 1996a, 14)

Yancey posits that such a new genre would provide a "place where multiple ways of knowing are combined collage-like, a place where alternatives are at least as valuable as single-voiced, hierarchically argued master narratives"(7).

What has become apparent to me from observing students writing in computer classrooms is that most students are eager to become competent in this new environment and to participate in the new literacy— including new kinds of essays, new genres, and multimedia. Students are battling the old academic system to an extent. But their resistance to old processes and genres appears to be more than matched by their enthusiasm for the new processes and genres which computer polylogue appears to engender.

Note

1. The expression, "polylogue" was apparently coined by Gary Waller, Kathleen McCormick, and Lois Fowler on page 4 of *The Lexington Introduction to Literature: Reading and Responding to Texts*, Lexington, MA: D.C. Heath, 1987. Since the Greek origin of *dia* is "between" and not "two," as in *di*, the word "dialogue" already implies "two or more" and the substitution of *poly* for *dia* is not logical. However, the term polylogue has been used to convey a multiplicity of voices, and I therefore find it useful in referring to LINC.

@25

The_Last_Day_of_Class

There is a brief period of twilight of which I am especially fond, lit-
tle more than a moment, when I see what seems to be color without
light, followed by another brief period of light without color.
—Robert Grudin, *Time and the Art of Living* (1982, 166)

ON THE LAST DAY OF CLASS, LESS THAN THREE WEEKS BEFORE CHRISTMAS, many students arrived early as was always the case on a day that papers were due. Students sent their final drafts to the network and printed up hard copies with ease.

When David arrived, we chatted for a few minutes, and it was clear that he was disappointed with Burns's response to his last paper. "He didn't like it," he said, "but I think I'm learning to develop my own sense of what I want to write anyway." He was still looking forward to writing a book on race relations as soon as he graduated. He would be quitting his job at the supermarket which would give him more time.

When I mentioned to Todd that I liked his paper, "The Guitarist Tunes Up," he said, "That wasn't really my best work. I didn't have enough time. Would you like to see my final paper?" I of course responded in the affirmative, and Todd printed up a copy and presented it to me with obvious pride.

Tim was in his usual state of panic, trying to do several things at once, including filling out a questionnaire for Kara. Kara had passed out this questionnaire to her classmates weeks ago as part of a project she was doing for a language acquisition course she was taking. Everyone else had completed this promptly; but not Tim the procrastinator.

Irene looked weary, but said she was relieved that the semester was over. She said that it didn't appear that she would be going home for Christmas. Lora said she hadn't yet decided if she'd go home or not.

Burns gathered the group at the "center donut" for some final administrative details. He passed out envelopes for students to self-address; he would mail to them the grades and evaluations of their final papers.

Burns made some closing remarks and then went to the room across the hall while I conducted my survey and Steve conducted the course evaluation. Students filled out the surveys, posted and printed their papers, and chatted.

Lora and Irene talked together about their future plans as writers. Lora said that if she became a writer, she would invent a more alliterative pseudonym than her own name. "I could use my mother's maiden name," she said. "Garcia." She laughed and added, "That would never do, would it?" Irene said she would write under a man's name so that she could get published.

Most of the students went across the hall to say their good-byes to Burns. Todd mumbled some awkward farewells and sauntered down the hall. Lora and Irene wished me luck on my project and left together.

By 4:30, the room was empty except for Tim. He was still checking his files on the computer and didn't leave till 5:15.

The community was officially disbanded.

Postlogue

A week later, Burns found the following message in his email, sent via modem by Jake. (The strange formatting resulted from an incompatibility between Jake's system and the class system.)

```
JAKE  |  HUGH BURNS  |  FINAL PORT
DR. BURNS,_ i HAVE BEEN UNABLE TO FIND THE COMPUTER LAB
OPEN._ IF YOU NEED AN ELETRONIC COPY OF MY PAPER, I CAN BE
REACHED_ AT EITHER [XXX-XXXX] IN AUSTIN OR [XXX-XXX-XXXX] IN
HOUSTON _ DURING THE BREAK. I WILL CONTINUE STOPPING BY THE
LAB AND _ TRYING TO POST IT, BUT IF I AM UNABLE AND YOU NEED
ONE CALL _ ME AND I CAN SEND YOU A DISK. I REALLY ENJOYED THE
COURSE,_ AND I THINK THAT MY WRITING REALLY DID IMPROVE.
WOW! IT'S _ NOT EVERY DAY THAT YOU ACTUALLY LEARN SOME-
THING USEFUL_ AMYMORE.HAVE A GREAT CHRISTMAS AND A
HAPPY NEW YEAR._ JAKE
```

@26

Closing_Thoughts

As we approach the new millennium, our institutions, once considered bedrock, now seem to be in flux. As if this weren't enough, personal identity is no longer seen as something solid, forged, like metal, but rather something fluid and ever-changing. Our written language, which we used to equate with stable print on tangible paper, increasingly is experienced as ephemeral pixels on a screen—appearing or disappearing through the flick of a switch or the click of a mouse. And new generations are finding it less necessary to encode meaning in words since they can now use pictures and sound for this purpose.

Students who enter college classrooms are cynical about school and determined to show their peers that they are not taking this game of school seriously. Many are burned out on the five-paragraph essay and resist writing anything that remotely resembles it. These students are caught up in popular culture which is created locally, but also constructed internationally through the dizzying advances of technology. They grew up with the mature media of television bringing them amazing windows into world events—and also bringing mind-numbing trivia.

Meanwhile, even as our students are coming of age, a new medium is coming of age along with them—the medium of computer networks. It's no wonder that students think of this medium as theirs—a space where they can bring their own language and concerns. Whether on campus or off, students are discovering the kaleidoscope of ideas and images that is only a few keystrokes away every minute of every day on the World Wide Web. On computer networks, whether local or wide, students pursue learning on their own terms.

A computer network will not transform a mere composition classroom into a democratic utopia. Nor will it lessen the uncertainties and challenges of teaching and learning. What this environment will do, as Myron Tuman observes, is "put our students deeply in tune with the central tonality of their time" (Tuman 1992, xv).

We are all mired in tradition to some extent, and change is worrisome and risky. One way to stay anchored in the turbulence of change is to recognize that at least some of the changes affecting us flow from streams of thought that sprang up a long time ago. For example, in 1916, John Dewey wrote, "Democracy is more than a form of government; it is primarily a mode of associated living, of conjoint communicated experience" (87). Dewey also said, "Only gradually and with a widening of the area of vision through a growth of social sympathies does thinking develop to include what lies beyond our direct interests" (148). Burns's pedagogy was in harmony with these notions. The World Wide Web also appears to offer unprecedented opportunities for people to expand their social sympathies beyond the close-at-hand and to see the connections between the immediate and the distant.

Most network users concur that there is something fundamentally democratic about the way classroom networks are configured, even though negative sanctions can still be applied by a teacher or by peers. Because there are multiple, essentially simultaneous, responses not only to the teacher's messages but to all the messages, the typical evaluative pattern is replaced by a web of multiple perspectives. While this makes dialogue more chaotic, it also makes communication more exciting and multifaceted. It propels even the most recalcitrant student into an active mode of thinking. It allows students and teachers to, in Spiro's (1987) words, "criss-cross" differing domains of knowledge as well as to construct new knowledge.

This book focused on a particular local area network in which students communicated only with others in their class who, for the most part, were physically present. As classrooms become linked to the Internet, the very necessity for a physical classroom is being questioned. Moreover, students are increasingly joining conversations outside of their own group of local peers. To some, the classroom-based local area network described here may seem outmoded. My own take on this is that local conversations will always be important.

I think it is critical that we maintain a healthy balance between local and distant conversations. Physically coming to a common meeting place will always be important. Throughout this book, the concept of linking has been foregrounded. It is important to continue to link physical people with conversations by combining real spaces with virtual spaces. And it is important to continue to link local conversations with long-distance ones. We must not get carried away with technology to the extent that we forego local links with our neighbors. Sherry Turkle talks of the "cycling through identities" that occurs on networks (quoted in McCorduck 1996, 164). I would urge that we also promote a sort of cycling between the local and the remote, never choosing one *instead* of the other.

The networked classrooms appearing on campuses across the country can be treated as laboratories for pedagogical renewal. This ethnography has explored the experience of just one writing class at a large university. While every situation is different, it appears that networked classes have much in common. Here students and teachers negotiate curriculum, meaning, control, and identity on a daily basis. Certainly, we in the humanities will continue our commitment to democratic and humanitarian ideals. At the same time, this moment in history, this "link age" calls upon us to foster a certain tentativeness and playfulness in the face of change.

The power of electronic media, combined with the power that students gain when they use this media, can be daunting. Yet, despite the complexities and challenges of networked classrooms, I believe their introduction to college and high school campuses is timely and provides students and teachers with something far more significant than a "new tool." Computer networks introduce new metaphors into our thinking.

As literacy moves online, we must address problems with inequitable access. We must also help students understand the shadow side of a networked society. Throughout their lives, they will be making choices which will either foster or thwart panopticon-type uses of computer networks. In schools we have unique opportunities to preserve and build upon the democratizing potential of electronic text forums.

Paradigms or world views emerge within societies as part of humankind's need to understand and interpret reality. Paradigms are double-edged; like all perceptual constructs, they help us to make sense of some things while at the same time precluding our ability to even notice other things.

The Newtonian paradigm helped us notice and understand the part of our world that can be described with mechanistic, deterministic, "either-or" constructs. But it failed to consider that which is uncertain, unpredictable, emerging, "both-and."

Just as scientific notions are prompting us to turn our gaze toward complexity, our colleges are facing new challenges in the way we respond to the complexity of social diversity. Quantum metaphors appear to offer useful models. Instead of thinking of people as isolated individuals, each blindly pursuing self-interest through collision and confrontation, quantum metaphors can help us envision a community in which individuals share their unique points of view in a complex, ever-emerging pattern. Through dialogue, we share multiple points of view in a sort of verbal dance. Afterwards, no one is quite the same, and in this way complexity brings about change holistically rather than mechanistically. Logic is still in the mix, but so too is intuition, humor, imagination, and situatedness.

In this new type of dialogue, the goal isn't to determine winners and losers, but to enhance our understanding and appreciation of complexity. A new aesthetic seems to be emerging, one which celebrates a sense of community in which otherness is experienced not as a threat but as a new element adding richness and variety to the dance—the pattern. This is what the "link age" is all about. To paraphrase Todd's metaphor, perhaps there was something important germinating in the "dungeon" of the University of Texas English Department Computer Classroom.

@27

Epilogue_in_Three_Parts

Where are they now?

THE STUDENTS WHOSE EXPERIENCES HAVE BEEN CHRONICLED IN THESE pages have now graduated from, or dropped out of, college. When they took this course, they reported it was the first time they had encountered computers in a humanities course. The computer revolution was in its infancy, and students displayed a wide range of attitudes toward it. At one end of the spectrum was Jake, already using a modem, and accessing class from his fraternity. At the other end of the spectrum was Irene who preferred to write in small books of unlined pages, and who had decidedly mixed feelings about using computers at all. Although a couple of students used computers outside of class and were experimenting with the state-of-the-art ability to transport "papers" via disk, most of the students had minimal experience with computers. I was curious to see if computers now played a more pivotal role in their lives. I also wanted to get a sense of literacy practices in their lives. With these questions in mind, I located several of Burns's former students and interviewed them—either in person, by phone, by mail, or email. I did this once in 1993 and again in 1996.

Irene followed up on her desire to explore foreign countries by moving to Germany shortly after graduating. She works at a patent office where she types dictated letters to American, English, and Japanese clients, using a headset and an "IBM compatible computer." She still aspires to be a professional writer and writes poems by hand on unlined paper in small books. She answered my query in a handwritten letter which included the statement that she wasn't yet "financially nor emotionally" ready to own a computer:

Emotionally, because it takes Herculean patience to learn how those things work, and when you finally do, there is an exception which throws you off and/or breaks you down. I also believe that computers have personalities. In other words, computers can dislike you and you can dislike them. (Computers are people, too.) . . . I think that part of the creative process, or explosion, as it were, is mood. And I personally feel very little when sitting opposite a computer. It's so hard to inscribe it, and you can't have anything getting in the way.

Todd returned to his home town and worked as account executive of the daily paper, later moving to a smaller town to become advertising director of another paper. In this position, Todd could occasionally publish editorials he himself had written. He asked me if I'd like to see some of his recent writing. His offer to share his writing reminded me of that day in class when he asked, "Would you like to see my final paper?"

A short time later, I received an envelope packed with clippings of Todd's published columns, most of which dealt lightheartedly with local issues such as no-smoking ordinances and proposed road repairs. After a few years of small-town newspaper work, Todd moved to Dallas to work with a friend who manages a Hispanic radio station. In this position, Todd now sells commercials and, using the office computer, writes "spec" spots to get new clients. He also plays guitar in a band and downloads musical charts from the Internet. In an email message he wrote: I use [my home] computer not only to find and to store the lyrics of songs, but to print them out in large font to facilitate ease of reading during a live gig . . . in case our singer forgets.

Jake worked in technical support for Apple Computers and then switched to inside sales—helping clients with third-party add-ons to meet their technology needs. All his communication with customers is through the phone or email: "I don't do anything on paper at all. I don't have a piece of paper on my desk." He says he has "about four" computers at home, including his laptop, and is on several listservs relating to his hobbies of tinkering on cars, mountain biking, and shooting:

> My hobbies are somewhat unusual and it is hard to find a lot of other people that have been there, done that and have knowledge of hindsight. On the Net I can find hundreds of people doing the same thing and I can get all sorts of cool information. No telling how much money I've saved on my car, doing repairs myself.

When he was recently diagnosed with an eye disease, Jake looked for information on it within the Net and discovered an "incredible" discussion list which included researchers, doctors, and patients. He tends not to play computer games or to read books because he says he has little self discipline and would just get engulfed for several days and let everything else slip. (Using the jargon of *Wired Magazine* [2.01], he would become a "Mouse Potato.") A few years ago he wrote some articles and letters to shooting and biking magazines which were published, but he doesn't find time anymore for writing except for email and listserv comments.

Tammy received a M.S. in Education and went on to teach middle school in a small town in Texas. Her school district constantly submits proposals for more computers and computer training, but they have only about one stand-alone computer per class which some students use for reports. She bought herself a personal computer three years ago and a modem within the last year so she could exchange personal email messages with her friends all over the state and country. She uses the Net to download lesson plans and to find graphics and other "stuff" to use with her classes. Of her fiancé, she said, "His ambition is to play spades with someone on the other side of the globe."

After graduation, David accepted a legislative assistant position at the Capitol Building and quit his job as a supermarket bagger. Later, he enrolled in computer science classes, with plans to get a second degree. However, when he got a job with a national credit card company, he dropped out of school. He was soon promoted to a management position—working in the executive inquiry department. He said he uses the computer all day—for looking up records, sending intra-company email, etc. (Companies use the term "intranet" to refer to intra-company mail.)

David has a computer at home and on occasion telecommutes. He is also subscribed to America Online and does some random surfing, visiting the Dilbert and Simpsons sites just for fun. He also has an email correspondence with six or seven friends, including Austinites as well as a friend who lives in the Northeast. He still plans to write his book on race relations and says, "I've always thought that affirmative action was holding us back. I have a problem with people feeling that if you're black and you got a scholarship that's the only way you got ahead."

Josh is working for a computer company and hoping to get into programming. Sandra is pursuing a Ph.D. in math.

It was fairly easy to locate and interview the students who had graduated. This was not the case with Lora who had dropped out and moved to the West Coast. Every year or so I would try to phone her family, but to no avail.

What about Burns and the lab?

The Computer Research Lab has been renamed the Computer Writing and Research Lab (CWRL), and now serves as a research and training facility for the teaching assistants who staff and teach in one of the four computer classrooms. These classrooms resemble the one described in this book; in most cases the computers line the perimeter of the room, and a large table—for face-to-face interaction—occupies the center of the room. Professor John Slatin has been the director of the CWRL since 1989. This constellation of classrooms is now a part of the Division of Rhetoric and Composition (DRC), directed by Lester Faigley, within the College of Liberal Arts. Classes still use LINC and email but also use a "panoply of applications, including multimedia and a wide range of Internet applications such as newsgroups, email and listservs, and more recently, the World Wide Web" in both literature and writing (Slatin, in press). The DRC's goal is to teach 85 percent of the undergraduate writing courses online by 1999, and it is thus adding computer classrooms on a continuing basis. Burns is director of educational technology at Smith College.

Lora's (Generation X) literacy

In June, 1996, I finally reached Lora by phone at her workplace in Berkeley—an upscale organic grocery store. I briefly reintroduced myself and asked, "Are computers a part of your life now?" "Oh, my God, yes!" said Lora. Since I had an upcoming trip to the West Coast, I asked Lora if it would be possible for me to visit her at her job, and possibly at her home, to see how she uses computers these days. Lora readily agreed to this and even got me a reservation at the Red Victorian, a bed and breakfast in the Haight-Ashbury neighborhood of San Francisco only a block from the apartment she shared with her boyfriend, Adam.

After flying into Oakland, I climb into a taxi and head for the Berkeley grocery store where Lora works. It is hot, but I notice that none of the cars have air conditioning. Or at least they don't use it. The driver does not speak English well, and I hope he understands my directions. Weaving effortlessly between trucks on the freeway, he exudes confidence, so I sit back and relax, taking in the scene. All the windows are open and the air blasts through the cab, throwing my hair into my face and whipping the loose manuscript pages emerging from my briefcase. The images of the

Bay Area swirl around me: a huge billboard of Snoopy on the phone with METLife, Kinko's print shops, bridges, bead shops. The traffic, the wind, the weirdly dressed people hurrying or meandering down crowded streets, all form one turbulent pattern. The postmodern always seems most evident when one travels through an unfamiliar city in a careening taxi.

And suddenly the turbulence stops. The taxi has pulled up in front of the store. The driver jumps out and pops the trunk. I assemble my luggage on its wheels and soon feel out of place rolling it through a grocery store as if I were in an airport. I ask where the wine and cheese section is and head toward a back corner. Smells of bread, curry, and apples remind me that I am hungry, and I look forward to having lunch.

Behind the cheese counter a small man with a mustache is cutting cheese for the display case. (I later find out this man is Santiago and that Lora is his boss.) He is expecting me and tells me how I can get to Lora's office by going through the stock room and up the stairs. Still pulling my suitcase with the briefcase piggybacked on it, I walk past case upon case of wine until I get to a narrow wooden staircase leading upstairs.

Lora rushes up to greet me and help me with my luggage. She is dressed much the same as she was six years ago, a sort of punk look: gray jumper over a white T-shirt, clunky shoes. Her straight hair is dyed dark reddish-brown and some of it is pulled back haphazardly and caught in a tortoise-shell clip. Because Lora manages the wine and cheese department of the store, her office is right next to the store manager's. She introduces me to the manager who has apparently been informed about my project. He tells Lora he needs to talk to her sometime before she leaves. (Lora later tells me this is about stock options in light of recent expansion of the store at the national level.) Lora stuffs my suitcase under her desk, asking me where I want to eat. We spend a few moments discussing this, during which time she is interrupted about three times by co-workers who move up and down a hallway which overlooks the sales floor below. No one actually *sits*; instead everyone sort of bounces around like molecules in a heated solution. The noise of shoppers, stockers, office workers, and music all merge into one friendly, wheaty cacophony.

"We need to pick a restaurant that's quiet," I say, "because I want to tape you if that's all right." Lora instantly asks someone where would be a quiet place to go. On the Meyers-Briggs, Lora would definitely be considered an Extrovert on the energy scale ("Preference for drawing energy from the outside world of people, activities, or things." Web site, YAHOO, Meyers-Briggs). Someone recommends a Mediterranean restaurant. It's a bit of a hike, but it should be quiet. Lora grabs her black leather backpack and hoists it over her shoulder just as she did her canvas one six years ago. We walk briskly down the street, and I am amazed at the huge orange poppies growing with abandon on this urban turf—especially in contrast to drought-stricken Texas.

The restaurant isn't quiet after all: A polished mahogany cavern of noise. We take a table on the sidewalk, trying to ignore the rumbling trucks and wailing sirens. After ordering the Mediterranean plate for two, I set up my tape recorder and we begin.

Joan: What do you remember about Burns's class?

Lora: I remember part of it being sort of like being on the Internet. We talked back and forth in class. I don't remember what I wrote. It's sad but I don't. I sort of remember this guy Todd but not totally.

Joan: Do you remember Irene?

Lora: No. Not at all. No. Since that class I took probably ten more classes. I don't remember . . .

Joan: Was this the first time you had used a computer?

Lora: Definitely. That's why I took it—because of computers. I needed to know it. I don't like them that much now. I do use them, and I do enjoy what I have to do, but I get bored quickly.

Joan: When you say, quickly, what do you mean?

Lora: After about two hours. When I first got the computer, I had walking pneumonia, and I was out of work for a month so I had all the time in the world to surf the Net and play games. I don't have that kind of time anymore. But Adam [her boyfriend] uses it so much for work and to play games I don't get a chance to get on it. His jobs are both computer-related. In the evening he manages a band and he books a nightclub, so he does that.

  We bought it together. We did a whole bunch of research. He wanted a PC and I wanted a MAC so that I could do work things at home. So we decided on the 6115 Power Mac at that point because it's PC compatible. Of course now they're obsolete—a day later. Anyway, all of our friends had America Online, so we got that. Then Netscape.

Joan: You do work-related things at home?

Lora: Yes, I check out the Epicurious page from *Gourmet* and *Bon Appetit*. Oh, and Adam found this wine page for me. I use it to try to find more stuff about organic wines. I also use it to try to find out more about organic cheeses, especially like French organics. And I get recipes sometimes. I also use it to do spreadsheets and to write the "talkers" that we display over some of our newer products.

Joan: It sounds like you're really into your job.

Lora: Yes, I love it. I would like to own my own business some day, I just don't know what kind of business yet. But for now [the grocery store] is great because I'm just learning so much about retail and about what works and what doesn't.

Joan: When you were in Burns's class, you wanted to be an English teacher?

Lora: Yes, I don't know why. I don't even remember why that sounded appealing to me. I think it's because Kate Frost made such an impression on me. What an amazing woman! She was really into Shakespeare and I don't know, I don't know what that period was. What? Renaissance? Like John Donne and oh I don't know, all those writers. I don't really remember. She just made you want to read Shakespeare and things that I probably never would have wanted to read ever. Because I couldn't understand them or hated the language or whatever. It's like now when I read it's like very bizarre written-language kind of stuff and it's because of her.

Joan: Do you remember her speech about papers like yours, undergraduates saying Beowulf is definitely a hero?

Lora: Oh, yes, I know. I guess it really bothered me then, but now I think it's funny. It is! It's really funny! She could take something, some kind of reading that I probably never would have done on my own and make it that interesting and make me feel that passionate and great about it. Maybe that's why I wanted to teach. I don't want to be an English teacher now, that's for sure. I'm way more number oriented. I love—like this whole thing with the stock going up. We're all in there just trying to figure out how much money we can make.

Joan: But you do still read?

Lora: All the time.

Joan: What was the last book you read?

Lora: Andrew Vachss. It's called *Shella*. He's a—he lives in New York; he's a New York writer. I have these friends that work at the *New Yorker* and they told me to read him. And right now I'm reading Harry Crews, do you know him? I'm reading *Scar Lover*. I think the book he has out now is *The Knockout Artist*. Have you heard of that?

The waitress arrives and delivers bowls and plates of dolma, sarma, beurek, jajoukh, olives, and pita bread. I move my tape recorder over to make room for the delicious-smelling Mediterranean delicacies. Then I resume my questioning:

Joan: Do you remember Grudin? Grudin was the author some students hated. Do you remember *Time and the Art of Living*? It was a book with about 300 hundred little one-paragraph sections—very introspective.

Lora: Oh, I loved that book! I remember that book. I loved that! I love little—that's why I love the two books I'm reading right now. They're short chapters. And the language. These people make a statement and then it's done and they go to the next statement. It's not like this long, narrative thing that goes on forever. I have a really hard time with long narrative stuff. I lose interest quickly unless it's just something amazing. I like short bold statements. And later I'll show you the book I just finished reading. You'll see what I mean. It was a 300-page book and I finished it in three days.

Joan: Do you remember the paper you wrote on Grudin? Because his book was *Time and the Art of Living*, everyone was supposed to substitute a word for time. So, I'll tell you what some of them were. One girl wrote "Chaos and the Art of Living." Somebody wrote "Happiness and the Art of Living," another "Places and the Art of Living." Do you remember what concept you chose?

Lora: I didn't say food, did I? It would be food now, which is hilarious, but that's what it would be! I don't remember.

Joan: It was kind of opposite of happiness.

Lora: Kind of? I keep wanting to say *sarcasm*.

Joan: It was "Pain and the Art of Living." Do you remember?

Lora: No, I don't remember. Wow! What a depressed person I was! I remember writing a paper on vegetarianism. Boy, I'll bet that was a boring paper!

Joan: Do you watch TV?

Lora: Yes, I watch *ER, X-Files,*—I admit it—*Friends*.

Joan: It used to be that shows just had one plot, but now they have all these interwoven plots. Have you noticed that?

Lora: Yes, I like that. I used to like soap operas, I don't any more, but when I was younger, I used to like them because there was so much stuff going on. It's the same in my life—the more going on the better. In fact just a month ago my beer and wine buyer had a hernia and then he broke his leg. So I was literally doing five or six jobs at once and doing them all beautifully.

Joan: So tell me how you use your computer at home?

Lora: There's a friend of mine. We talk to each other on the phone almost every day anyway, but we email stuff to each other. She's a copy-editor. She'll say "I've got this funny joke here." And this friend Jeannie who works for a start-up company, I converse with her. Oh, and then this guy who's a senior buyer for a magazine distributor in Austin.

Joan: Any relatives who use email?

Lora: No, my family doesn't do that. My mother reads all the time, but she hates that she has to use the computer at work. She hates email.

Joan: Are you on any listservs?

Lora: There's a record store that I really like. Just the other day, I emailed Wendy to see if they had a certain album and she emailed me right back. And this woman who sends out all these recipes.

Joan: So it sounds like you are on listservs that share information. Are there any where you share ideas?

Lora: Only the book club. It was a Website, it was this woman who enjoyed Southern writers who would tell us, "Hey, if you enjoyed so and so, you'll enjoy so and so." I typed in what's-her-name, the author of *The Liar's Club*—she's from East Texas.

Joan: Mary Carr.

Lora: Yes! So I typed her name in, and I said I was looking for other stuff she'd written. And then at the bottom it had this whole thing that said other Southern writers, or other similar authors—something like that, and I clicked on that. A lot of Web pages have that. Especially a lot of music sites say, "If you liked this, click on here and you'll like this, too," or whatever.

Joan: So, how did you happen to read *The Liar's Club*?

Lora: My bookstore down the street. The people there know what to read.

Joan: Would you say most of your reading is still offline—books?

Lora: Yes, Kate Frost made me want to read. I mean I really didn't read a book till I got to UTexas. My high school was a joke. I read all of *Sybil* and wrote a paper on that. That was the first book I read all the way through. In Kate Frost's class, if you were feeling like you didn't understand the language, you could say, "What does this mean?" and she would explain in a way that didn't make you feel like an idiot. She would make you really excited about it and want to keep reading it. She would ask these essay questions that were very open-ended and you could just go for it. And if you didn't go off on some rambling rampage and you actually made some sense, it didn't have to be so eloquent. You had to—what's that called?

Joan: Defend it?

Lora: Defend it! That's what she liked. She just made you not afraid.

Joan: She also talked about how the university should be changed.

Lora: Yes, I totally agree.

Joan: You dropped out of UT. Why?

Lora: To be with Adam. I was planning to transfer to Berkeley, but too expensive.

Joan: So, it wasn't that you didn't like UT?

Lora: Not really. I remember at UT all those classes where there were 600 people in the class. They weren't showing you anything in those classes. It was like you were an ant in the room. I don't know. I didn't enjoy those kind of classes at all. I enjoyed the smaller classes.

Back at the store, Lora shows me some of the spreadsheets she does on the computer. She shows how she records anticipated sales, actual sales, number of hours worked by employees, bonuses earned, etc. She navigates through the programs with remarkable dexterity, telling me more than I wanted to know about the figures she is responsible for recording. She says she has learned these programs from a "computer genius boy" who used to work there.

Next Lora gives me a tour of the wine and cheese department. As she rattles off the names of various wines, beers, and specialty olives, it appears that she takes pleasure in sheer names. At the cheese case, she says: "We call this the coffin case. It has the specialty cheeses. Soy cheese, fat free cheese, swisses, goudas, cheddars, jacks, goat, mozzarella, ricotta, pate. Teleme." She leans over to read the "talker" which had been printed and hung over the teleme: "Try it with a peppery sausage." She laughs, "That's Santiago's quote. We write up these 'talkers' and sometimes we'll add a recipe."

Pointing to a bulletin board on which a handwritten schedule is thumbtacked, Lora says, "I don't attempt to do the schedule on computer. There's too many changes. As you can see I've already whited out several times. I work Sunday nights because that's our second busiest night and I try to be fair to my peons. Just kidding, Santiago. We all kind of do everything."

Later, when we leave the store, her co-workers call out good-byes to her. Lora has definitely found her niche. Her red Honda is parked in the back.

She unlocks the car, removes the Club from the steering wheel, pulls the "face" of her sound system out of her backpack, snaps it onto the dash, and turns on the radio which is tuned to National Public Radio. All of this occurs in one fluid movement, the routine of five years.

Lora drives through the crowded streets of Berkeley, deftly shifting gears. We listen to the news and Lora mentions that she listens to it every day on the way to work and home again. She says she doesn't read newspapers—just gets news from NPR and occasionally watches local news on TV. As we cross the Bay Bridge, the newscaster is talking about the Unabomber. He was finally indicted today. A former Berkeley math professor who went off the deep end resisting technology.

When we get to Haight-Ashbury, Lora drives down Haight Street and points out her apartment on Ashbury, then drives on to the Red Victorian. She is planning to go home, take a nap, and call me around seven o'clock for part two of our interview, to take place at her home computer.

The Red Victorian is an historic bed and breakfast owned by an artist, Sami Sunchild, whose artistic and social visions affect every nook and cranny of the renovated turn-of-the-century building. After checking in, I haul my luggage upstairs. Pausing to catch my breath, I read a framed message on the wall: "The unleashed power of the atom has changed everything save our modes of thought, and we thus drift toward unparalleled catastrophe.—Albert Einstein, 1946." Next to this, another framed quote: "The purpose of this business, these paintings, my life is to provide a gentle demonstration of how businesses, professions, human relationships can work in the world at large to promote change in human consciousness.—Sami Sunchild"

I make my way through labyrinthine hallways to my room, The Flower Child Room—a delightful room with blue sky and clouds on the ceiling and a rooftop flower garden right outside the oversized window. I munch on cheese and crackers I'd bought at the store and wait for Lora's call.

Later, I walk to her apartment. She rings the buzzer to let me in and then escorts me to the kitchen where the computer is set up on a desk occupying the small space obviously intended for a kitchen table. The desk is actually wedged between the refrigerator and a huge bookcase filled with books. She pulls kitchen chairs up to this desk, and I set up my tape recorder. The computer hums and the refrigerator growls. Lora's cat vies for our attention. We can hear Adam on the phone right outside the back door on the fire escape. "He makes his calls out there where he can smoke," she explains. "He's using his cell phone so we can use the line."

Lora dials into her server and accesses the Web. She scans the bookmarks to show me the sites she visits regularly, including the Punk Page, several food and marketing oriented pages, and the Southern Writer's page. Lora suddenly loses her connection to the server, and decides to wait a few minutes before dialing in again.

I take this opportunity to begin the second interview:

Joan: Have you done any MOOs or MUDs?

Lora: No, except about the Southern writers. At one point she would have like three people in a chat room, and we all kind of conversed. For me to get on MOOs, this kind of thing happened all the time [referring to the fact that she was disconnected]. Either you couldn't connect or there wasn't a line available or something like that. It's really hard to get on. That's the only time I did that though.

Joan: Do you play games?

Lora: Adam does all that stuff—the games. He'll hook up with some friend down the street, and they'll both be in the computer at the same time playing this game. He has the speakers, and so it's like going through the whole house. I hate it. I mean it drives me insane. I'm not into the game thing. I mean he has the most amazing stuff for this machine! You know, the games are just incredible. They give me headaches because it's that 3-D kind of thing, and it's hard enough for me to stare at words for this long. Actually it's easier for me to stare at the words. I can't deal with pictures moving. One time when we first got it, we went into one of those silly kind of nasty chat rooms; that's the only time I've ever done that, and it was really hilarious. We just did it for the fun of it. We wanted to see what kind of smut people were talking. Got bored with that quickly and never did it again.

Lora then turns to the bookshelf against the kitchen wall and pulls *Shella* off the top.

Lora: See, here's the book I was telling you about. It has these short, short sections. But it was so easy to read because of these tiny sections. It jelled altogether, but it was like he would have one thought and it would end and he would go on to something else. It was great. He made each point so succinctly. You know these very short, blunt kind of out-there ways of communicating—speaking—and that's just what I relate to.

The book I'm reading now, *Scar Lover*, half of it is written in Rastafarian language so you talk about "hard to read"—I don't know—it's getting harder for me to read. It's based in Florida, so there's this guy from Jamaica and he's working on this train car with this total white guy from Georgia. And it's about their interaction together. So I'll be reading in totally English language and then they'll be this Rastafarian language. "Dat man funt bak." It's really hard to understand. [She pulls out *How the Garcia Girls Lost Their Accent*.] This was good; kind of silly, but good. And speaking of writing in different ways, I was going to show you *Shipping News*. Talk about a totally different use of language! I loved that book! I know a lot of people who couldn't get through it because of the language.

Joan: It began each chapter with how to tie a certain kind of knot, didn't it?

Lora: Yes, I loved that!

Lora checks to see that she is connected again and continues looking through her bookmarks. She carries on a monologue in front of her screen just as she had done in Burns's class.

Lora: What happened? What did I do? Okay. Get me out of there. No. No. TV Movies. What happened? "Welcome to Epicurious." There's one of mine!

[Continuing] Net Girl was another [site] I [visited]. It was a bunch of just girl bands. It was interesting because my best friend is a lead singer of a band out here, and so we'd go in there and we could download songs. She's a copyeditor by day, rock star by night. I can show you some of her comical email that we send back and forth. Here's a bunch of my emails. Here's a bunch of jokes I get from friends of mine that work at this start-up company and have nothing better to do on some days but email people silly things, disgusting pick up lines, Homerisms, all these silly things.

[Continuing] Now it's going to act up. This is from Jeannie. This is just blabbing. We haven't emailed in about a week or two. When we first started to be friends, she was in two bands, so she didn't have time to get together. So we would email. Adam manages her band, so its easier now for us to see each other. This is the record store list. I'm looking for something, and she'll write back and say Yes, she can get it or No, she can't get it.

By now, Lora has about twelve windows open, overlapping each other in a geometric stack of perimeters. She continues her monologue.

> . . . Adam emailing me. How long ago is this? Oh this is when we were being nice to each other. Just kidding. This is all Adam's stuff. His phone list, his calendar. I don't know what stuff it is. Shrink wrap. I have no idea what this is. I didn't know what I was getting myself into when we got this. We got the modem, a lot of the software and then he bought the zipdrive and this gadget. [She gestures toward the refrigerator, but I realize she is pointing to a gadget on top of it.]

Joan: Why do you think men like these games and women don't?

Lora: I think it's a whole different chemical in men or something. I don't even know—something bizarre! [She laughs.] But seriously, Jeannie likes these games and there's these women I've met who like them.

Joan: Does Adam read?

Lora: All the time. He's always been an avid reader. We just read totally different things. He's really into science fiction books. And his computer books. We've got tons of computer books. We've got tons more books in the bedroom. Like *Islands in the Net* and all these crazy books.

Joan: Do you do work things at home?

Lora: All the time. The other day I had to compose a manager's wish list. I did a really nice schedule. All done out with sales and labor percentages.

Joan: Do you ever use the word processor to write letters for snail mail?

Lora: No, the only thing like that I send is postcards.

After this, I talk briefly with Adam. He says he likes competitive strategy games. Also, he likes "random surfing" by which he means, "I look for shareware. I'm sort of a software collector freak. I look for demos for new things. I go to lots of FTP sites and just look around." He uses the computer to organize bookings for nightclubs. He says he doesn't use it for conversation because he prefers the telephone.

As I am leaving—

Lora: I have a question. Were you in the class?

Joan: I lurked. But every once in awhile I would take one of you out across the hall and interview you.

Lora: Oh, I remember that! That tiny little room! I remember the yellow hallway! That I remember. That cream—beige colored hallway. And it

was like an office, kind of like a newspaper or yearbook office. I'm starting to remember!

In the early morning, I go to a coffee shop which is the only shop open
at that hour. The coffee is good, and the sound system is playing Leonard
Cohen: "Suzanne takes your hand / and she leads you to the river . . . "
Young urban professionals and a few musician types stop in for coffee.
There are brief, friendly conversations between and among the customers
and the sales clerk. It has the makings of a Great Good Place. These early
morning people are dressed in dark, almost tailored clothes—but beaded
earrings, sandals, or a Guatemalan bag seem to signal their allegiance to
the sixties and perhaps explain why they choose to live here. Lora said she
chose to live here because she could come home at any hour, and the
streets would still be populated and therefore safe.

I think about Lora, her literacy, and her lifestyle. I realize that she was
never a "typical student" any more than her lifestyle and career are now
typical of her generation. On the other hand, she seems to embody many
of the elements that I have come to associate with her generation. She has
chosen to enter the business world rather than the worlds of academia or
the service professions. She is connected closely to popular culture
through both music and literature—seemingly equal parts of each. She
doesn't write personal letters to friends, but stays in touch through email,
visits, and phone calls. She lives comfortably with many overlaps between
her career and her "private" life. Although she holds a management position, she resists hierarchy in such moves as sharing unpopular shifts—and
occasionally working "the floor" alongside the people she supervises.

Perhaps most encouraging to the readers of this book is the fact that she
reads and enjoys literature. Her Net surfing doesn't seem to substitute for
reading books but rather to supplement and feed into her reading of
books. And, Lora takes obvious pleasure in discussing literature. She has a
keen interest in literary style, but never once mentioned symbolism, fore-
shadowing, or those other literary elements which literature teachers
drone on about even in the face of massive underlife revolts. Her joy in
reading seems to derive from the sounds of words and the resonance of
style with rhythms in her own life. What she learned from Kate Frost was,
above all, that the struggle to construct meaning is worth it, even in the
face of prose which at first seems obscure or inaccessible.

Later I head for the bookstore Lora had recommended. On the way, I
stop in a T-shirt shop to get a Bob Marley shirt for my younger son, Alex,

a high school senior. The shop walls are flocked with tie-dyed shirts, and the voice of Janis Joplin pierces the air. Back on the street, it occurs to me that the whole neighborhood, in true postmodern fashion, is a simulation of life in the 60s. Four tourists jump from a car that has come to an abrupt halt at the corner of Haight and Ashbury. Three of them clamber onto the roof of the car, then pose by leaning as close as they can get to the street sign marking this 60s landmark. First one, then another takes a snapshot of the others next to the sign, Haight/Ashbury. For a moment, snapshots render reality as a series of particles. Afterwards, all climb back in the car, which soon disappears in the traffic, caught up again in the dynamic flow of time.

At the bookstore, I buy Clifford Stoll's *Silicon Snake Oil*. I try to read it on the plane, but quickly grow impatient. Shortly after getting home, I mention the book to my older son, Nicholas, a junior at MIT and a computer engineering student. I say, "This guy thinks that the Internet is overrated."

Nicholas says, "He's probably wrong."

Works_Cited

Adams, Anthony. 1984. Talk and Learning in the Classroom. *Language Arts.* 61, 2: 119–24.

Aldrin, Buzz. 1994. Signature of Our Century. *U.S. News & World Report,* (July 11): 48–49.

Atwell, Nancie. 1987. *In the Middle: Writing, Reading, and Learning with Adolescents.* Portsmouth, NH: Heinemann, Boynton/Cook.

Au, Kathryn. 1980. Participation Structures in a Reading Lesson with Hawaiian Children: Analysis of a Culturally Appropriate Instructional Event. *Anthropology and Education Quarterly.* 11: 91–115.

Bakhtin, Mikhail. 1981. Discourse in the Novel. In *The Dialogic Imagination,* translated by C. Emerson and M. Holquist, ed. M. Holquist, 259–404. Austin, TX: Univ. of Texas.

Baldwin, Beth. 1996. Evolving Past the Essay-a-saurus: Introducing Nimbler Forms into Writing Classes. *RhetNet: A Cyberjournal for Rhetoric and Writing.* [Online] Available website: http://www.missouri.edu/~rhetnet/baldwin_snap.html.

Balestri, Diane. 1988. Softcopy and Hard: Wordprocessing and Writing Process. *Academic Computing,* (Feb): 14–17, 41–45.

Barnes, Douglas. 1990. Language in The Secondary Classsroom. In *Language, The Learner, and the School,* ed. D. Barnes, J. Britton, and M. Torbe, 9–87. Portsmouth, NH: Heinemann.

Batson, Trent. 1985. *ENFIlog 13.* (12/13/85).

———. 1989a. In *ENFI Report #3,* eds. E. G. Solis and J. K. Peyton, Washington, DC: The ENFI Consortium.

———. 1989b. Teaching in Networked Classrooms. In *Computers in English and the Language Arts: The Challenge of Teacher Education,* eds. C. Selfe, D. Rodrigues, and W. Oates, Urbana, IL: NCTE.

———. 1993. The Origins of ENFI, *Network-Based Classrooms: Promises and Realities,* ed. B. Bruce, J. K. Peyton, and T. Batson. Cambridge, MA: Cambridge University Press.

Belenky, Mary, Blythe Clinchy, Nancy Goldberger, and Jill Tarule. 1986. *Women's Ways of Knowing: The Development of Self, Voice, and Mind.* New York, NY: Basic Books Inc., Harper Collins.

Berthoff, Ann. 1981. *The Making of Meaning: Metaphors, Models, and Maxims for Writing Teachers.* Portsmouth, NH: Boynton/Cook.

Bishop, Wendy. 1995. If Winston Weathers Would Just Write to Me on E-Mail. *College Composition and Communication,* Vol. 46, No. 1 (February): 97–103.

Bizzell, Patricia. 1982. Cognition, Convention, and Certainty: What We Need to Know about Writing. *PRE/TEXT,* 3: 213–43.

———. 1987. What is a Discourse Community? Transcript from Penn State Conference on Rhetoric and Compostion. University Park, (July): 18–19.

Bohm, David. 1951. *Quantum Theory.* London, England: Constable.

Bolter, Jay David. 1991. *Writing Space: The Computer, Hypertext, and the History of Writing.* Hillsdale, NJ: Lawrence Erlbaum Associates.

Bridwell-Bowles, Lillian. 1992. Discourse and Diversity: Experimental Writing Within the Academy. *College Composition and Communication,* Vol. 43, No. 3, (October): 349–368.

Brodkey, Linda. 1987. *Academic Writing as Social Practice.* Philadelphia, PA: Temple University.

Brooke, Robert. 1990. Underlife and Writing Instruction. In *Rhetoric and Composition: A Sourcebook for Teachers and Writers,* ed. R. Graves, 96–107. Portsmouth, NH: Heinemann Educational Books.

Bump, Jerome 1990. Radical Changes in Class Discussion Using Networked Computers. In *Computers and the Humanities,* 49–65.

Burns, Hugh. 1979. Stimulating Rhetorical Invention in English Composition Through Computer-Assisted Instruction. Unpublished PH.D. dissertation, University of Texas at Austin.

————. 1992. Teaching Composition in Tomorrow's Multimedia, Multinetworked Classrooms. In *Re-imagining Computers and Composition Studies: Teaching and Research in the Virtual Age,* eds. G. Hawisher and P. LeBlanc, 115–130. Portsmouth, NH: Boynton/Cook.

Butler, Wayne and James Kinneavy. 1991. The Electronic Discourse Community: God, Meet Donald Duck. *Focuses, IV,* 91–108.

Catano, James. 1985. Computer-based Writing: Navigating the Fluid Text. *College Composition and Communication,* 36: 309–316.

Cazden, Courtney. 1988. *Classroom Discourse: The Language of Teaching and Learning.* Portsmouth, NH: Heinemann.

Chafe, Wallace. 1985. Linguistic Differences Produced by Differences Between Speaking and Writing. In *Literacy, Language, and Learning,* ed. D. Olson, N. Torrance, and A. Hildyard, 105–123. Cambridge, England: Cambridge University Press.

Cintorino, Margaret. 1993. Getting Together, Getting Along, Getting to the Business of Teaching and Learning. *English Journal,* 82, No. 1: 23–33.

Cohn, Carol. 1987. Sex and Death in the Rational World of Defense Intellectuals. *Signs: Journal of Women in Culture and Society,* Vol. 18 No. 4: 687–718.

Crump, Eric. 1996. *RhetNet: A Cyberjournal for Rhetoric and Writing.* [Online] Interactive Historiography page. Available website: (<http://www.missouri.edu/~rhetnet/ih>).

Daily Texan, (April) 1990.

Day, Michael. 1996. Pedagogies in Virtual Spaces: Writing Classes in the MOO, CoverWeb OverView, *Kairos: A Journal For Teachers of Writing in Webbed Environments,* 1.2, (July). [Online] Available website: (http://english.ttu.edu/kairos/1.3/).

DeBerry, Stephen. 1993. *Quantum Psychology: Steps to a Postmodern Ecology of Being.* Westport, CT: Praeger.

DeCurtis, Anthony. 1991. An Outsider in This Society: An Interview with Don DeLillo. In *Introducing Don DeLilllo,* ed. F. Lentricchia, 43–66. Durham, NC: Duke University.

Dewey, John. 1916. *Democracy and Education.* New York, NY: Macmillan Publishing Co.

Dillard, Annie. 1989. Schedules. In *The Best American Essays,* ed. G. Wolff and R. Atwan, 71–79. New York, NY: Ticknor and Fields.

Doherty, Mick, ed. 1996. *Kairos: A Journal For Teachers of Writing in Webbed Environments.* [Online] Available website: (http://english.ttu.edu/kairos/1.3/).

Doll, William. 1987. Foundations for a Post-Modern Curriculum. Paper presented at the Annual Meeting of the American Educational Research Association, Washington, DC, (April).

Elbow, Peter. 1981. *Writing with Power: Techniques for Mastering the Writing Process.* New York, NY: Oxford University Press.

Eldred, Janet. 1989. Computers, Composition, and the Social View. In *Critical Perspectives on Computers and Composition Studies: Questions for the 1990s,* ed. G. Hawisher and C. Selfe, 201–218. New York, NY: Teachers College Press.

Elmer-Dewitt, Philip. 1994. Bards of the Internet. *Time Magazine,* (4 July).

———. 1995. Welcome to Cyberspace. *Time Magazine,* (Spring), Vol. 145, No. 12: 4–11.

Emig, Janet. 1982. Inquiry Paradigms and Writing. *College Composition and Communication,* Vol. 33, No. 1: 64–75.

Epstein, Joseph. 1989. Confessions of a Low Roller. In *The Best American Essays,* eds. G. Wolff and R. Atwan. New York: NY, Ticknor and Fields.

Faigley, Lester. 1986. Competing Theories of Process: A Critique and a Proposal. *College English,* 48 (6): 527–540.

———. 1989. Subverting the Electronic Workbook: Teaching Writing Using Networked Computers. In *The Writing Teacher as Researcher: Essays in the Theory of Class-Based Research,* eds. D. Daiker and M. Morenberg, 290–311. Portsmouth, NH: Heinemann.

———. 1992. *Fragments of Rationality: Postmodernity and the Subject of Composition.* Pittsburgh, PA: The University of Pittsburgh.

Ferrera, Kathleen, Hans Brunner, and Greg Whitemore. 1991. Interactive Written Discourse as An Emergent Register. In *Written Communication,* Vol. 8, No. 1 (January): 8–34.

Fillmore, L. W. 1990. Now or later? Issues related to the early education of minority-group children. In *Early Childhood and Family Education: Analysis of the Recommendations of the Council of Chief State School Officers.* Orlando, FL: Harcourt Brace Jovanovich.

Foley, Vernard. 1976. The Social Physics of Adam Smith. West Lafayette, IN: Purdue University.

Frost, Robert. 1969. What Fifty Said. In *The Poetry of Robert Frost,* ed. E.C. Latham, 267. New York, NY: Holt, Rinehart, and Winston.

Foucault, Michel. 1979. *Discipline and Punish: The Birth of the Prison,* translated by Alan Sheridan. New York, NY: Vintage.

Gatto, John. 1991. The Exhausted School. Speech given at LBJ Auditorium, University of Texas, (12 September).

George, Laurie. 1989. *ENFI Report #3.* Carnegie Mellon University, Gallaudet University, University of Minnesota, New York Institute of Technology, and Northern Virginia Community College.

Gerrard, Lisa. 1995. The Evolution of the Computers and Writing Conference. *Computers and Composition,* Vol. 12, No. 3: 279–292.

Goffman, Erving. 1961. *Asylums: Essays on the Social Situation of Mental Patients and Other Inmates.* New York, NY: Anchor.

———. 1973. *The Presentation of Self in Everyday Life.* Woodstock, NY: The Overlook Press.

Goodlad, John. 1984. *A Place Called School.* New York, NY: McGraw-Hill.

Goodman, Ellen. 1994. *The Austin American Statesman,* (26 July): A-11.

Goodwin, John. 1993. Elements of E-Text Style. Version 1.0. (August). St. Charles, IL: John E. Goodwin, P.O. Box 6022, ZIP 60174. Also at: jegoodwin@delphi.com.

Grudin, Robert. 1982. *Time and the Art of Living.* New York, NY: Ticknor and Fields.

The Hacker's Dictionary: A Guide to the World of Computer Wizards. 1983. New York, NY: Harper and Row.

Hairston, Maxine. 1982. The Winds of Change: Thomas Kuhn and the Revolution in the Teaching of Writing. *College Composition and Communication,* 76–88.

Hammer, Michael, and James Champy. 1993. *Reengineering the Corporation: A Manifesto for Business Revolution.* New York, NY: Harper Collins.

Handa, Carolyn, ed. 1990a. *Computers and Community: Teaching Composition in the Twenty-First Century.* Portsmouth, NH: Boynton/Cook Publishers.

Handa, Carolyn. 1990b. Politics, Ideology, and the Strange, Slow Death of the Isolated Composer or Why We Need Community in the Writing Classroom. In *Computers and Community: Teaching Composition in the Twenty-First Century*, ed. C. Handa, 160–184. Portsmouth, NH: Boynton/Cook Publishers.

Hanson, Norwood. 1958. *Patterns of Discovery.* Cambridge, England: University Press.

Harris, Joseph. 1989. The Idea of Community in the Study of Writing. *College Composition and Communication,* 40: 11–22.

Harvey, David. 1989. *The Condition of Postmodernity: An Enquiry into the Origins of Cultural Change.* Oxford, England: Basil Blackwell.

Hawisher, Gail. 1991. Electronic meetings of the minds: Research, electronic conferences, and composition studies. In *Re-imagining Computers and Composition Studies: Teaching and Research in the Virtual Age,* eds. G. Hawisher and P. LeBlanc, 81–101. Portsmouth, NH: Boynton/Cook.

———, and Cynthia Selfe. 1991. The Rhetoric of Technology and The Electronic Writing Class. *College Composition and Communication,* 42: 55–65.

———, and Cynthia Selfe. 1994. From the Editors. *Computers and Composition: An International Journal for Teachers of Writing.* Vol. 11. No. 1: 1–2. Norwood, New Jersey: Ablex Publishing Corporation.

———, and Charles Moran. 1993. Electronic Mail and the Writing Instructor. *College English,* 55: 627–43.

———, Paul LeBlanc, Charles Moran, and Cynthia Selfe. 1996. Eds. *Computers and the Teaching of Writing in American Higher Education, 1979–1994: A History.* Norwood, New Jersey: Ablex.

Hayles, N. Katherine. 1984. *The Cosmic Web: Scientific Field Models and Literary Strategies in the Twentieth Century.* Ithaca, NY: Cornell University Press.

———. 1990. *Chaos Bound: Orderly Disorder in Contemporary Literature and Science.* Ithaca, NY: Cornell University Press.

———, ed. 1991. *Chaos and Order: Complex Dynamics in Literature and Science.* Chicago, IL: The University of Chicago Press.

Heath, Shirley Brice. 1983. *Ways with Words: Language, Life, and Work in Communities and Classrooms.* New York, NY: Cambridge University Press.

Heim, Michael. 1987. *Electric Language.* New Haven, Connecticut: Yale University Press.

Hill, G. Christian. 1994. All Together Now. *The Wall Street Journal* (14 November): R1, R8.

Holdstein, Deborah. 1996. Power, Genre, and Technology. In Counterpostings on a Genre of Email. *College Composition and Communication,* 47, No. 2 (May): 279–284.

Hymes, Dell. 1972. Introduction. In *Functions of Language in The Classroom*, ed. C. Cazden, V. John, and D. Hymes, xi–lvii. New York, NY: Teachers College Press.

Joyce, Michael. 1992. New teaching: Toward a Pedagogy for a New Cosmology. *Computers and Composition,* 9: 7–16.

Kemp, Fred. 1993 The Origins of ENFI, Network Theory, and Computer-Based Collaborative Writing Instruction at the University of Texas. In *Network-Based Classrooms: Promises and Realities*, ed. B. Bruce, J. K. Peyton, and T. Batson. New York, N.Y.: Cambridge University Press.

———. 1995. *Megabyte University List (MBU),* (3 March).

———. Writing Dialogically: Bold Lessons from Electronic Text. In *Reconsidering Writing, Rethinking Writing Instruction*, ed. J. Petraglia, 179–194. Mahwah, NJ: Lawrence Erlbaul Associates.

Kinsley, Michael. 1996. Welcome to Slate. *Slate.* [Online] (3 July). Available website: http://www.slate.com/Readme/Current/r2.asp#objec.

Kramarae, Cheris, and Paula Treichler. 1990. Power Relationships in the Classroom. In *Gender in the Classroom: Power and Pedagogy*, ed. S. Gabriel and I. Smithson, 45–59. Urbana, IL: University of Illinois.

Kremers, Marshall. 1990. Sharing Authority on a Synchronous Network: The Case for Riding the Beast. *Computers and Composition,* 7: 33–44.

Krupnick, Catherine. 1985. Women and Men in the Classroom: Inequality and Its Remedies. In *On Teaching and Learning: The Journal of The Harvard-Danforth Center,* 18–25. Cambridge, MA: Harvard University Press.

———. 1992. In *Who Needs Boys?* A. L. Rockmore (Producer). 20/20 television broadcast.

Kuhn, Thomas. 1970. *The Structure of Scientific Revolutions, Second Edition.* 1962. Reprint, Chicago, IL: The University of Chicago Press.

Lanham, Richard. 1990. Foreword in *Computers and Community: Teaching Composition in the Twenty-First Century*, ed. C. Handa. Portsmouth, NH: Boynton/Cook.

———. 1993. *The Electronic Word: Democracy, Technology, and the Arts.* Chicago, IL: The University of Chicago Press.

Long, Joan. 1986. The Effects of Teacher Sex Equity and Effectiveness Training on Classroom Interaction at The University Level. Unpublished Ph.D. dissertation, The American University.

Lu, Min-zhan. 1987. From Silence to Words: Writing as Struggle. *College English,* 49, (April): 437–47.

Lyotard, Jean-Francois. 1984. *The Postmodern Condition: A Report on Knowledge,* Translators Geoff Benington and Brian Massumi. Minneapolis, MN: University of Minnesota Press.

Marshall, James 1988. *Patterns of Discourse in Classroom Discussions of Literature: A Report for the Center for the Learning and Teaching of Literature.* Office of Educational Research and Improvement. U.S. Dept. of Education.

McCorduck, Pamela. 1996. Sex, Lies, and Avatars. *Wired* (April): 106–111 and 158–165.

McLuhan, Marshall. 1987. *The Medium is the Massage: An Inventory of Effects.* New York, NY: Simon and Schuster.

Mehan, Hugh. 1979. *Learning Lessons: Social Organization in The Classroom.* Cambridge, MA: Harvard University Press.

Miller, Carolyn. 1996. This is Not an Essay. In Counterpostings on a Genre of Email. *College Composition and Communication,* 47, No. 2 (May): 284–288.

Miller, Robert K. 1990. "Class" Acts: On Teaching Computer Assisted Writing. In *Harbrace College Handbook, Instructor's Manual,* Eleventh edition: 20–28.

Moran, Charles. 1991. We Write, But Do We Read? *Computers and Composition,* Vol. 8, No. 2 (August): 51–61.

Mossberg, Walter. 1995. Is Technology the Enemy of Literacy? Speech given at Conference on College Composition and Communication. Washington, DC, (25 March).

Moyers, Bill. 1993. *Healing and the Mind.* New York, NY: Doubleday.

Murray, Denise. 1985. Composition as Conversation: The Computer Terminal as Medium of Communication. In *Writing in Nonacademic Settings,* ed. L. Odell and D. Goswami, 203–228. New York, NY: Guilford.

The New Hacker's Dictionary. 1991. Cambridge, MA: MIT Press.

———. 1993. Compiled by Eric. S. Raymond. Cambridge, MA: MIT Press.

Oldenburg, Ray. 1991. *The Great Good Place: Cafes, Coffee Shopts, Community Centers, Beauty Parlors, General Stores, Bars, Hangouts, and How They Get You Through The Day.* New York, NY: Paragon House.

Ong, Walter. 1982. *Orality and Literacy: The Technologizing of the Word.* New York: Methuen.

Pang, Valerie. 1990. Asian-American Children: A Diverse Population. *The Educational Forum,* (Fall). West Lafayette, IN: Kappa Delta Pi.

Papert, Seymour. 1980. *Mindstorms: Children, Computers, and Powerful Ideas.* New York, NY: Basic Books Inc., Harper Collins.

———. 1993. *The Children's Machine: Rethinking School in the Age of the Computer,* New York, NY: Basic Books Inc., Harper Collins.

Pari, Caroline. 1996. From La Famiglia to Academia: A Dutiful Daughter Becomes an Academic Doubter, unpublished speech given at CCCC, Milwaukee, WI, (29 March). (Part of session J.16: Invisible Working Class: Claiming Our Roots and Inventing a Class-Conscious Pedagogy, chaired by Ira Shor.)

Philips, Susan. 1972. Participant Structures and Communicative Competence: Warm Springs Children in Community and Classroom. In *Functions of Language in the Classroom,* eds. C. B. Cazden, V. P. John, and D. Hymes, 370–394. New York, NY: Teachers College. Reprinted by Waveland.

Prigogine, Ilya. 1996. Chasing the Arrow of Time. *On Campus.* Austin, TX: Office of Public Affairs, University of Texas (June 20): 1, 6–7.

———, and Isabelle Stengers. 1984. *Order out of Chaos: Man's New Dialogue with Nature.* New York, NY: Bantam Books.

Probst, Robert. 1984. *Adolescent Literature: Response and Analysis.* Columbus, OH: Charles E. Merrill.

Quinn, Clark, Hugh Mehan, James Levin, and Steven Black. 1983. Real Education in Non-Real Time: The Use of Electronic Message Systems for Instruction. *Instructional Science,* 11: 313–327.

Regan, Allison. 1993. "Type normal like the rest of us": Writing, Power, and Homophobia in the Networked Composition Classroom. *Computers and Composition,* 10: 11–24.

Reynolds, Nedra, A. Benson, M. Cardinale, H. Castline, C. Felix, J. Hudson, K. Kennedy, K. Moffitt, H. O'Grady, J. Regan, B. Saez, M. Satran, T. Stuart, and L. Faigley. 1994. Fragments in Response: An Electronic Discussion of Lester Faigley's Fragments of Rationality. *College Composition and Communication,* 45: 264–273.

Rheingold, Howard. 1993a. *All Things Considered,* National Public Radio, Reporter: McChesney, (12 July).

———. 1993b. *The Virtual Community: Homesteading on the Electronic Frontier.* Reading, MA: Addison-Wesley Publishing Co.

RhetNet: A Cyberjournal for Rhetoric and Writing (e-zine). [Online]. Available website: http://www.missouri.edu/~rhetnet.

Rich, Adrienne. 1979. *On Lies, Secrets and Silences: Selected Prose 1966–78.* New York, NY: Norton.

Richards, Bill. 1994. The Virtual Company. *The Wall Street Journal,* (14 November): R12, R18.

Rickly, Rebecca. 1996. Syllaweb Value. *Electronic Conference: ACW.* [Online] (12 April). Available email: LISTERV acw-l@unicorn.acs.ttu.edu.

Romano, Tom. 1987. *Clearing the Way: Working with Teenage Writers.* Portsmouth, NH: Heinemann.

Romano, Susan. 1993. The Egalitarianism Narrative: Whose Story? Whose Yardstick? *Computers and Composition,* 10(3): 5–28.

Rose, Mike. 1989. *Lives on the Boundary: A Moving Account of the Struggles and Achievements of America's Educational Underclass.* New York, NY: Penguin.

Sadker, Myra, and David Sadker. 1986. Sexism in the Classroom: From Grade School to Graduate School. *Phi Delta Kappan,* (March).

Sandberg, Jared. 1994. Net Working. *The Wall Street Journal,* (14 November): R14, R33.

Schoenbaum, Bernard. 1996. Cartoon. *New Yorker,* (18 March): 77.

Selfe, Cynthia. 1989. Redefining Literacy: The Multilayered Grammars of Computers. In *Critical Perspectives on Computers and Composition Studies: Questions for the 1990s* ed. G. Hawisher and C. Selfe, 3–15. New York, NY: Teachers College Press.

———. 1990. Technology in the English Classroom: Computers Through the Lens of Feminist Theory. In *Computers and Community: Teaching Composition in the Twenty-First Century*, ed. C. Handa, 118–139. Portsmouth, NH: Boynton/Cook.

———, and Gail Hawisher. 1991. The Rhetoric of Technology and the Electronic Writing Class. *College Composition and Communication*, Vol. 42: 55–65.

Shor, Ira. 1986. *Culture Wars: School and Society in the Conservative Restoration, 1969–1984.* Boston, MA: Routledge.

Sky Magazine. 1996. Nothing But 'Net.' (May): (70–71).

Slatin, John. 1990. Reading Hypertext: Order and Coherence in a New Medium. *College English,* 52: 870–883.

———. In press. This Will Change Everything. *Computers and Composition Studies.* Norwood, NJ: Ablex.

Sontag, Susan. 1966. *Against Interpretation and Other Essays.* New York, NY: Dell.

Sosnoski, James. 1996. Notes on Postmodern Double Agency and the Arts of Lurking. *College Composition and Communication,* 47, No. 2 (May): 288–292.

Spiro, Rand, W. Vispoel, J. Schmitz, A. Samarapungavan, and A. Boerger. 1987. Knowledge Acquisition for Application: Cognitive Flexibility and Transfer in Complex Content Domains. In *Executive Control Processes,* eds. B. Britton and S. Glym. Hillsdale, NJ: Lawrence Erlbaum Associates.

Spitzer, Michael. 1989. Computer Conferencing: An Emerging Technology. In *Critical Perspectives on Computers and Composition Instruction,* eds. G. Hawisher and C. Selfe. New York, NY: Teacher's College.

Spooner, Michael, and Kathleen Yancey. 1996. Postings on a Genre of Email. *College Composition and Communication,* 47, No. 2 (May): 252–278.

Sproull, Lee, and Sara Kiesler. 1986. Reducing Social Context Cues: Electronic Mail in Organizational Communication. *Management Science,* Vol. 32, No. 11 (November): 1492–1512.

Steinmann, Martin. 1982. Speech-Act Theory and Writing. In *What Writers Know: The Language, Process, and Structure of Written Discourse,* ed. Martin Nystrand, 291–325. New York, NY: Academic Press.

Steiner, Peter. 1993. Cartoon. *New Yorker,* (July 5).

Sterling, Bruce. 1995. In *Time,* (Spring). Vol. 145, No. 12: 10.

Takayoshi, Pamela. 1994. Building New Networks From the Old: Women's Experiences With Electronic Communications. *Computers and Composition,* Vol. 11, No. 1: 21–36.

Tannen, Deborah. 1985. Relative Focus on Involvement in Oral and Written Discourse. In *Literacy, Language, and Learning,* eds. D. Olson, N. Torrance, and A. Hildyard, 124–147. Cambridge, MA: Cambridge University Press.

———. 1990. *You Just Don't Understand: Women and Men in Conversation.* New York, NY: William Morrow and Company.

Taylor, Paul. 1992. Social Epistemic Rhetoric and Chaotic Discourse. In *Re-Imagining Computers and Composition: Teaching and Research in the Virtual Age,* eds. G. Hawisher and P. LeBlanc, 131–148. Portsmouth, NH: Heineman, Boynton/Cook.

———. 1993. Computer Conferencing and Chaos: A Study in Fractual Discourse. Unpublished Ph.D. dissertation, University of Texas at Austin.

Technology Review. 1996. Session with the Cybershrink: An Interview with Sherry Turkle. (February/March).

Tornow, Joan. 1993. Discussing Literature in High School English Classes Using a Local Area Computer Network. Unpublished Ph.D. dissertation, University of Texas at Austin.

Toulmin, Stephen. 1982. *The Return to Cosmology: Postmodern Science and The Theology of Nature.* Berkeley, CA: University of California Press.

Tuman, Myron. 1992. *Word Perfect: Literacy in the Computer Age.* Pittsburgh, PA: The University of Pittsburgh Press.

Turkle, Sherry. 1984. *The Second Self: Computers and the Human Spirit.* New York, NY: Simon and Schuster.

———. 1995. *Life on the Screen: Identity in the Age of the Internet.* New York, NY: Simon and Schuster.

Valacich, Joseph, Alan Dennis, and Terry Connolly. 1994. Idea Generation in Computer-Based Groups: A New Ending to An Old Story. *Organizational Behavior and Human Decision Processes,* 57: 448–467.

Vygotsky, Lev. 1962. *Thought and Language.* Translators E. Hanfman and G. Vakar. Cambridge, MA: MIT Press.

Welch, K. 1984. Sex Differences in Language and The Importance of Context: An Observational Study of Classroom Speech. Undergraduate thesis (referred to in Krupnick 1985), Yale University.

Wired Magazine, 1.4. 1993. Journal Watch: (Sept/Oct).

———. *2.01.* 1994. Journal Watch: (January).

———. *4.10.* 1996. Journal Watch: (October).

Wittig, Rob. 1994. *Invisible Rendezvous: Connection and Collaboration in the New Landscape of Electronic Writing.* Hanover: Wesleyan University Press.

Wolff, Geoffrey, and Roberta Atwan, eds. 1989. *The Best American Essays, 1989.* New York, NY: Ticknor and Fields.

Written Communication. 1991. Vol 8, No. 1 (January).

Yancey, Kathleen. 1996a. In Search of Net/Intertext. Unpublished speech given at the Computers and Writing Conference, Logan, Utah (May).

———. 1996b. The Place I Write: Woman. Unpublished speech given at the CCCC, Milwaukee, WI (March).

Yoder, Stephen. 1994. When Things Go Wrong. *The Wall Street Journal,* (14 November): R16.

Zinsser, William. 1988. *Writing to Learn.* New York, NY: Harper and Row.

Zohar, Danah and Ian Marshall. 1994. *The Quantum Society: Mind, Physics, and a New Social Vision.* New York, NY: William Morrow and Company.

Zuboff, Shoshana. 1988. *In the Age of the Smart Machine: The Future of Work and Power.* New York, NY: Basic Books, Inc., Harper Collins.

———. 1995. The Emperor's New Workplace. *Scientific American,* (September), Vol. 273, No.3: 202–204.

Zukav, Gary. 1979. *The Dancing Wu Li Masters:An Overview of the New Physics.* New York, NY: Bantam Books.

Index

About_the_Author

JOAN TORNOW lives in Austin, Texas, with her husband John. Their sons, Nicholas and Alexander, are away at college, but occasionally write home via email. Joan received her Ph.D. from the University of Texas in 1993. She is associate professor of Humanities at Austin Community College, where she teaches writing online and heads the writing department at the Riverside Campus. Joan's previous publications include *Every Child is a Writer* (Heinemann, 1984).